Convert!

Designing Web Sites to
Increase Traffic and Conversion

Ben Hunt

WILEY

Wiley Publishing, Inc.

Convert! Designing Web Sites to Increase Traffic and Conversion

Published by
Wiley Publishing, Inc.
10475 Crosspoint Boulevard
Indianapolis, IN 46256
www.wiley.com

Copyright © 2011 by Wiley Publishing, Inc., Indianapolis, Indiana

Published simultaneously in Canada

ISBN: 978-0-470-61633-8
ISBN: 978-1-118-03692-1 (ebk)
ISBN: 978-1-118-03693-8 (ebk)
ISBN: 978-1-118-03694-5 (ebk)

Manufactured in the United States of America

10 9 8 7 6 5 4 3 2 1

For general information on our other products and services please contact our Customer Care Department within the United States at (877) 762-2974, outside the United States at (317) 572-3993 or fax (317) 572-4002.

Wiley also publishes its books in a variety of electronic formats. Some content that appears in print may not be available in electronic books.

Library of Congress Control Number: 2010932422

For Oliver, Madeleine, Alanna, and Henry

CREDITS

PROJECT EDITOR
Brian MacDonald

TECHNICAL EDITOR
Todd Meister

SENIOR PRODUCTION EDITOR
Debra Banninger

COPY EDITOR
Kim Cofer

EDITORIAL DIRECTOR
Robyn B. Siesky

EDITORIAL MANAGER
Mary Beth Wakefield

FREELANCER EDITORIAL MANAGER
Rosemarie Graham

ASSOCIATE DIRECTOR OF MARKETING
David Mayhew

PRODUCTION MANAGER
Tim Tate

VICE PRESIDENT AND EXECUTIVE GROUP PUBLISHER
Richard Swadley

VICE PRESIDENT AND EXECUTIVE PUBLISHER
Barry Pruett

ASSOCIATE PUBLISHER
Jim Minatel

PROJECT COORDINATOR, COVER
Katie Crocker

COMPOSITOR
Maureen Forys,
Happenstance Type-O-Rama

PROOFREADER
Nancy Carrasco

INDEXER
Robert Swanson

COVER IMAGE
© Dietmar Klement/istockphoto.com

COVER DESIGNER
LeAndra Young

ABOUT THE AUTHOR

Ben Hunt has been designing web sites since 1994. He rode the bubble in the late 1990s as Head of Design for Freeserve, the first mass-market free ISP. He has been a director at brand consultancy Poulter Partners and at youth marketing specialists Dubit. As principal consultant at UK web design consultancy Scratchmedia, Ben has helped corporations, government agencies, and NGOs all over the world achieve greater success through better design and usability. In Ben's blog on webdesignfromscratch.com, he teaches skills to create simple and effective web design. These articles have been read by millions. As a result, Ben has been listed as one of the most influential figures in web usability. In 2007 Ben condensed his design philosophy and techniques into an ebook, "Save the Pixel—The Art of Simple Web Design," which has sold more than 8,000 copies.

ABOUT THE TECHNICAL EDITOR

Todd Meister has been working in the IT industry for more than 15 years. He's been a technical editor on more than 75 titles ranging from SQL Server to the .NET Framework. Besides technical editing titles, he is the Senior IT Architect at Ball State University in Muncie, Indiana. He lives in central Indiana with his wife, Kimberly, and their four sharp children.

ACKNOWLEDGMENTS

I'd like to thank:

- ▶ Ken McCarthy and Drayton Bird for setting the scene for this book back in October 2008.
- ▶ All the clients of Scratchmedia who were willing to let us experiment on their web sites over the past year.
- ▶ Dan Johnson, web production wizard at Scratchmedia, for his skill and dedication in running a huge range of valuable tests.
- ▶ Scott, Brian, and the editorial team at Wiley for making it all happen.

Most of all, I would like to acknowledge my wife, Lizzie, and my kids, whose support made it possible for this book to be written.

CONTENTS AT A GLANCE

CONTENTS

PART II Designing for Conversion

FOREWORD

Just about every business organization with any sense nowadays has a web site.

You've got to, because just about everybody with any sense goes on the Internet when they want to find out about something—especially if they are thinking of spending money.

Unfortunately, most websites are appallingly bad at what they are supposed to do: inform, influence or persuade as many people as possible.

But even if your site is a blessed exception, it isn't much use if hardly anybody ever visits it—which is true of the overwhelming majority of sites. As my old boss David Ogilvy observed, "You can't save souls in an empty church."

That is why this book is a tremendous bargain.

First of all it is written in plain English, unlike a great many business books which seem designed to display the writers' polysyllabic dexterity rather than help the readers.

Second, it takes you logically through all the things you need to know to get more business—and more of the right kind of business—at the least cost.

Third, it is full of practical examples so you can easily relate to what the writer is talking about.

Read it once and you will learn a lot. Read it twice and you will start to think about many ways you can do better.

Then read it again and act upon what you have discovered. You will not regret it.

DRAYTON BIRD
Drayton Bird Associates

FOREWORD

It wasn't that long ago that all the people who had confidence that the Internet could become a "real" medium fit around a small table.

I know because I was one of them.

You can't imagine how hard it was back in the early 1990s to interest Silicon Valley and "interactive digital media" types in the Internet's commercial potential.

Of course today the Internet's impact and influence has far outstripped even the most wild-eyed predictions from those early days.

But a huge disconnect remains.

The Internet is a trackable medium, which means unlike print, radio, TV or just about any medium you can name, designers, and producers can actually *see* how their creations impact users.

Strangely, it's a very rare web designer who takes advantage of this simple, but game-changing fact.

The biggest reason for this is that—until now—no one has shown them how to track and test different approaches and made the case for why they should do it.

In writing this book, Ben Hunt has undertaken a task that few professionals in any field have the guts to tackle. He set aside his preconceptions about web design—ones that made him highly successful—and looked at the subject with beginner's eyes.

The result—this book—is as exciting as anything I've seen since Marc Andreessen added the image tag to HTML.

Internet design fads come and go.

The book you hold in your hands is a rock solid foundation you can build your future on.

KEN MCCARTHY
Founder, The System Seminar
Organizer and sponsor of the very first web marketing conference

INTRODUCTION

In 2007, I wrote an ebook called "Save the Pixel—the Art of Simple Web Design," which teaches that simplicity is the key to designing web pages that work. The book has sold more than 8,000 copies, and my agency Scratchmedia has become well known for the clean, spacious design style.

After I presented on simple web design at Ken McCarthy's System Intensive seminar in 2008, I was asked what evidence I could share that proved the effectiveness of my approach. I was shocked to realize I had no numbers to prove that simplicity works!

I made a commitment to discover what really makes the difference between an ordinary web site and a great site. I devised a plan to make design fixes to a range of web sites. These fixes would address 50 common web design mistakes, which I thought would have a positive, measurable impact on the *conversion rates* of web sites (that is, what proportion of people took the action the designer intended).

I planned to test each of these changes across multiple sites and then to compare the results. These experiments would generate data that would prove which design factors make the most impact on conversion. I would publish the results in this book, to give other site owners a checklist of guaranteed fixes. I found several site owners who were willing to let my team experiment on their sites, and we set to work.

The project did not work out in the way I had envisaged. When I started out on this journey, I thought this book would be about graphic design. I discovered that graphic design is only one factor in what makes your site work—and a relatively minor one.

After running about 100 experiments on dozens of web sites, I discovered that it is possible to improve success rates on every web site—in many cases significantly! My team has *more than doubled* the conversion rates of several web pages on a range of sites, often through simple fixes to common problems.

My extensive research, and the results of our own experiments, have taught me that optimizing a web site goes much deeper than just simplifying its design. Yes, graphic design has a part to play in the success of your web site, but I have also discovered some *far more powerful techniques*, which you can start to implement today, and which don't require graphic design skills!

Who This Book Is For

This is not the "50 Proven Design Fixes" book I intended to write. This is a guide you can use to *transform the success rate of any web site*. Its lessons will be useful to every web site owner, every marketeer, every web developer, and every designer.

You need no particular creative or technical skills to apply the lessons in these chapters. Crafting web sites that work comes down to a few simple disciplines, which I set out for you in a simple step-by-step guide.

This book is for everyone who has a web site that is failing, is just "doing okay," or even doing pretty well. If you own a web site, or you are in charge of one, and you suspect it could be doing more, I think you are right.

Most web sites do not perform *anywhere near* their potential. They are not seen by enough of the right people. And when folks do visit the site, the vast majority leave again without getting what they want, or fulfilling the site's goals.

Do not assume that this is the way it has to be.

Some web sites are found by more of the right people, and when those people come they take action. These sites do really well for their owners. Do they succeed because they look fantastic, or because they have had thousands invested in *search engine optimization*? No, that is usually not the case.

Web sites that work do a couple of things well: get seen by the right people, and make it easy for those people to find what they are looking for. This book tells you how you can do the same.

How to Use This Book

This book is organized into two parts. Part I shows you a simple process you can use to multiply the traffic to your web site. Part II gives you the techniques you need to get visitors to engage with your web site, and to continue to interact until they achieve what you want them to do.

I encourage you to start at the beginning and read through. There are hundreds of tips and tricks in these pages, but none of them alone will give you breakthrough results. When you understand the complete process of web site optimization, you will be ready to make a few critical changes that will transform your web sites, and have a platform on which to build ongoing optimization.

Part I: Designing for Traffic

The way you structure your web site is the most important factor in attracting visitors. The first part of the book shows how most web sites do it wrong, and gives you a new approach to creating web sites that's guaranteed to bring you much more traffic.

> ▶ *Chapter 1: How to Transform Your Web Site's Success* describes what is wrong with the familiar approach to web design and why it is set up to deliver poor results. It introduces a new model for creating web sites that target more markets with greater precision.

> ▶ *Chapter 2: Search Engine Optimization Fundamentals* shows you how search engines work, and how to get your web site seen by more people.

> ▶ *Chapter 3: Expanding Your Reach* explains how to get out of your own point of view and take your customers' perspective, multiplying the scope and impact of your web site's message.

> ▶ *Chapter 4: Using the Awareness Ladder* gives you a simple but extremely powerful tool for visualizing your markets, addressing groups of prospects you have never reached before, and giving them exactly what they need to keep engaged with your site.

> ▶ *Chapter 5: Working through the Awareness Ladder* takes you through eight real-world case studies, and shows how you can apply the Awareness Ladder model to any marketing challenge.

Part II: Designing for Conversion

Getting people on your web site is great—but only if they complete your site's goals. I have spent two years researching and testing to discover what causes people to choose to say "yes." Part II of the book gives you all the techniques you need to turn prospects into customers, including a simple three-step structure that gets people to take action.

> ▶ *Chapter 6: Making Your Site Sell* shows you how to model your site using conversion funnels so that you can spot where you are losing visitors, and what to do when you find leaks.

▶ *Chapter 7: Get Their Attention* gives you a toolkit of techniques for creating web pages that engage people's attention and encourage them to believe they are going to find what they want. This chapter addresses basic graphic design techniques, including layout, getability, and imagery, as well as essential tips for effective copywriting.

▶ *Chapter 8: Keep Them Engaged* is packed with techniques for ensuring people stay interested and carry on interacting with your web site, so that you can deliver a complete message. You will discover why you must present positive signs, build trust, and resolve concerns, so that visitors have no reason not to keep reading. It also explores ways to craft web pages that work for visitors with different personality types.

▶ *Chapter 9: Call Them to Action* highlights the critical difference between a web site that just engages and one that sells. Most web sites simply do a bad job of asking people to take action in a way that is timely and powerful. And it is no surprise that not enough people take action. Effective calls to action must be crafted. This chapter gives you six tips for crafting effective calls to action. It explains how to build momentum leading to each call to action, how to keep visitors moving forward from each page to the next, and how to get them over the crucial finish line. The tips are reinforced with examples of how you can use copy and graphics to maximum effect.

▶ *Chapter 10: Executing Your Web Site Strategy* gives you the complete step-by-step guide you need to put into action all the techniques in this book. Whether you are creating a new site, or working with an existing site, it tells you exactly what to do, in the right order, to start transforming your success.

▶ *Chapter 11: Optimizing Your Web Pages* shows how to test your web site's ability to convert visitors, using Website Optimizer, the popular free tool from Google. I give you a set of practical tips that we have learned the hard way, using these approaches on more than 70 of our own experiments over the past year.

How You Can Start to Transform Your Web Site's Success Today

The radical system I set out in this book will deliver incredible results. It will also challenge you. It will require you to look at web sites in a new way, and then you must put the lessons into action.

Most of your competitors will never take on the challenge to transform their web sites, because it is easier to keep doing things the way we have always done them. Right now, you have a great opportunity to gain a competitive advantage, which you can build upon every day. But it takes action.

The sooner you learn the lessons in this book—and apply them—the sooner you will start to see amazing results. They are just a few steps away. I invite you to turn to Chapter 1 now and take the first step.

PART I

Designing for Traffic

CHAPTER 1

How to Transform Your Web Site's Success

How well is your web site doing? What does success mean? Maybe you have goals you can measure. How many of those goals does your site achieve, and what does that mean for your business?

Whether you know your site's current performance, or it's currently a mystery, I want to help you make it far more successful. This book shows you how. Using the process I teach you in this book, you will get more value for each dollar or each hour you invest in your web marketing.

Does This Sound Like Your Web Site?

Do you remember how your web site was created? The process probably went something like this. The web designer was briefed. The designer used her experience, insight, and what she knows about the market to create her best guess at a design that would please the client. There was some back and forth about the design, taking into account different people's insights and preferences. Finally, the successful design was built and launched.

The result is a web site that has all usual content you would expect. Your home page tells people who you are and what you do. The site talks about all the products and services you offer and their features. There may be an FAQ page to answer other questions prospects may have. There is some means to purchase or to take the next step, like a "Contact Us" page.

The site may have analytics set up, which tells you how many people are visiting the site, what they searched for when they arrived, and where they go on the site. You probably do not do anything with that information.

You may even have set up pay-per-click advertising, or done some link-building activity.

It all seems pretty complete. But I bet it doesn't produce great results. I frequently hear web site owners tell that they have paid thousands for a web site that has delivered no business in years.

Here's the problem. Most site owners—even most web designers—don't realize how much more powerful their web sites could be. The vast majority of sites on the Web today could attract far more visitors, and convert far more of those visitors to take desired actions and complete the site's goals.

The reason why most people don't know how to make their web sites perform better is because they are being built the way they have always been built (which is badly). In this chapter, I describe this old model of designing web sites, explain why it is insufficient for your needs, and introduce the new way to go about marketing your business on the Web.

The good news is, it is actually quite easy to achieve significant success online. You just need to know the steps and put them into practice. All the steps you need to know are in this book, together with a complete worked example, case studies, samples, and a wealth of tips and advice. Follow the steps I give you, and I guarantee you will make your web site more successful.

The "First Best Guess" Method of Web Design

I describe the approach to web design that you're probably familiar with as the "First Best Guess" method. The decisions that drive the structure and design of sites is based mainly on guesswork, or on looking at the competition's sites, which were designed based on guesswork.

When it comes to delivering results, this method has a poor track record. It is fundamentally flawed, because it is ignorant about what factors really influence success and how to optimize those factors.

Bad at Attracting Traffic

With regard to attracting visitors, the old method takes the view, "If you build it, they will come." The client and designer assume that all you can do is sum up what you do as clearly as possible, ensure the search engines find the site, get links from relevant directories, and wait for visitors to turn up.

If you need more visitors, you can buy traffic through advertising, which does not always pay off. You might also hire a *search engine optimization (SEO)* firm to generate better search rankings through an extensive link-building campaign. This also does not always work.

The fundamental flaw with this approach to getting visitors is that it is far too narrow. It takes a singular approach. You have a home page, which says what the company does and what you're about. You have a page for your services or products, and maybe another page that describes each one.

The result is that you get a generic home page that gives several weak and mixed messages. The product or service pages give more detailed information that might attract people looking for those things. The "frequently asked questions" page might add a few more useful terms that stand a chance of matching the occasional search engine query.

It isn't that there is anything *wrong* with this approach. The problem is that it isn't *enough*. It falls far short of what is possible. The rest of Part I of this book will show you how much farther it is possible to reach, and exactly how to do it for your own web site.

Bad at Conversion

When it comes to converting visitors into customers, again the traditional approach is pretty ineffective. The site talks about what you do and how you do it. It tells visitors about the features of your products, and provides the information they need. And it gives them a way to buy, to request more information, or to contact you. What more could it do?

The answer is: a lot more! When a web site is designed correctly, it can engage directly with many more different types of visitors and lead them to find exactly what they want.

A site that is at once too narrow and too generic will fail to attract the right people. When search engines find a page that talks about a bunch of different things, they will identify that the page is *about* several topics (but none with much strength). Search engines match pages to people's searches, so generic pages will only be matched to generic searches. But no one is searching for a bunch of different topics together. When someone searches, they search for a specific thing, and they will get the result that is most relevant to that thing.

Say your business is tax advice. You may attract someone looking for "tax advisor" in your local area. But how many people who need tax advice are looking specifically for "tax advisor"? Only a minority. Many more will be looking for a range of more specific needs, such as "managing tax on saving for child's college fund."

For those who are searching for your generic offering, how much competition is there for that term? If your web site does not appear on the first couple of search engine results pages, it is unlikely to bring you much business.

If visitors do arrive at your "tax advisor" home page, they will find a broad message that describes all the different things you can do. If they do not connect quickly with a message that tells them they are in the right place to get what they want, they are unlikely to persevere. They will go back to the search results and try again to find a better fit.

Part II of this book is all about optimizing your conversion rates for visitors who do come to your web site. It breaks down in detail the steps for generating conversions, and gives you clear steps to get the maximum value from every visitor.

A New Perspective on Web Design

The methods I teach you in this book require a new perspective on what "web design" means.

Design does not mean creating stuff that looks good. That's art. Someone who creates web pages that look good, whether or not they work, is not a web designer but an artist, or a graphic designer at best.

You should view design as *the creation of a new solution to a problem*. That often means creating an experience for people, whether it be a lecture, a dinner menu, a ceremony, a sales pitch, a perfume, or a charity campaign.

Unlike art, design always has a purpose. In web design, you always have goals to achieve. An e-commerce site should sell stuff. A marketing site should gather leads or communicate a message. A web-based application should allow people to carry out certain tasks.

Your goals define the problem you need to solve. Design is the process you follow to create the best possible solution to that problem. So web design does not start with graphics. It starts with understanding the challenge. Who am I communicating with?

What do they want? How can I attract them? And how can I get them to do what the site needs them to do?

> **NOTE** *What are your web site's goals?*
> *What is the value of each goal to your organization?*
> *How many goals does the web site need to deliver in order to be a success?*

This high-level vision of web design places it in the broader realm of *marketing*. Marketing is the discipline of defining markets and offerings that deliver what the markets need in order to achieve a result (which is usually to make a profit).

So a web designer should be a marketer who operates in the web medium. In addition to the functional tasks involved with creating a web site, the design process must include techniques to target markets, to reach out to them, and to lead them from wherever they are to the point of taking action. For most web designers, this requires a new set of skills.

The new skills I will show you go beyond creating appealing graphic designs and beyond search engine optimization. You will learn how you can proactively structure your web site to reach more new markets, and to reach deeper into those markets. You will discover a step-by-step process that continually builds your web site into a conversion machine!

The New Approach

It should be becoming clear that to achieve its goals, your web site needs to do only two things:

1. It needs to get the right number of the right kind of people to visit it.
2. It then needs to get as many of those people as possible to take action.

If a web site does not address the right needs in the right markets, it will not get the visitors it needs to succeed. If it fails to appeal to its visitors, and to lead them powerfully along the path to get what they want, the traffic will not be converted into business success.

Success = Traffic × Conversion

If your web site sells peanuts, the number of peanuts you sell is exactly the number of visitors that visit your site multiplied by the site's conversion rate. Clearly, if you have no visitors to your site, you can't sell any peanuts.

If you have a bricks-and-mortar peanut store, it doesn't matter how great your product is, how pleasant your service, and attractive your prices, if your store is hidden in a back street where nobody knows about it.

> **WARNING** *Zero Traffic × Any Conversion Rate = Zero Success*

Likewise, if your conversion rate stinks, any traffic you get will only generate poor results. This would be like establishing your peanut store in a great location on a busy street, putting up great signs and never opening the doors, then wondering why you didn't sell any peanuts.

> **WARNING** *Any Traffic × Zero Conversion Rate = Zero Success*

This means that both traffic and conversion rate are critical for success. It is unwise to neglect either your traffic or your conversion rate. You can prove this pretty easily. A number that's the result of multiplying two other numbers can be represented by a rectangle. The optimal result (greatest area) is achieved when the factors are more balanced, as shown in Figure 1-1. So you need to invest effort both in methods that increase your targeted traffic and methods that optimize your conversion rate.

Your Major Advantages

Today, you have a number of serious advantages over previous generations. With the Internet, it is easier to generate business than at any other time in history. More people are doing more online than ever before. And it is cheaper and quicker to reach them than ever before.

On the flip side, there is also more competition than ever before, which means the greatest rewards will go to the sites that do the best job of attracting and converting traffic. You have this book, so the know-how is in your hands, which gives you a competitive advantage.

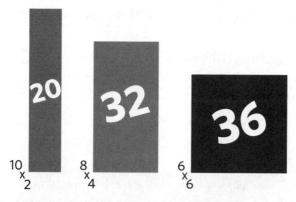

FIGURE 1-1 Investing effort in both traffic and conversion delivers the best results.

DIRECT RESPONSE MARKETING

The Internet is also the world's most powerful *direct response marketing* medium. (The pioneer in this area is Ken McCarthy, who has been teaching business owners how to use direct response techniques in the new media in his seminars since 1994.) Direct response marketing was created in the late nineteenth century, when people started marketing directly to householders using mailed product lists. Customers could choose and order what they wanted, which could be delivered directly to them using the railroads and the new U.S. Postal Service.

Direct response introduced two crucial factors entirely new to marketing:

▶ The marketer communicates *directly to the consumer.*
▶ The consumer orders *direct from the marketer.*

Aside from cutting out the distributors and traditional retailers, the reason direct response was so successful is that it allowed marketers to do something they could never do before: measure the results of every communication.

Unlike branding and advertising, which deliver fuzzy feedback at best, now marketers could change the product lines, prices, or descriptions they offered from one week to the next—or even at the same time—and learn first-hand how their customers would respond.

TEST TO FIND "WHAT WORKS"

Instead of having to *guess* what price point would make the most money, or which payment option would sell the most seed, the ability to gather data directly from the market made it possible for these marketers to test and measure the impact of any choice (or guess), with lower risk.

Before sending out hundreds of thousands of catalogs to households across the U.S., direct marketers could test *multiple options* on samples of their customer base, and change their approach in response to what worked best.

The big difference for you is, what took the early direct marketers weeks to learn, you can learn almost instantly. You can set up a new offer, get it seen by people, and test the responses, all within a day, and at low cost.

The practice of direct marketing has fueled massive economic growth through the twentieth century. You can easily apply the same principles to your online marketing, to drive traffic and conversion.

The fundamental principle is to commit to testing different approaches, measuring the results, and altering your campaigns in response to what you learn about the way that people really respond.

The catch-phrase is "what works?" Very different to "first best guess"!

COMBINE CREATIVITY AND ANALYSIS

The new approach requires a combination of creativity and analysis. In marketing, and in web site optimization, just as in the scientific method, both processes are vital for making advances.

Creativity is forward-looking, asking "What could we do?" The creative process can only generate new future possibilities. It cannot tell you for sure which is best. Analysis looks backward and asks "Did that work?" It examines existing options and tells you which seems to work best. It cannot show the way to what might work even better.

The new approach to web design also calls you to think creatively about the scope of the problem. Challenging the singular approach is a typical example. Take the example of selling ice cream from a cart at the beach. If you were to test your market, asking which flavor people prefer, and discover that half your market likes vanilla best, would you stop selling any other flavors? Of course not.

Without sufficient creative exploration, site owners can sometimes go down a similar path. If you are stuck in viewing your site in singular terms, you may (quite rationally) find better results when your home page focuses on one particular feature over another.

For example, let's say you offer counseling services, which are useful for business professionals and for private clients who want success in some area. If you find that the professional market is the more profitable, would you just stop offering your other services? No, it would be foolish to turn away good business.

The same goes for your web site. If you were placing a newspaper ad, it might make sense to focus on one service, but on the web you can easily create a page to address each market. The fact that a few more people respond to one angle than to another does not validate or invalidate any approach. The right approach is to reach out to all your markets, using multiplicity.

Multiplicity

Whereas the old approach to designing web sites was singular and generic, the key to transforming your success lies in *multiplicity*.

Imagine you go to a cocktail party. During the course of the evening, you meet twelve different people who, you discover, could benefit from the services your company offers. How many different conversations would you have with those people? Twelve! It would be crazy to give each person the same sales pitch, before you understand their problems and what their needs are.

Some of the people you speak to may know exactly what they want. Others may only have a problem with no idea how best to solve it. One may have heard of your business before. Others may not even know your industry exists.

That is how most web sites do business today. You have a singular home page, one single page for each product or service, usually a single page of frequently asked questions, and maybe another one for testimonials. All are woolly and generic, all telling the same story over and over.

As I mentioned earlier, there is nothing intrinsically wrong with these pages. They each have their place, providing one bundle of information to one type of inquirer. If that is all you have, one type of inquirer is all you'll get.

In the old approach to web design, most designers are still making web sites as though they are like advertisements or brochures.

In the old approach, we would treat web design as though space is expensive. Space is not expensive. It is very cheap. You can make as many pages as you have things to say.

In the old approach, we would design web sites as though they are fixed structures. They should not be fixed. They will usually have a fixed core of pages, but they should grow and adapt continually.

In the old approach, we would use the classic model of client-agency relationship. You need a designer to produce your ad or brochure. You brief the designer, he does the work, you pay him, and the job is done. This is not the best way to build web sites. A web designer who really gets it will help his client create a content strategy, to build a platform the client can use to add and update their own content continually, and to establish a relationship for ongoing design support. This benefits both client and designer.

The new approach does it very differently. Instead of relying on a small number of generic pages, you will create a range of specialized *landing pages*, each one designed to be found by specific types of visitors with their own specific needs. Each landing page can be an entry point into a different conversation.

All these conversations are arranged into a logical structure, which lead all types of inquirers to a selling proposition. And because people arrive at pages that *match closely what they need*, they will be more engaged, will have a higher level of trust, and will feel more optimistic about following the path forward that you provide for them.

If you want advice on saving for your child's college education, are you going to be more interested in a page that says "Tax advisor" or one that says "Advice on saving for your child's college education"?

You will see that, in order to follow the multiplicity approach, you will need to publish more pages. Fortunately, publishing online today is so cheap that cost is almost negligible, compared to the results that are available to you. The more you publish, the more conversations you can have with more different people, which is the key to optimization.

Steps for Optimizing Your Traffic

Put all these techniques and benefits together and you get a new picture of online marketing that is fluid and expansive. Instead of getting a web site built and hoping that people will arrive and buy, the new approach is an ongoing discipline that constantly looks for new marketing opportunities, creatively explores what the market responds to, and builds an ever-expanding network of content that continually reaches both wider and deeper to find new customers.

The sooner you start implementing these methods, the sooner your business will start to grow.

The best time to plant a tree is twenty years ago. The second best time is now.

CHINESE PROVERB

The rest of Part I of this book sets out the steps to follow to optimize the traffic coming to your site. It will lead you through every stage in order.

▶ Chapter 2 gives you a grounding in the principles of how search engines work, and how to optimize your pages for chosen terms. Basic search engine optimization is essential for a successful web site, and appreciating how search engines match queries to results will help you target and attract more visitors.

▶ Chapter 3 addresses the fundamentals of marketing. You will learn easy ways to identify new profitable markets that you can target using the multiplicity method.

▶ Chapter 4 introduces the *Awareness Ladder,* a model that you will find invaluable for further expanding your reach by addressing target markets in greater depth. Combining the Awareness Ladder with multiple markets gives your web site far greater reach.

▶ Chapter 5 includes worked examples that show you exactly how to combine all the methods of multiplicity and the Awareness Ladder, using real online businesses.

CHAPTER 2

Search Engine Optimization Fundamentals

To design your site for good search rankings, it is vital to understand how search engines work. In this chapter, you learn the fundamentals of how search engines like Google do their job, what they look for, and how to give them what they want.

At the end of the chapter, you will know what your site needs to do in order to rank well and to attract more traffic. When you combine this knowledge with the other methods in Part I, you will be able to boost *dramatically* the number of visitors to your site. You will also start to realize the full power of multiplicity.

When you type a query into Google, it will probably have millions of potential pages in its index that match your query. Google's job is to arrange those millions of pages into a single file, starting with what it thinks is the best match, followed by the second and third best matches, and so on.

How does the search engine work out what is the best match? It basically uses only two main criteria:

1. What *the page* says it's about.
2. What *the rest of the Web* says the page is about.

Of these two main criteria, the second has by far the greatest impact on where a page ranks in the *search engine results pages* (SERPs). It probably has ten times the weight of the first factor.

Before I explain how these factors are calculated, and how to make use of them, there is an initial step to take, which is to figure out *what terms you want to rank for*.

Keyword Research

Keyword research is the exercise you go through to identify attractive target keywords for your web pages. These are the terms (single words or phrases) that you want your page to appear to be *about*.

The goal of keyword research is to find terms for each page that balance three important criteria:

1. High relevance
2. High traffic
3. Low competition

High Relevance

There is no point attracting people who are looking for something you don't offer. Though it may be possible to identify search terms that could bring a lot of traffic, if the traffic does not match the proposition they find on the page, they will go away again and cannot be converted into customers.

The starting point for your keyword research is always to identify what each page is offering, so that visitors to that page will find what they expect when they click the link.

From that starting point, you may consider alternative terms that people may be searching for. This is very important, and not as easy as it may sound. You may have worked in your own business area for years, and it is likely that you will use particular terms that may not be the same terms your customers use.

For example, one of our clients teaches rock climbing. They could use the term "learn rock climbing" or they could focus their page around "rock climbing course." Which is best? In fact, six times more people are looking for "rock climbing course" than "learn rock climbing."

A quick and easy way to identify terms that people are searching for is to start typing some starting-point keywords into the regular Google search field. Google has a feature called "Suggest," which shows a menu of related searches as you type. Figure 2-1 shows what Google.co.uk tells me people are searching for that includes the words "garden furniture."

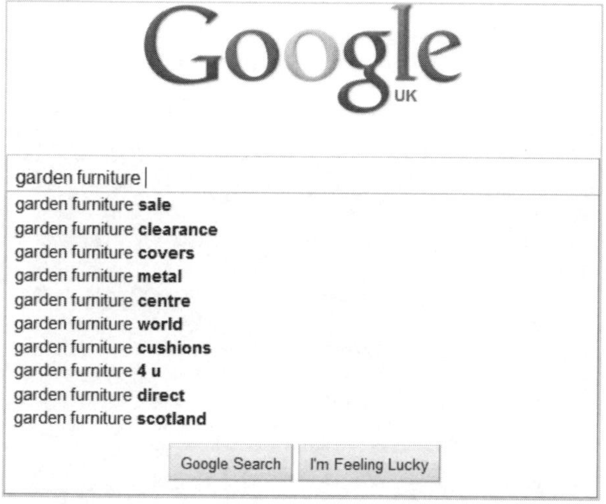

FIGURE 2-1 Google's suggestion feature is a very quick way to find alternative terms that people are typing in today.

High Traffic

It is pretty easy to find terms for which you can get to #1 on Google. You could get to the top spot for the term "automated translation pixie dust" just by publishing a page that features those words, but it wouldn't bring you any traffic, because nobody's looking for that term.

Before you go to the effort and expense of creating a new landing page, you need to be confident that you will get the maximum benefit from that page in terms of visitors. It is important that you know the subject the page focuses on is a subject that people are searching for.

Google provides their AdWords research Tool, a free tool that will indicate the most popular search terms related to keywords you enter (`https://adwords.google.co.uk/select/KeywordToolExternal`). Figure 2-2 shows terms around "simple web design," together with an estimated number of monthly searches.

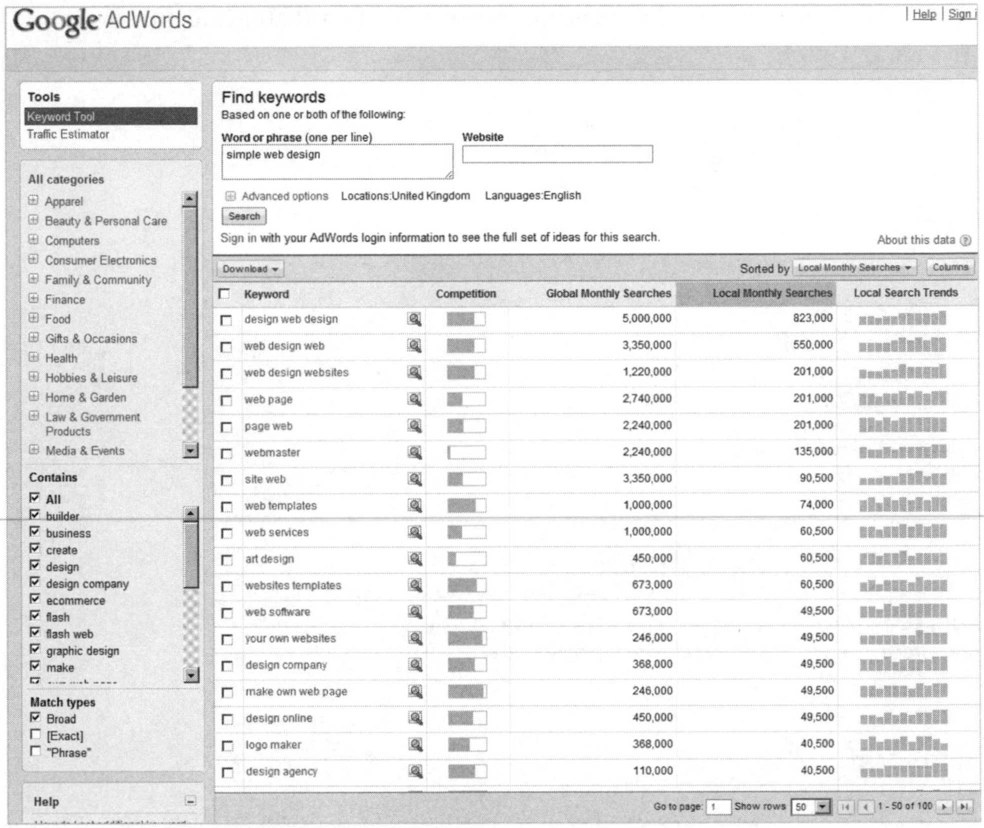

FIGURE 2-2 Using the Google AdWords Research Tool to discover search volumes for keywords

Low Competition

If you identify target search terms that are relevant to your offering and get a lot of searches, you have to take into consideration how much competition there is for that term.

I cannot stress enough the importance of getting high up in the search rankings for the terms you choose.

WHY YOU HAVE TO RANK HIGH

As a rule of thumb, on average the top search result will typically get about 40% of the clicks, the second result will get just over half that number (26%), the third around 14%, and so on.

The result, as shown in Figure 2-3, is that the top ten rankings will get more than 99% of the clicks. Being on page two of the search results will give you slim pickings.

What this suggests is that SERP ranking position is absolutely critical. So much so that it overrides the popularity of the search term. Unless you can get onto the first page of the search engine results, you may be wasting the investment in creating the page.

It is a critical aspect of keyword research to *try to identify the best terms for which you think you can get on page one*. Even if those terms get less traffic, it is better to get a big slice of a small pie than to get a crumb from a big pie.

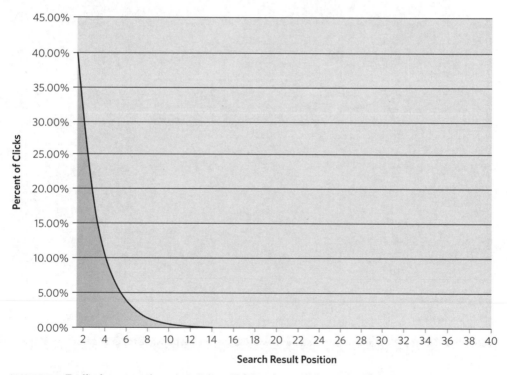

FIGURE 2-3 Traffic from search engines is heavily biased toward the top ranking results.

It is easy to imagine that most of your web site's traffic comes from the terms for which you rank highest. That is often not the case. Although the most popular search terms can get into very high numbers, they still account for a minority of searches carried out.

Most searches on the Web are not for the most popular search terms.

Figure 2-4 shows the top 20 search terms on our web site from a recent month, in order of the number of visits each term brought in. The top term "web 2.0 design" was responsible for more than 3,400 visits. And, yes, one of my articles currently tops the Google rankings for that search term. But this web site gets hundreds of thousands of search visits each month.

Keyword ⌄	None ⌄	Visits ↓
1. web 2.0 design		3,409
2. web design		1,205
3. css block		972
4. css inline		941
5. inline javascript		923
6. css inheritance		590
7. web design process		477
8. best designed websites		456
9. web design from scratch		433
10. web 2.0 designs		415
11. web 2.0 style		360
12. modern web design		347
13. inline css		322
14. web 2.0		280
15. web designing		280
16. web 2.0 design examples		279
17. css block inline		276
18. web designer		271
19. website architecture		256
20. best web design		229

FIGURE 2-4 The top 20 search terms for a busy web site may be responsible for only a fraction of the site's search traffic.

Upon analyzing the stats, it turned out that the top 500 search terms for our site accounted for less than 45% of the total search traffic. In other words, the majority of your traffic will come from "the Long Tail."

THE LONG TAIL

Figure 2-5 shows the search results from the month's analysis plotted on a graph. It would seem that the thick top end of the graph must be responsible for the majority of the visits, but the reverse is true. Most of the traffic is in the Long Tail. The Long Tail is very, very long!

Does this contradict the idea that you should aim to top the rankings for your preferred search terms? Absolutely not! Think of your top search terms as the bow of a boat. It breaks the water and helps bring the Long Tail in its wake. The better you rank for its primary terms, the higher your page will rank *for any terms on that page*.

The real lesson of the Long Tail is the importance of having *diverse content* on your pages. A page should focus on its own target term, but should also include a healthy, natural variety of other words. This is what feeds the *Long Tail* searches.

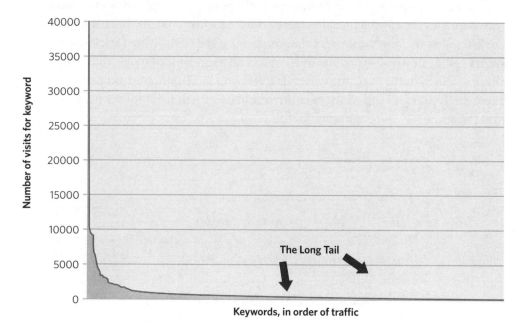

FIGURE 2-5 The *Long Tail* will provide most of your search visits.

FINDING ALTERNATIVE TARGET SEARCH TERMS

If you find yourself in a highly competitive market segment, where the top searches are responsible for extremely high traffic levels, consider what may be typed into the search engines.

This lateral thinking is the key skill in keyword research. If you find that the search market for "New York City lawyers" is sewn up, what other terms may folks be searching for? Public defenders? Divorce attorneys? Personal injury specialists? Spend a few minutes browsing the Web for your initial target terms to discover a range of different terms that people are using. In this case, "New York lawyers" might get you five times the traffic of "New York City lawyers" if you could top the Google rankings, but there is more than ten times the competition, making the less popular term a more realistic option.

Do not make the mistake of thinking that every potential customer has the same language skills that you have. Particularly in competitive search segments, it can prove valuable to deliberately target misspelled or mistyped words.

Most web pages are carefully prepared and are likely to be spell-checked, so you may find that few competitors would leave misspellings on their pages. However, most search queries are entered quickly, so they can frequently contain "mispelings." Figure 2-6 shows the results for pages that compete on the term "New York lawyers." The syntax "allintitle:+new +york +lawyers" shows all pages in the Google index that have all three words in the page title (which is a very good indicator of strong relevance). There are 177,000 results, which means it would be very difficult (or very expensive) to get near the top of the rankings for this term.

FIGURE 2-6 Using "allintitle:" syntax in Google to estimate search competition

Figure 2-7 shows the results of a similar search for a simple typo: "New York layers" returns just 1,990 competing results. It would be much easier to get on page one for this term. (Notice that the sponsored ads are all for New York lawyers!) Of course, that would mean having to put misspelled words on your web page, which may not be appropriate (especially in a law firm).

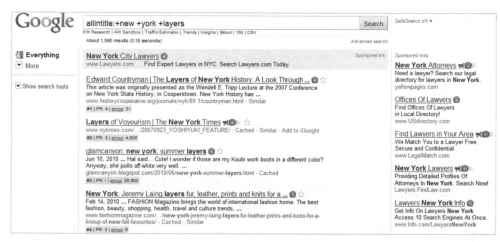

FIGURE 2-7 A simple typo could reveal a viable niche in competitive search markets.

Using Keyword Research Tools

Clearly, it would be useful to combine your research for relevance, traffic, and competition in a single interface. Several good solutions are on the market that will save you hours of time. I mentioned the AdWords Research Tool earlier, which is free. I will briefly introduce two other good tools that we use in our SEO work.

MARKET SAMURAI

Market Samurai (`www.marketsamurai.com/`) is a desktop application that combines a range of useful SEO and marketing tools. Its keyword research module, shown in Figure 2-8, is excellent. It combines data from a number of sources to give you useful insight into potential target niches.

Here, I have entered a range of search terms, to compare the appeal of the "New York layers" niche. I will explain what some of the columns show:

- ▶ "Searches" estimates the number of daily searches for the term (either globally or for a geographical range you specify).
- ▶ "SEOT" is an estimate of the number of clicks per day you could expect for placing at #1 on Google for the term (that is, around 40% of the daily searches).
- ▶ "SEOC" shows how many pages on the Web contain the words (equivalent to typing the term into Google and seeing how many results are returned).

- "SEOTC" is a measure of how many pages use the term in their title tag (that is, which are focused on the term). This is a good indicator of the strength of competition.
- "SEOTCR" is a calculation that compares the popularity of a term on the Web to the number of pages that feature the term in their titles. A lower percentage score may suggest low competition.

These results, unsurprisingly, show that "New York lawyer" and "New York lawyers" are competitive terms, with around 200,000 competing pages (SEOT). They also get a good number of searches. You would need to invest heavily to get to the top of the list on these terms.

"New York layer" and "New York layers" get far fewer searches, only 33 and 16 per day, respectively. However, there is far less competition, so it would be far more feasible to get onto page one for these terms, even taking into account that some of those searches are not looking for lawyers.

In this situation, I would consider the typo route, but would also explore a range of more specific search terms.

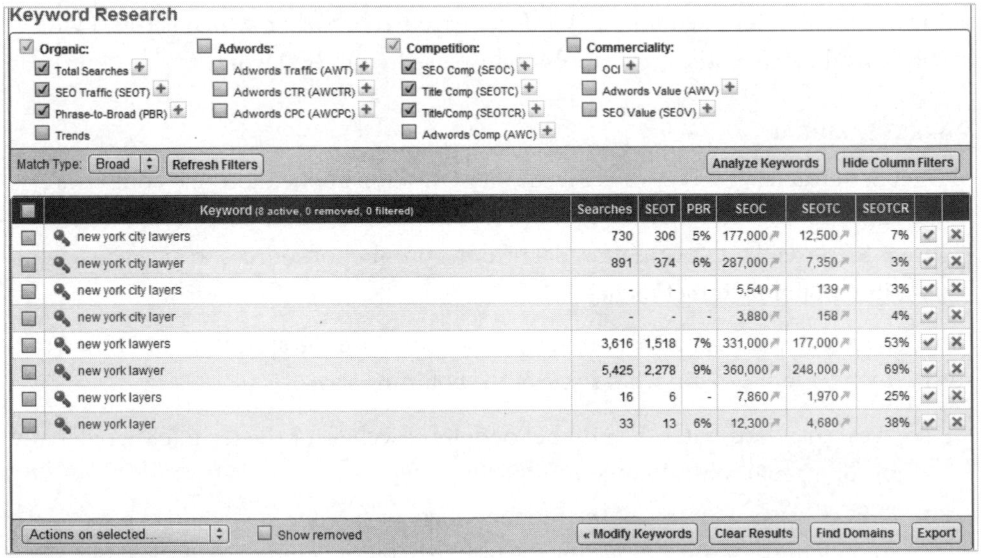

Keyword (8 active, 0 removed, 0 filtered)	Searches	SEOT	PBR	SEOC	SEOTC	SEOTCR
new york city lawyers	730	306	5%	177,000	12,500	7%
new york city lawyer	891	374	6%	287,000	7,350	3%
new york city layers	-	-	-	5,540	139	3%
new york city layer	-	-	-	3,880	158	4%
new york lawyers	3,616	1,518	7%	331,000	177,000	53%
new york lawyer	5,425	2,278	9%	360,000	248,000	69%
new york layers	16	6	-	7,860	1,970	25%
new york layer	33	13	6%	12,300	4,680	38%

FIGURE 2-8 Market Samurai's keyword research interface

WORDTRACKER

WordTracker (www.wordtracker.com) takes a different approach to keyword research. It is an online application, so you can log in from anywhere.

Figure 2-9 shows some results from WordTracker. I have entered a starting search of "redesign web site," and WordTracker has returned a long list of results (part of which is shown). Like Market Samurai, it shows "Searches," but also features "In Anchor And Title," which is a strong indicator of competitiveness. This gives the number of pages that have the phrase in their titles *and also* have links pointing to the pages that include the same phrase.

WordTracker has its own calculations for predicting the competitive attractiveness of keywords, called "KEI" and "KEI3." One thing I like about WordTracker is that I can click any words that look interesting and browse around to find interesting target search terms.

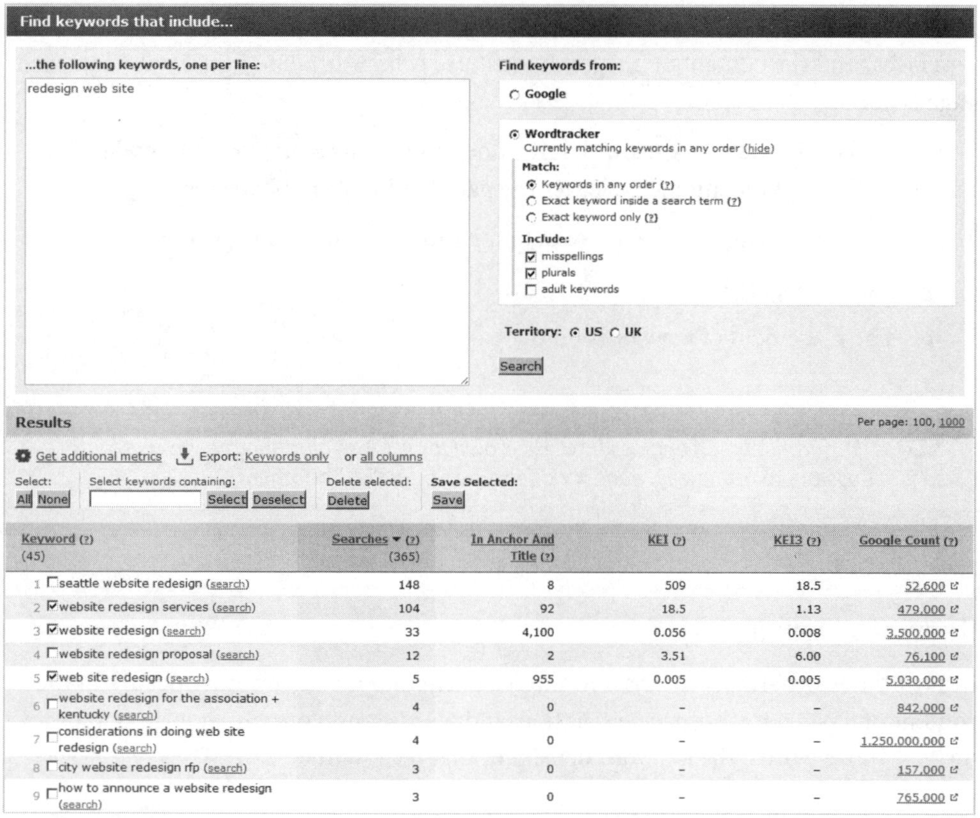

Keyword (?) (45)	Searches ▼ (?) (365)	In Anchor And Title (?)	KEI (?)	KEI3 (?)	Google Count (?)
1 ☐ seattle website redesign (search)	148	8	509	18.5	52,600 ↗
2 ☑ website redesign services (search)	104	92	18.5	1.13	479,000 ↗
3 ☑ website redesign (search)	33	4,100	0.056	0.008	3,500,000 ↗
4 ☐ website redesign proposal (search)	12	2	3.51	6.00	76,100 ↗
5 ☑ web site redesign (search)	5	955	0.005	0.005	5,030,000 ↗
6 ☐ website redesign for the association + kentucky (search)	4	0	–	–	842,000 ↗
7 ☐ considerations in doing web site redesign (search)	4	0	–	–	1,250,000,000 ↗
8 ☐ city website redesign rfp (search)	3	0	–	–	157,000 ↗
9 ☐ how to announce a website redesign (search)	3	0	–	–	765,000 ↗

FIGURE 2-9 WordTracker's keyword research results

These are just two of the keyword research tools on the market. Both tools will suggest alternative words based on your initial suggestions, to help you find terms that may perform better but that were not obvious to you.

The two tools each get their data from a different combination of sources and present their results differently. I suggest trying both to find which suits you best.

Once you have identified a target search term for a page, you should ensure that page appears to be *strongly about that term*. The first step is to make sure the content of the page itself tells the search engines that the main subject matter of the page is the term you have selected.

On-Page SEO

Search engines are getting smarter all the time, but they are still not very smart. A search engine spider does not assign meaning to visual factors, such as layout, color, typefaces, and the content of images. It must use *computation* to figure out what each page is about.

To view a page in the way a search engine does, look at its source HTML code. This removes all visual meaning, and leaves the page's content in its raw form.

The factors search engines use to evaluate the subject focus of a page are:

▶ *Keyword density*
▶ The placement of keywords on the page

> **NOTE** *Different search engines have their own logic for evaluating the various factors, so it is possible to optimize a page for one search engine or another.*

Keyword Density

Keyword density simply means how often a particular word or phrase occurs in the content of a page. If your page has a thousand words, and your target term makes up forty of those words, the keyword density of that term will be 4%.

If you want your page to rank for a certain term, that term should occur with a density that is *neither too low nor too high*.

Clearly, a page that does not mention a term very much will not seem to be about that term, so it cannot compete. On the other hand, a page that has one term taking up half of the words on the page will have a very high density. But that page would be viewed as artificially stuffed with the keyword, which is unnatural and unlikely to be readable or useful. Search engines like to see a natural balance of language.

As a general guide, Google will tolerate a keyword density of *between 2% and 4%*. Other search engines such as Yahoo and Bing may accept higher densities, so bear this in mind when you are optimizing your pages.

A handy free tool for testing keyword density is the Keyword Density Checker (keydensity.com/keyword-density-checker-calculator). Figure 2-10 shows the tool in action. Here, I have asked it to look at the home page of my ebook site (www .savethepixel.org) and fetch the density of a target search term "web design ebook." The results show the phrase appears only once in the page contents, which is not going to help the page get to the top of the search engines.

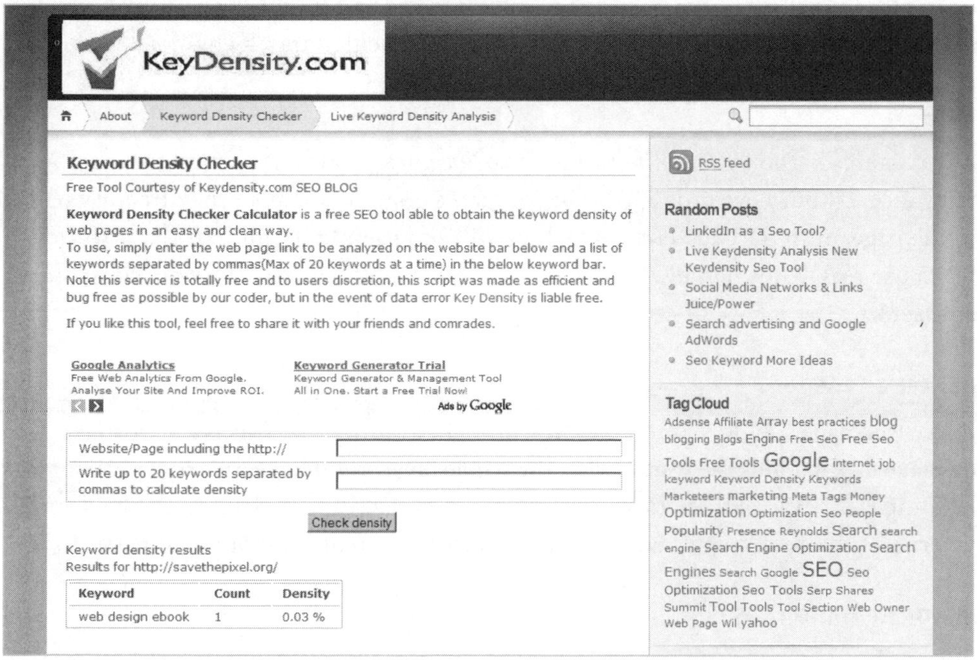

FIGURE 2-10 The low keyword density of only 0.03% may help explain why this page ranks at only position 13 for the term "web design ebook."

Placement of Keywords

HTML (Hypertext Markup Language) is the tagging language that gives a web page its structure. HTML tags identify structural elements, some of which assign meaning to their contents.

Where search engines are concerned, some HTML tags give more relevance to the subject focus of a page's contents.

TITLE TAG

The `<title>` tag is probably the most important tag for identifying a page's subject focus. Every page should have one title tag. This belongs in the `<head>` section of the page, which means it is not part of the visible content on the page.

The contents of the title tag are displayed in the window or tab of the page, in the browser's back/forward navigation menus, and in the bookmark when the page is saved.

Keyword density and length are relevant to your page titles. Keep to natural language and do not repeat keywords too often. Google only recognizes about the first sixty characters of a title tag, whereas Yahoo may read the first hundred and twenty characters (also useful when optimizing a page for a particular search engine).

URL

The contents of the *URL (Uniform Resource Locator)* are also important for search relevance. If your keywords appear in your site's domain name, in the directory path to the page, or in the page's filename, they will add useful relevance. It is always better to use real words in the URL, which may be separated by hyphen or underscore characters.

HEADING 1 TAG

Every web page should feature one `<h1>`, or main heading tag. This is the primary on-page tag that tells the visitor what the whole page is about. In an article, the main heading is the title of the article. Ensure your `<h1>` tag contains your target keywords where possible, but keep it meaningful, interesting, and only as long as it needs to be.

MINOR HEADING TAGS

Your web pages may feature several minor headings, typically `<h2>` and `<h3>`. These tags describe the contents of a subsection of the page, so they give relevance but are less important than the main <h1> tag. It is advisable to repeat your target search terms, or variations on those terms, in your minor tags, but always keep them readable and useful.

BODY CONTENT

As mentioned, the rest of your page content should feature keywords in a natural proportion. However, content that is *higher up the page* (in the HTML source) will be viewed as introductory, which means it is more likely to describe what the page is about. Relevance decreases the farther down the page you go.

The alt (alternative text) and longdesc properties of images also carry relevance. Treat these like you would other body text. They also describe the subject matter of images to search engine spiders and screen readers (which translate the contents of web pages to audio so they can be understood by people with vision impairment).

META CONTENT

Meta tags are tags which, like the <title> tag, belong in the <head> section of the page, so are not displayed on the web page itself. They are used to describe properties of the page to other *user agents* (that is, not browsers, but search engines and so on).

The most common meta tags are the keywords and description tags. Google does not seem to assign relevance to the contents of these tags, but some other search engines do, and may use the meta description in the search result listings themselves, so ensure your meta description gives an accurate description of what's on the page.

When you have optimized your web pages to feature your target search terms in reasonable proportions wherever possible, you should see them feature higher in search rankings. However, as I mentioned earlier, on-page SEO plays a relatively small part in the overall ranking calculation (particularly for Google).

To get really competitive, a web page must be validated by the rest of the Web, which is where off-page SEO comes into play.

Off-Page SEO

In 2006, I wrote an article on my tutorials site that described the current style in web design at the time. It highlighted the main design features that were prevalent, and explained why they worked.

The page was a huge success, generating a significant amount of additional traffic. Looking at the analytics logs, I noticed a high proportion of visitors were coming to the site from web searches for the phrase "web 2.0 design." (Figure 2-4 shows that this phrase still brings the most visitors to the web site.)

When I tried a Google search for the phrase, my "Current Style" article ranked in the top spot, and it has remained up there ever since (more recently pushed into second place by another article I wrote with the title "Web2.0 Design How-To Style Guide").

What is most interesting about this story is that the "Current Style" article *did not mention the phrase "Web2.0 design" in its content*! So why did the page get to #1 on Google? The answer lies in the power of inbound links.

The Power of Inbound Links

Inbound links are simply links to your web page from other pages. In the early 1990s, search engines used only on-page factors to judge what pages were about. The pages that mentioned terms most frequently were viewed as more relevant to the term. At that time, it was quite easy to game the search engines by stuffing keywords into the page content and into meta tags.

Then Google came along and changed the game. Google took a novel approach to calculating relevance. It recognized on-page factors, but it introduced the concept of inbound links from other pages. These links are seen as votes for the linked-to page. And the content of the link, such as "Check out this great guide to Web2.0 design," provided the context of the vote.

Google's approach immediately delivered better results than the other search engines, and established Google as the world's favorite search engine. Today, all the search engines use similar tactics.

Today, to get a high ranking, you need the subject focus of your page to be validated by the rest of the Web. As my "Current Style" article story proves, on-page factors play only a marginal role in search success. If the rest of the world says that your page is about a certain topic, that's good enough for Google and the other engines.

How do you get your pages to rank well when you do not control the factors directly? First, I need to describe the mechanics of how Google might use these factors to establish relevance.

How Google Calculates Inbound Link Value

I will describe the general method Google uses to establish which page is most relevant for a given term. The exact workings of any search engine's algorithm are closely guarded secrets, but we know the principles at work.

Three main factors are involved:

1. Number of inbound links
2. Relevance of linking pages
3. Link juice

NUMBER OF INBOUND LINKS

When considering how search engines work, a useful phrase to start with is, "All other things being equal..."

All other things being equal, a page with more links from the rest of the Web will be viewed as more popular, and more relevant, than a page with fewer inbound links. That said, the value of any inbound link can vary enormously.

RELEVANCE OF LINKING PAGES

All other things being equal, a link to a page about web design from another page about web design will be more relevant than a link from a page on a different subject. Because search engine spiders evaluate the subject matter of all the pages they visit, they can figure out how closely the subjects relate. Links from related pages are far more valuable than any links from unrelated pages.

LINK JUICE

For Google, the most significant of the three factors is the amount of *link juice* a linking page gives to the linked-to page.

WARNING *The information in the following paragraphs almost certainly* does not *accurately describe how Google actually works. It is based on assumptions, and is for general illustration only.*

Google gives every page on the page a *PageRank (PR)* value. This is a general indicator of the importance of that page on the Web. The more inbound links a page has, the higher its PageRank is likely to be.

PageRank is a number between zero and ten, with ten being the highest. But it is not a linear scale. A PR5 page is *far* more important than a PR4 page, which is far more important than a PR3 page. (Let's assume that an increase of one PR point is equivalent to a fifty-fold increase in importance. So a PR5 page will be 2,500 times as important as a PR3 page, and so on.)

Generally speaking, when a page links out to another page, the link juice is a factor of the PR value of the linking page, which is divided between all the outbound links from that page.

If the link is described as "nofollow" in the HTML markup (which indicates to the search engines that the link is not viewed as important by the linking page), the PR value is not carried over.

What all this means is that it is far more valuable to get inbound links from pages with higher PageRank than lower PageRank. Links from pages that are both relevant and have high PageRank have by far the greatest impact on establishing search relevance.

To sum up, the inbound link value for a certain term might be understood as: the sum of (PageRank value multiplied by relevance) for all inbound links.

INTERNAL LINKS

Links that come from other pages on your own site do provide value. You can use this to your advantage. For example, let's say you want one particular page to rank highly for a certain target search term. If you use that search term on every page on your site, each time linking back to the page you want to promote, these internal links can help boost the relevance of that page.

In this example, all the pages on a site are working together to boost the rankings of one particular page for one term. You can't use a lot of major phrases in this way, so it is important to choose one that is more contested than your individual target phrases, that is relevant across every page on your site, and for which you still stand a chance of getting to the top of the rankings.

If the competition on a particular term is moderate, you may even be able to dominate the search market, if you have enough pages. For example, if there are 2,000 pages that mention your target phrase in their titles (which the "allintitle:" search syntax on Google will tell you), if you put the term in the title tags of 20 pages or blog posts on your site, you would immediately own 1% of the pages that compete on that term. Link all those pages to one page that focuses on that term and you could find that term quickly moving to the top of the rankings.

A common approach, which suits many medium-sized or large sites, is to group your pages into thematic sections, known as *silos*, with all the pages in each silo supporting one particular search term.

The objective of off-page SEO is to get as many relevant and important pages as possible to link to your page. I will describe two approaches: link-building and what I call "ultimate SEO."

Link-Building

Link-building is the practice of actively trying to get other sites to link to yours. Tactics include:

▶ Contacting the owners of other pages and asking them for a link.

▶ Offering the owners of other pages a link, in return for a reciprocal link back to their page.

▶ Manually creating other pages yourself, on a similar topic, and placing a link to your own page from those pages.

▶ Adding comments to articles or blog posts on other sites, which contain links back to your page.

▶ Posting messages on social networks (like Twitter, Facebook, LinkedIn, Digg, del.icio.us, Reddit, and so on) with backlinks to your page.

▶ Submitting articles to other sites, which contain backlinks.

You will notice that the factor all these methods have in common is that they are time-consuming! You can actually get a web page to start ranking (particularly in an uncompetitive sector) using a bit of manual link-building, but to get to the top of the results for even a moderately competitive search phrase would take a significant amount of effort.

Many site owners outsource their link-building to specialist companies, often based in countries like India or the Philippines, where labor costs are lower. This can produce results, but is still far more expensive than my preferred method.

Ultimate SEO

For me, the best form of SEO is—no SEO at all!

The overriding goal of search engine design is to distinguish between sites that are *naturally liked* by the rest of the Web and those that are *artificially promoted* to look as though they are liked. Teams of very clever people are working right now on finding ways to make it harder for you and me to game the system.

The ideal approach is to play the game the way the search engines want you to play. That is, to make better content, which the rest of the Web really does see as valuable, and wants to link to.

I learned this lesson with my online articles and tutorials, which I just wrote and posted online. Before I knew it, my content had thousands of daily visitors. Of course, the world still needs to find out about your content, so some promotion will always be necessary.

Thinking from the journalistic perspective, people want to read content that is valuable, interesting, and original. People writing on blogs and social media are more likely to link to stories that have a clear and original theme than pages that offer a generic treatment of a subject.

Pages don't have to be long. In fact, a good blog post or news story could be just a few paragraphs.

If your web site relies on one main page to describe your offerings, there will be a strong tendency to play safe, which will result in a page much like competitors' pages, and which is unlikely to be original or noteworthy. However, when you commit to creating a range of pages that deal with various specific subjects, you can make each one short, punchy, unique, and genuinely valuable: all useful factors for making good *link bait*.

At its highest level, then, SEO actually becomes PR. If you create content that is genuinely newsworthy, interesting, and valuable, your only task is to get the word out. I did this when I redesigned my tutorials site by searching for "web design blog" on Google, and personally e-mailing the top 20 web design bloggers, simply asking them to check out my site and tell me what they thought. Enough of them posted links to the new site to cause a ripple that's still rippling today.

It may seem that the Web is flooded with content. It is. However, the more noise there is, the more important it is for people to find trustworthy channels that can help them filter out what's really relevant. Where we used to go to the mass media for our news, more web sites are offering this kind of service than ever before. And their owners are desperate for news. They love to be the first to find out something interesting and to post it for their readers.

I could tell you about hundreds of SEO tricks, but any of them could stop working tomorrow, resulting in your site suddenly losing ranking, or—worse—getting banned by Google altogether!

For me, ultimate SEO comes down to creating content that has value. This requires a different set of skills. It requires insight into marketing and psychology, and the ability to create story value from the raw materials you have in front of you. To win at the traffic game, to get the greatest number of visitors to your site, you just need to think like a marketer and a journalist.

If you don't think you have these skills, don't worry. Most of your competitors don't either. In the next three chapters, I give you ways to visualize and to create new channels that will funnel more people to your content than you may now think possible.

CHAPTER 3

Expanding Your Reach

This chapter expands on the concept of *multiplicity*, and shows how it should be the central principle of your online marketing strategy. I take you through a few simple steps to start widening the scope of your web presence.

Marketing is the process of defining markets and matching them to solutions. The better the match, the greater the demand for the solution, and the easier it is to make money.

What Are You Really Selling?

Do you sell your products and services? No. What people buy from you are *solutions to their needs.* Your products and services themselves are not the solutions—they are a means to an end. Whatever people buy, they are not really buying the thing. They are buying some benefit that the thing gives them.

> *A man who goes into a hardware store to buy a quarter-inch drill bit does not need a quarter-inch drill bit—he needs a quarter-inch hole.*
>
> UNKNOWN SOURCE

All you sell is *solutions to needs.* This is the first step to unlocking more selling opportunities. When you focus on the solutions that you sell, instead of on the products and services that deliver them, you take a big step closer to your prospects.

If your web site talks about your products, what queries will the search engines match it to? People looking for the subject matter of the page—in other words, your products!

If you have a product that a lot of people want and which your keyword research reveals a lot of people are searching for, you may expect good results from that market. But most web sites do not offer specific products like that. Most web sites are trying to market or sell things to people who don't yet know the exact solution they need. They may not be ready to choose, or to hand over money. They are thinking about their problem and how to solve it.

If someone is looking online for a solution to a problem, the way to draw them to your web site is to address them *using the same language*. It is language that search engines use to match queries to content. And your site will engage visitors more effectively if they see their present thoughts addressed on the page in front of them.

Researching Your Markets

Every problem that every one of your products or services could solve is a potential market. The ultimate question is whether you can make a profit selling to that market. Eugene Schwartz, one of the twentieth century's great copywriters, puts it succinctly:

> *It is the moment when a private desire is shared by a statistically significant number of people large enough to profitably repay selling these people, that a market is born.*
>
> EUGENE M. SCHWARTZ, BREAKTHROUGH ADVERTISING

Of course, you have an advantage over Eugene Schwartz. You are marketing online, whereas he sold his products by mail order. Whereas he wrote only one ad for each product he sold, you can create as many web pages as you like. And unlike printed ads, you can easily and quickly improve or remove web pages that don't perform.

The first step in identifying new markets, then, is to list the possible problems or needs that your product or service could solve. Then, you research the size of all markets so that you can prioritize your marketing activities.

What Problems Do You Solve?

Let's go back a few years and say your product is a sharpened flint hand tool. This tool has no intrinsic value. All its value comes from what it enables people to do. Here are just a few problems that your tool may solve:

- ▶ How to carve meat from a kill more quickly
- ▶ How to sharpen sticks (for weapons or cooking)
- ▶ How to scrape hides quickly and cleanly
- ▶ How to improve your chances in a hand-to-hand fight

You can see that several different groups are already here. Both males and females carrying out various roles could all benefit from your product.

What attracts them is not the product itself, but *how it helps them solve a need*. They get more meat for their family. They get to make weapons and cooking sticks with less effort, which means they get more rest. They get a better quality of hide, also with less work. And they get to improve their survival options in a conflict. These are all valuable benefits.

> **NOTE** *Do the same exercise for your own products or services. Instead of looking at the tool, describe how it solves a need or problem for the person who buys it. List as many problems as you can, and state the solution to each problem.*

A great place to start looking for insight into the needs your products actually solve is just to ask your existing customers. People like to tell their own stories, so ask them what their concerns, priorities, and needs were when they were looking at the market. Ask them what other benefits they have discovered. The answers to these questions may highlight new needs that you were not previously aware of. You can also ask your own sales and customer service people for their stories from the front line.

Flip Products to Propositions

People don't buy products; they buy solutions to their needs. These needs may be functional (enabling you to do something you could not do before), time-saving, money-saving, or emotional (such as the need to look good, to belong, or to feel secure). It is our needs that motivate us to buy.

Each of your products may address multiple needs. However, there is a gap between the needs and the product. You need to bridge that gap and connect each need with the solution you offer.

What bridges the gap is a *proposition*. It is the way you present a solution to a prospect's need: "This is how this thing will give you what you need."

Nobody buys a flint hand tool. They buy a "how you can carve more meat in less time before the wolves show up," or a "how you can make better hides to help your family get through the winter." These are propositions.

There may be many solutions to any given problem. The solutions may be equally good. It is the best proposition that wins the day.

Let go of the idea that you sell products, and flip it to "I sell propositions." Your products and services have no value in themselves. People do not care about them. They only care about their problem at hand. It is your job to present propositions that show how your products solve the problems.

Flip Features to Benefits

If the only thing we ever buy is *benefits to us*, why does so much marketing still talk about *features*? Here's the distinction:

- ▶ A feature is what something does.
- ▶ A benefit is what it does for me.

No one ever bought a feature. No one would pay for a lighter or sharper hand tool. They bought what the lightness or sharpness *means to them*. Either they can carry one with them wherever they go, or do their work quicker, or just have the social status that comes with having the latest "gadget."

Behind every product are multiple propositions. Behind every feature are multiple benefits. That's one reason why the long tail is where the action is. Because any product can solve many needs, the people who need what the product can do for them will be searching for many different things. They are searching for the potential benefits to them, in their own context, and those benefits cover a much wider range.

To attract the largest possible audience, you need web pages that are *about the things that people are looking for right now*. Each page can capture people looking for a specific benefit, and present a proposition that shows each group how the features of your products or services fulfill their need.

This will already seem like a daunting amount of work, but these pages do not need to be made today (that's the old approach). They can be developed over time, and they do not have to do a complete selling job. They only have to catch the attention of a certain type of visitor. The following two chapters give you a method for arranging all your landing pages into a logical structure that will give you the maximum marketing reach for the minimum possible effort.

Flip "Us" to "You"

Here is some news, which may be surprising: Your customers are not interested in you, in your company, in what you do, or even in your products.

Your customers (and prospects) are only interested in one thing:

"What's in it for me?"

Every proposition you offer is nothing more than a way of translating your features into their benefits. If everyone is really only interested in themselves, we should endeavor to present our propositions in a way that makes sense *from their perspective*, not from our own.

Most web sites built with the old approach today come from the *internal perspective*. This is like the view from the inside of the store looking out. But your potential customers are outside looking in. They have an *external perspective* of your business, which may be totally different.

From our internal perspective, we are interested in the features of our products and our competitors' products. That will come through in our communication.

From the external perspective, prospects are interested in benefits to them. They just want confidence that they can find a solution to their needs.

From our internal perspective, we use the language of our own industry, vocabulary that everyone understands inside the office. When we use this language on the Web we wonder why our site does not attract more visitors.

From the external perspective, your prospects use their own language to describe what they want. This language may be incorrect (to someone on the inside), but it is the language being typed into Google right now by someone who wants what you can deliver.

One of our customers provides good quality, low-cost web hosting. Their keyword research revealed some fascinating results:

▶ The term "low cost web hosting" could deliver 250 daily visitors for a #1 placement, but the title competition is over 27,000.

▶ An alternative "Affordable web hosting" is worse, with good potential traffic around 1,000 per day, but almost half a million competing pages.

▶ Compare "cheap web hosting package," which could deliver 200 daily visitors, but has under 2,000 competing pages.

Very few hosting providers want to identify themselves as "cheap," yet that's what people are looking for. The internal perspective is "low cost," but the language being used outside in the real world is "cheap." I would expect that a good proportion of the pages that mention "cheap web hosting package" are not competing providers but people discussing recommendations. Good opportunities exist for providers who are willing to let go of their self-image and to use the language of the external perspective.

Anywhere we talk about us, we are missing an opportunity to address our prospect's needs directly. This is why legendary copywriter Drayton Bird advises using *three times more space* talking to your visitor *about them* than talking about yourself.

Each of the needs you have identified could be a market that you can address with the solutions your products offer. The next step is to evaluate each market to estimate which are the most attractive.

If you express the needs in terms of "how do I?" or "how to," these can give you starting points for keyword research. Throw a range of variations on these terms into your keyword research software and see how many people are typing in queries relating to the theme.

To help broaden your search, I would recommend typing the starting phrases into a search engine and browsing the first few pages. When searching on problems, you are likely to find forum discussions. Look for alternative phrases that people are using to describe their real needs. Try pasting those terms into your keyword research tool, and keep thinking laterally until you are confident you have a good idea of the size and competitiveness of the market.

To show how you can expand the markets your web site addresses, I will present a fictional worked example, which I'll use throughout the book.

Marketing Joe's Miracle Hair-Gro

Joe is our fictional web marketer. His product is a treatment for male pattern baldness called "Joe's Miracle Hair-Gro."

Joe's current web site (shown in Figure 3-1) has a simple structure that is typical of the "first best guess" method:

- ▶ His home page tells visitors about his product, talks about how it came about, and invites you to purchase a bottle.
- ▶ He has a page of frequently asked questions.
- ▶ A "Buy it now" page allows you to buy the product.
- ▶ He has a contact page where prospects or customers can get support or submit queries.

FIGURE 3-1 The Joe's Miracle Hair Gro home page communicates some useful points, but does not get results.

Joe's web site does not perform well. Nobody is searching online for "Joe's Miracle Hair-Gro." He presents all the features of his product, like the fact that one tub of the cream will give you 20 applications, and that it contains natural plant extracts, but nothing seems to bring him more traffic.

Joe's product is not a known brand, so nobody is looking for it by name. If he focuses his site's keywords around "Joe's Miracle Hair-Gro," those words will be of no use to him. Although the features of his product may be interesting to some, are they what people are actually looking for? Do people need "natural plant extracts" or "20 applications from a bottle"?

Joe needs to stop talking about what his product *is*, and focus his language on "what it does for you." Let's flip Joe's marketing to the external perspective, using real data, and see what's possible.

The general problem area that Joe addresses is wanting hair where you don't have hair. Let's look at the keyword research landscape to see what other problems Joe's product may address—or other terms people might use to describe their problems.

Joe's Keyword Research

I started by entering "hair loss treatment" into Market Samurai and clicked the "Generate Keywords" feature, which uses the Google Synonym Tool to find related search terms. I then exported the results into a spreadsheet so that I could manipulate the data.

I created my own column that shows the SEO Traffic (how many visits you could get at #1) divided by the Title Competition (a good indicator of how many pages you have to beat to get there). Figure 3-2 shows the results ordered by that figure.

My starting phrase "hair loss treatment" is near the top of the list, and it gets a lot of traffic, but 36,700 competing pages would be a tall order for Joe's small budget. What I'm looking for are terms that are relevant to Joe's product and which have fewer than 1,000 competing pages.

I have highlighted some likely looking target phrases. There are a few surprises in this list:

▶ Interestingly, the typo "hair thining" seems to be quite common. With only 409 competing pages, it could still help bring a hundred daily visitors.

▶ "Hairloss" (one word) is another surprising option, with two entries in the top ten.

▶ Another surprise is the profile of terms about hair loss in women. About half of the most attractive target phrases mention "women" or "female." Joe should certainly take that market seriously.

▶ The fifth result in this list is "reasons for hair loss," which is a fairly popular topic that is not hotly contested. Clearly, anyone searching for this phrase has a concern about hair loss, and could be in the market for a restorative treatment.

	Searches (Exact)	SEO Traffic (Broad)	SEO Comp	Title Comp	Traffic / TC
hair thining	29	136.5	4920	409	3337
hair loss vitamin deficiency	29	111.72	2700	468	2387
hairloss treatment	79	167.16	24200	717	2331
hair growth shampoo	325	683.34	27300	3100	2204
reasons for hair loss	178	136.5	58900	664	2056
hair loss after pregnancy	178	111.72	16000	548	2039
hair growth products	595	683.34	53800	3450	1981
receding hair	62	306.6	58400	1580	1941
hairloss women	43	74.76	903	399	1874
hair lose	95	835.38	37200	4630	1804
thinning hair men	79	204.54	50700	1160	1763
hair loss treatment	1989	6213.9	670000	36700	1693
loss treatment hair	2	6213.9	246000	37100	1675
hair loss hormones	16	60.9	16200	365	1668
alopecia women	29	167.16	4300	1100	1520
alopecia	4438	11364.36	9260000	76600	1484
regain hair	62	136.5	13700	941	1451
vitamins for hair loss	266	204.54	32300	1430	1430
female thinning hair	62	91.14	5620	645	1413
premature balding	29	22.26	19300	164	1357
hair loss children	33	111.72	32200	841	1328
female hair loss products	29	18.06	3450	136	1328
balding	487	3396.96	4270000	25700	1322
hair regrowth	730	2775.36	498000	21300	1303
hair loss vitamins	118	456.96	26200	3570	1280
how to prevent hair loss	217	136.5	232000	1110	1230
cause hair loss	24	1021.86	611000	9200	1111
cause of hair loss	53	111.72	48600	1080	1034
laser hair regrowth	62	91.14	9290	900	1013
causes female hair loss	13	60.9	30400	613	993
hair loss shampoos	145	111.72	13700	1140	980
prevent hair loss	178	456.96	203000	4930	927
female pattern baldness	118	111.72	71100	1210	923
hair regrowth products	118	111.72	20100	1210	923
androgenetic alopecia	145	204.54	132000	2260	905
excessive hair loss	53	74.76	36800	847	883
thinning hair treatment	95	204.54	13800	2320	882
hair loss treatments	398	1021.86	214000	11700	873
women hair loss treatments	43	49.56	117000	569	871
women hair loss treatment	62	204.54	128000	2380	859
laser hair loss treatment	43	111.72	9870	1300	859
hair loss men	145	835.38	82400	9760	856
hair loss female	43	1021.86	21200	12400	824
best hair loss product	79	60.9	11400	741	822
new hair loss treatment	118	74.76	162000	947	789
stop balding	33	39.9	22200	526	759
causes of female hair loss	43	22.26	25500	295	755

FIGURE 3-2 Keyword research results for Joe's hair loss campaign

Choosing Joe's Target Keywords

What benefits might Joe notice in this list, which he can promote in place of the general features of his product? Although Joe currently promotes his product as a treatment for male pattern baldness, the phrase "pattern baldness" does not appear until the 33rd item in the list, and only then in the context "female pattern baldness"! In fact, the words "bald," "baldness," and "balding" occur only ten times in 177 results.

It seems that people take an interest earlier in the process, going online to find solutions to combat hair thinning, or to promote hair growth. This insight alone, from only a few minutes' work, could transform the fortunes of Joe's web site.

The outcome of flipping Joe's perspective is that he realizes he can market his existing product as the solution to a range of problems. Instead of being exclusively a "male pattern baldness treatment," his Hair-Gro can now help with "hair thining," "hairloss," and "women hair loss," among others.

In Joe's case, I might consider "hair growth products" as the main term to focus his site around, with 595 daily searches and 3,450 competing pages, in preference to "hair loss treatment" that has ten times the competition. The term "hair loss products," by contrast, would bring Joe only 835 visits per day, if he could beat 228,000 other pages to the top spot!

Joe can start to target certain markets, identify appealing keywords for each one, and create pages that really focus on those terms. These multiple landing pages will benefit Joe in several ways. This is putting multiplicity to work.

MORE CLICKS

If Joe can top the search results for just a few of his chosen phrases, the traffic to his web site will multiply. To get to the top, his pages need to be seen as *about* the phrase in question. The best way to do that is to have a separate page focused on each phrase, and to generate inbound links from other related pages.

Because the top-ranked search results get the lion's share of clicks, it is better to get twenty results onto page one for less popular terms than to get one result onto page ten for a popular term.

Though it's true that the high-profile generic keywords get the most searches and clicks overall, that is the wrong comparison. In fact, as we've seen, the long tail gets far more traffic. There are more searches for specific phrases than for general terms.

STRONGER ON-PAGE RELEVANCE

The more specific a page, the easier it is to maintain a high keyword density. If Joe creates a page on "female hair loss products," he can easily achieve a 2% keyword density and keep the content readable.

However, to make a useful page on a more generic subject like "baldness," Joe would need to cover a range of causes and impacts, which will naturally dilute the keyword density and focus of the page.

STRONGER LINK RELEVANCE

If Joe publishes a page on "hair loss" he is up against almost seven million other pages that mention the term in their title tags. Because it is a general topic area, any page that talks about hair loss will talk about a range of related issues, so its subject matter focus will be diluted among those issues.

However, if Joe writes a page around the phrase "hairloss women," he is competing against 400 other pages. Plus, he can look through the 900 pages that are on the same subject—and that use the same quirky spelling—for highly relevant inbound links. He will not need many to get to the #1 position.

Because of the tendency for a page on a more specific topic to have higher on-page relevance, a link from "hairloss women" to "hairloss women" is also likely to be more relevant than a link from "hair loss" to "hair loss."

MORE RELEVANT TO THE PROBLEM

Joe's keyword research shows that 178 people every day search for the exact phrase "reasons for hair loss." Only 664 pages exist with all those words in their titles, which makes it an attractive market for Joe.

If someone searches for "reasons for hair loss," and happens to arrive at Joe's page that has the title "Reasons For Hair Loss Explained" and which goes on to list all the major reasons, he or she is likely to be instantly engaged. A page that talks about the general issue of hair loss is less likely to hook the visitor's attention straight away.

Joe now has a distinct advantage. Because he knows that this visitor is concerned *right now* with "hair loss," as opposed to "balding," "alopecia," or "thinning," he can use that language in his proposition.

He can present Miracle Hair-Gro as a product that not only treats "hair loss," but that specifically addresses its major causes, which will be a perfect fit to the prospect's present need and language.

The next chapter describes how Joe can take all these groups of visitors, address all their various needs directly, and lead them through to take action, all using a simple, efficient, and logical process.

CHAPTER 4

Using the Awareness Ladder

In the previous chapter, you *widened* the reach of your web site by flipping your products and services into multiple propositions, which speak directly to people's needs.

In this chapter you go *deeper* into each market, to address your target markets at more levels. I introduce you to the *Awareness Ladder*, another powerful technique that lets you create even more entry points for each of your propositions. The Awareness Ladder is a simple model that can help you pitch every page on your web site at its target audience with precision.

Figure 4-1 shows how, in the old model, we expect visitors to arrive from the Internet through the front door. We spend a lot of time trying to balance all our messages into a home page (H). We create navigation that leads visitors from the home page to the product or service they require (p/s), and then we hope to get them to take action ($).

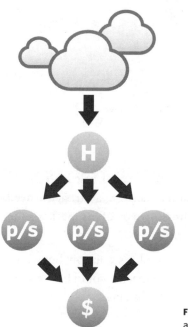

FIGURE 4-1 The simplistic architecture of the old model

The problem with this structure is that most people don't arrive via the front door. Most traffic comes through the Long Tail. (Of course, if you don't have much content on your site, the Long Tail may not be very long.)

When you flip your perspective, instead of expecting a generic home page to channel visitors to your products and services, you can create offerings (O) that expand your reach to target more different needs with greater precision, producing a model more like the one illustrated in Figure 4-2.

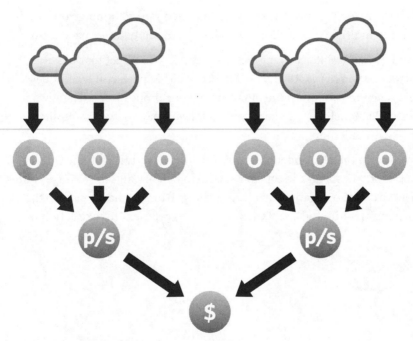

FIGURE 4-2 Multiple offerings ("O") can reach more markets and channel visitors to your products and services.

Yet this is only the beginning of your true reach.

Joe's old web site claimed, "Do you suffer from baldness? Buy my Miracle Hair-Gro and get a full head of hair in weeks!" At first sight, that may seem to address the needs of his market. And, in a way, it does. But it is only addressing part of his market—the segment that is *actively looking for a solution* to a conscious need.

What other groups could be out there who may benefit from Joe's solution, but who are not looking for it? More segments within Joe's potential market could be reached by extending his proposition to people at *multiple levels of awareness*.

Your Key to Reaching Deeper Markets

If Joe segments his market by its present level of *awareness*, he might identify the following groups:

0. At the outside are people who are experiencing hair loss and who may find it an annoyance, but do not consider it a problem.

1. There will be other people for whom hair loss is a problem, but who are not aware that treatments are available.

2. Some people are aware of some solutions, but do not yet know about Joe's Miracle Hair-Gro.

3. Others know about Joe's solution, but do not know how it is any better for them than other products.

4. Some people may be convinced of the benefits of Joe's product, but are not yet ready to commit to buy.

5. Finally, potential customers think that Joe's product is probably the best, and would like to buy it.

I call this progression in awareness *the Awareness Ladder*. Everyone who could possibly be in the market for Joe's product is at one point in this list. Each step represents a distinct market segment. Joe would love to be able to market his product to all of them—and he can. To do so, he will need to use a particular approach for each group.

In order to offer people the right proposition, it is important not only to segment them by their need but also by their level of awareness. There would be little point running an ad for "50% OFF Joe's Miracle Hair-Gro" to a market that is not aware of the product or its benefits. Similarly, an ad (or web page) proclaiming "Finally— A Treatment for Hair Loss!" would not catch the attention of a market that already knows of a dozen products on sale.

Because traditional advertising must carefully optimize the return on every dollar spent on page space, off-line ads must target the right people at the right awareness point with precision.

Again, you have a *huge advantage* marketing on the Web, thanks to the power of multiplicity. You can market to *people at every point of awareness at the same time.*

Understanding the Six Steps of Awareness

The Awareness Ladder (Figure 4-3) can help give you insight into any marketing or selling opportunity. To understand it fully, you need to be aware of a few simple laws about the buying process:

▶ Everyone, at some point, starts at Step 0 (before they realize they have a need).

▶ They can only ever buy from Step 5—when they are convinced by the proposition that the solution will address their needs.

▶ The sequence is logical. Prospects can only go up one step at a time.

▶ So, to achieve a sale, you must get people from their current level of awareness to the top of the ladder, one step at a time.

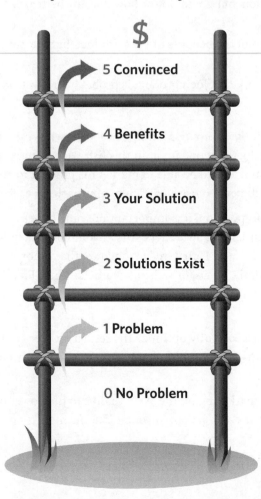

FIGURE 4-3 The Awareness Ladder has a set of simple principles that help you visualize any marketing or selling process.

Where Is Your Market on the Awareness Ladder?

Depending on your marketing environment, your market is likely to be focused around one point on the Awareness Ladder. If you are launching a new product, nobody will be above Step 2. So it is vital to invest in web content that speaks to people at Steps 2 and 1.

By contrast, there are many products that everyone knows about, like Coca-Cola. The bulge is around Steps 4 and 5. When you have a household name, in addition to reinforcing its benefits over the competition, the trick to increasing sales is to get more people to see it as a solution to new problems, or in new contexts.

In Joe's case, nobody knows about his product, so the market from Step 3 and upward is minimal. There may be plenty of people who have baldness and for whom it is not a problem (Step 0). You could expect to find some people at Step 1: those who would be interested in re-growing hair, but are not aware of a solution. And there will also be folks at Step 2, who are aware of some treatments. At this point, Joe can assume his market bulges at all three steps. Keyword research would give him more accurate data.

> **NOTE** *If you were to draw a graph next to the Awareness Ladder that shows the size of your market at each level, where would the bulge be?*

How to Use the Awareness Ladder

The key to getting people to move up the ladder is found in the answers to the following questions:

- ▶ What is their current level of awareness?
- ▶ What are they looking for right now?
- ▶ What are they open to at this point?
- ▶ What will get their attention?
- ▶ What next step can you invite them to take?
- ▶ What do you need to convince them of for the next step to make sense?

Let's look at how Joe could publish content on his web site that speaks directly to different market segments at each step on the Awareness Ladder.

STEP 0: NOT AWARE OF THE NEED

The "no problem" group is the hardest to market to, for two reasons. First, they do not need anything, so you cannot offer them a proposition. Second, because they are not looking for anything, you cannot attract them to your web site through regular marketing methods (such as SEO or pay-per-click advertising). If nobody is looking online for a solution, how can you serve them a page that addresses their nonexistent need?

The problem here is one of education, which is not a cost-effective way to market, because you have to invest in *creating a need* before you can offer a solution. To convince people to buy his product, Joe would first have to find people with a relevant condition and convince them that their condition is undesirable.

But how does he start? How can he reach people via the Web who aren't looking for anything?

The only approach is to *go where they are already,* which means publishing content in existing media that the target market is likely to use. This content would need to discuss the issue of hair loss or baldness and then go on to suggest that it is both undesirable and treatable.

Joe might run a survey of people in a certain age group, and write up the results into an interesting article that suggests that more people would like to regrow hair if they knew there was an affordable and reliable solution.

If you can open up the market this way, it is possible make good profits by being the pioneer brand that first gets into people's awareness. However, note that the education approach has its risks. First, it is costly. Also, by raising awareness of the condition, you can find yourself creating a market for competitors as much as for yourself.

Step 0 is most appealing when you suspect there is a large and untapped market waiting with an unexpressed need. Marketing to Step 0 would be an inefficient way for Joe to drive sales. He will get better results from focusing on the later steps. In his case, it is clear that there is a large enough market for Joe's product that he does not need to be concerned about developing new opportunities at Step 0.

STEP 1: AWARE OF A NEED (BUT NOT AWARE SOLUTIONS EXIST)

The segment on Step 1 is more accessible. These are people who already identify the condition as a problem, and who may be interested in discussing it. They want to learn about what options they may have.

The way for Joe to access this market is to publish articles that specifically match searches for his target "problem" terms (such as "hair thining," "hairloss women," and "regain hair" that were revealed by the keyword research in Chapter 3). Note how those terms are related to the problem only, and do not indicate the awareness of a solution.

Joe would optimize each page for its specific keywords. Each page could start by discussing the issue in general, acknowledge that it is somehow undesirable, and then lead to suggestions that treatments may exist.

Once he introduces the possibility of treatments, the prospects are now at Step 2. If they are interested, they will read on. Joe's "problem" articles could then link on to other articles that discuss what solutions are available.

STEP 2: AWARE OF SOME SOLUTIONS (BUT NOT YOUR SPECIFIC ONE)

At Step 2, people are actively looking for the right solution to their need. They may search for "cure for baldness" or "hair restoration options," for example. Or they may be asking for "best remedy for hair loss" or "which hair thinning treatments really work?"

For this audience, Joe simply creates more articles that match *each of* those specific terms. Of course, these pages already start from the assumption that the condition is both unwanted and treatable, and pick up the story with explorations of the various treatments available. They might cover multiple angles and mention alternative approaches before suggesting Joe's Miracle Hair-Gro as a good option.

After further keyword research, Joe might also find a significant number of people already searching on his competitors' brand names. This could prompt him to publish more articles that compare the effectiveness of different known treatments (and emphasize the particular strengths of his own solution).

When he has introduced Miracle Hair-Gro as a possibility, Joe has moved the visitors from Step 2 to Step 3. He should then link them through to Step 3 content. From this point, Joe's pages may start actively to *sell*.

STEP 3: AWARE OF THE SPECIFIC SOLUTION (BUT NOT OF ITS BENEFITS)

What kind of proposition would Joe present for people who are already aware of his product? Stepping into the shoes of people on the fourth rung, he just needs to ask what they will be searching for online.

Joe will get his answers using keyword research, and also by searching the Web for his product's name. He may come up with searches like "Does Joe's Miracle Hair-Gro Work?" or "Should I Buy Joe's Miracle Hair-Gro?"

The best pages to attract traffic for these questions are focused on the same language. So Joe should create a page called "Does Joe's Miracle Hair-Gro Work?" and another with the title "Should I Buy Joe's Miracle Hair-Gro?"

However they arrive, the job is always to get the visitors safely to the next rung on the Awareness Ladder. In this case, they need to be convinced of the *benefits* of Joe's solution over the competition. So Joe needs to answer the question on the page, giving the visitors evidence that his product does indeed do what it claims.

When he has communicated those benefits, he has moved his prospects up to Step 4.

STEP 4: AWARE OF BENEFITS (BUT NOT CONVINCED)

Simply communicating benefits is not usually enough to compel someone to take action and buy. To stimulate action, Joe must *convince* the visitors that his product will solve their need, and is worth trying. The best way to do this is to build the vision in their mind of how much easier or better their life will be once they enjoy the benefits.

At this point, Joe may encourage visitors to engage with a mental picture of life with a full head of hair. It is not the product, or even the hair, that will compel action. It is the vision of the *lifestyle* that the hair makes possible—the self-respect, the interested looks from women, the admiration of friends at the club, or reaching for a comb for the first time in years.

The visitor wants the fantasy, and the proposition is that Miracle Hair-Gro is the path to achieve that fantasy. So the visitor may become convinced he needs Joe's product. Joe should reinforce his own claims with third-party evidence, in the form of testimonials, press clippings, and "thank you" notes from happy customers.

When the content has done the job of convincing someone (who, let's remember, has arrived *ready to be convinced* that Joe's Miracle Hair-Gro is right for him) that the product is worth a shot, he is now a Step 5 prospect, and all that remains is to close the sale.

STEP 5: CONVINCED AND READY TO BUY

The purpose of Joe's selling page is to make sales. He can assume that people who arrive directly at this page, or this point, must already be convinced that Joe's product is for them. They may have searched for "Buy Joe's Miracle Hair-Gro" or "Hair-Gro best prices," or they may have clicked on an ad that mentions the product in its headline (which also identifies them as Rung 5 prospects).

Now, all Joe has to do is help them over the finish line. (Chapter 9 in Part II is dedicated to showing you how to achieve this final crucial result.)

Why the Old, Narrow Model Fails

Web sites built in the narrow model cannot possibly deal appropriately with every different type of prospect with every type of need at every step of awareness. They simply do not have enough pages.

Consider the structure of Joe's old site, and at what steps each of his pages belong.

Home Page

His home page discussed the issue of "male pattern baldness," and attempted to sell the product. From the search engine's perspective, it is about an issue and about a solution, so the page actually expects people who are aware of an issue and looking for a solution, so they are at Step 2 or Step 3. This is typical for a home page, and it is not wrong.

Because this is Joe's only Step 2/3 page, it has all the responsibility of funneling prospects through toward a sale, and it is unrealistic to expect it to do a good job of that.

FAQs Page

His "Frequently Asked Questions" page contains a range of long-tail content, but it is not focused on any step on the Awareness Ladder. It does not assume any particular level of awareness in arriving visitors, and does not aim to move them to any other level of awareness (other than generally upward).

Pages dedicated to "FAQ" and "Testimonials" really do not belong anywhere on the Awareness Ladder (and, I might argue, do not belong anywhere on your web site). FAQ and testimonial *content*, on the other hand, can be very helpful at several different points on the Awareness Ladder. For example, you could have a set of Q&A dedicated to discussing the merits of different solutions (at Step 2 or Step 3). You could have another set on the subject of benefits (Step 4), and another focused exclusively on resolving people's doubts before they enter their credit card details (Step 5).

I am a great believer in both FAQs and testimonials, but I advocate weaving them into your main content exclusively at points where they can positively support the prospects at their current level of awareness to get to the next level of awareness.

> **NOTE** *Most FAQ and testimonial pages are nothing more than places to file away some of a web site's most powerful content.*

"Buy It Now" Page

Clearly, a page for purchasing belongs at Step 5. It will only be effective if Step 4 has been achieved. If a site introduces a product, makes vague claims, and then expects people to buy without doing the necessary work to convince them, Step 5 will not see a good level of conversions.

Joe's site may only need one purchase page. However, I would like to see *at least one page* dedicated to Step 4. Remember, individual markets with different needs and different language will be best served by content that's dedicated to addressing their needs in their language.

> **NOTE** *If you have a web site today, go through and consider which pages belong at which steps on the Awareness Ladder. If a page does not seem to belong, what is its value? Are there steps missing altogether?*

The New Concentric Model

You see now that a web site that really hopes to reach the widest and deepest range of market segments must present a number of landing pages. These pages should be structured in a way that visitors are channeled efficiently up the Awareness Ladder.

Figure 4-4 illustrates the new landing page funnel in action for one market. Visitors may arrive at any step from 0 to 5. "O" represents an offering or proposition (where Steps 3 and 4 may often be combined).

When you combine all the funnels of landing and feeder pages into one web site structure, it helps to view it as a series of concentric rings (Figure 4-5). Visitors may arrive at any point in any ring. The only objective is to lead each visitor from their entry page to the next step, which is either the next ring up, or to complete one of the site's goals.

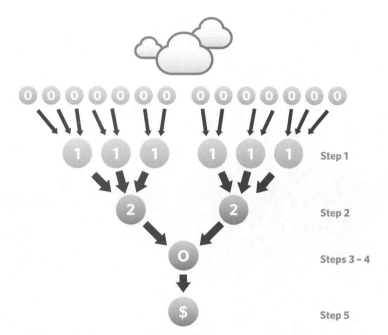

FIGURE 4-4 In the new model, each offering or proposition benefits from a structured funnel of pages that guide prospects up each step of the Awareness Ladder.

Any page may span more than one ring in the concentric model, if it leads the prospect through more than one awareness step.

Step 0 pages, if you have any, will not usually exist on your own site. (I address these more in following chapters.) Their job is to create the sense of a need, and then to lead to content that discusses the problem (Step 1) and maybe also how it may be addressed (Step 2). The pages should then link on to content for the next relevant step. Don't assume that Step 0 content has to be web pages. Because you have to go out to Step 0 prospects, a variety of media may be effective, including banner ads, direct mail, or even print, television, or radio ads.

Step 1 is the domain of "problem pages," which attract traffic looking for more information about problems. Their job is to communicate that solutions exist (Step 2), and may also introduce your solution (Step 3), and then link to the next step.

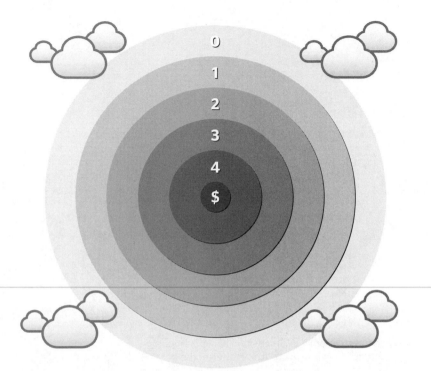

FIGURE 4-5 Bringing all your funnels together into a single model of concentric rings

Step 2 content may include "solution space" pages, which attract people who are searching for solutions, using either generic terms (such as "best ant repellent") or specifically (such as "Brand X ant repellent"). Pages that start with Step 2 content talk about existing solutions, and go on to present your offering as an option to consider (leading to Step 3).

Your home page will usually sit on Steps 2, 3, or both. Its job is to address the needs of people who are either already aware of your services (and need to find out more—Step 3), or those who are looking for services like yours (Step 2).

All your proposition pages belong at Step 3. These pages may also lead people through Step 4, or may send them on to further pages that deal with Step 4.

The purpose of Step 4 content is to convince the prospects that your proposition is the right one for them. To do this, they need to put forward a complete argument that resolves the natural fears and doubts and reinforces the proposition with reassuring evidence.

At Step 5, your only job is to close the sale (whether that is to facilitate a purchase or to get a prospect to make contact via the web site). As you move inward through these funnels, you will need multiple pages that lead into fewer pages. In the center you may only have one shopping cart or contact page. But if all the other steps are complete, your Step 5 should see good results.

Remember that you do not need a massive matrix of landing pages on day one. If you have a web site today, you probably have pages that you will always need, so build around them. Identify redundant pages and make them work. Identify missing steps, and start creating content to fill the gaps. Over time, you can work outward, adding more funnels that address more markets, constantly expanding your reach to explore new market segments.

The Semantic Matrix Method

We often find a range of alternative terms, any of which could be valid for landing pages. In this case, it helps to arrange the search terms into logical groups. The *semantic matrix method* simply means you group related types of meaning together, letting you express the solution in the form of a matrix, which can give you a structure for creating multiple targeted landing pages to cover a range of combinations of search terms.

In Chapter 5, I introduce one of our clients, Bridge Natural Health. They offer a wide range of therapies, each of which can treat a wide range of issues. Obviously, the Bridge site could benefit from a Step 2 page on each service they offer, a Step 1 page for every complaint they can treat, as well as more specialized Step 2 pages on the combination of complaint and treatment (such as "herbal treatments for insomnia").

I might express the range of possible searches in a semantic matrix like this:

$$(Problems) \times (Treatments)$$

I could then do keyword research to identify the most popular problems and the most popular terms describing treatments, which makes the process quicker and simpler.

You can find a useful online tool that I use to "seed" my keyword research at http://textmechanic.com/Permutation-Generator.html. Enter a range of first, second, third words, and so on and the generator will produce a list of every combination. Then, simply copy and paste the list into WordTracker or Market Samurai and see what combinations work. Figure 4-6 shows a semantic matrix I used to set up searches relating to web design agencies.

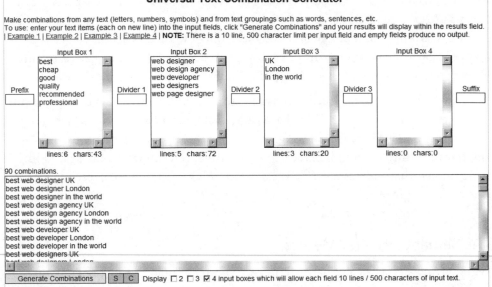

FIGURE 4-6 Use the handy text permutation generator to generate semantically meaningful phrases for keyword analysis.

Generating Large Amounts of Content

When you consider the number of pages this kind of landing page matrix demands, the first reaction is always, "How on earth are we going to generate all that content?"

You will usually find that the knowledge is already there within your organization. You just need to know, first, how to extract it, and then how to turn it into publishable content. There is no escaping the fact that it will take work. (There is also no escaping the fact that the return for that work could be enormous!)

To create landing pages focused on every possible combination would involve a huge amount of work. I suggested that the client hire a journalism student or recent graduate, and to give her the following brief:

▶ Arrange a 30-minute interview with one of our practitioners.

▶ Take a tape recorder. Ask the practitioner to list the ten most common conditions that the therapy treats most effectively.

- For each of the conditions, ask them to spend just a couple of minutes describing:
  - How their treatment works to address the problem
  - Why it is effective
  - Where it is most advisable, and where it may not be suitable
  - (Anonymous) examples of the way it has affected patients' lives
- Then sit down and write up the transcript of the interview, with minor edits as needed to make it suitable for the web site.
- Repeat with the next practitioner.
- After all the practitioners have been interviewed, repeat the whole process, this time with the next most common complaints.

The objective of this exercise is to extract the knowledge that is already in the practitioners' heads with the minimum of work for the expert. The questions should provide a natural and easy-to-read structure that can be translated to text with little editing required, and at relatively low cost.

Include Geographic References

If your offering is relevant to a particular geographic area, it makes sense to include geographic references on all relevant pages. This is most applicable to Step 1 and Step 2 pages, for example, to match people searching for "blocked drain Boston" (Step 1) or "drain clearing service Boston" (Step 2). Because search engines can only match the text you include, make sure you put all place names within the range you serve, including county, state, and neighboring towns or cities.

Here's a good tip for getting multiple place names onto a single page. Remember, there is little point getting visitors if the page does not come across as honest and useful. On one of our clients' sites, tile.co.uk (Figure 4-7), we made sure that every town within realistic driving distance was mentioned on every page of the site, by following the address with "easy distance from..." and a bunch of place names.

On the subject of local searches, it is worth mentioning Facebook advertising. Facebook takes a very different approach than Google AdWords and other major pay-per-click networks, and it can prove far more effective and profitable for certain markets. Whereas AdWords uses only the content of the page to display contextual ads, so it will show ads for hormone replacement treatment to every visitor on a page, even if the visitor is a 20-year-old man.

FIGURE 4-7 Mention all your target geographical locations in the context of "Easy distance from…" or "Less than 30 minutes by car from…"

Facebook, on the other hand, has access to far more powerful data—the profile of the person looking at the page! Facebook knows a lot about most of its members, including their age, location, gender, and job title. So, if you can define your market by these criteria, Facebook may be able to offer you incredibly accurate targeting, resulting in far higher click-through rates, and more profit.

The next chapter presents practical examples and case studies to show you how you can create content that builds a complete web site structure that is totally focused on reaching a wider range of prospects and guiding them to convert to customers.

CHAPTER 5

Working through the Awareness Ladder

In this chapter, I take you through eight real-world examples of sites that I have worked on recently, applying the Awareness Ladder model. These examples show how you can use the Awareness Ladder to create web site strategies for attracting more of the right kinds of visitors, and what to show them when they arrive.

I propose a variety of different strategies, each addressing the current level of awareness of real-world markets, which I estimate using keyword research. The case studies range across various marketing and e-commerce sites. Each one will provide new insights into the process, and may give you new ideas that you can apply to your own web site. At the time of this writing, many of these sites are still in development. The strategies I propose must be implemented over a period of time, which will generate real data that show which approaches are most effective.

You will see that every web site starts from a unique position. Some sites are in competitive markets, where they need to go head-to-head against established competition. Others offer new solutions, for which they need to go out and create markets. Relatively few web sites start with a significant market at Step 3 (already aware of your product). The majority of these case studies have a market that bulges at Steps 1 or 2.

Depending on the composition and maturity of your market, you will need to consider the right tactics for reaching the audience.

Save the Pixel

"Save the Pixel" is my first book, published as an ebook in January 2008. Now in its second edition, it teaches web site owners and designers how to use the principles of simple web design. The web site is currently a single sales page (see Figure 5-1), and does not attract a significant amount of search traffic.

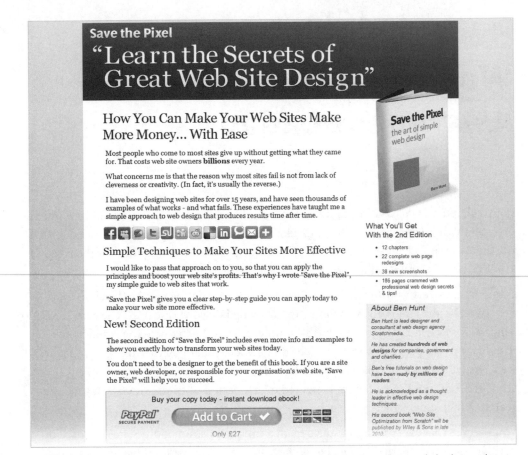

FIGURE 5-1 "Save the Pixel" currently has a single sales page, which means it can only be focused on one market.

Problem: Most Obvious Market Is Small

The most obvious key phrase is "web design ebook." However, the market is not very attractive. Figure 5-2 shows the keyword analysis. (The final column is calculated from the SEO Traffic divided by the Title Competition squared. It has also been multiplied by ten million to show meaningful numbers.)

The obvious target phrase "web design ebook" might deliver 75 visits per day with a top-place search ranking, but it is hotly contested with more than 50,000 competing pages. A few minor phrases, such as "web designing ebook," "website design ebook," and "web design ebook download," might deliver more than 10 visits per day each, but still have competition numbering in the thousands.

	SEO Traffic (Broad)	Title Comp	SEOT/TC2
free ebook for web design	1.68	870	22.2
web designer ebook	2.94	2390	5.15
web design for dummies ebook	0.84	1310	4.89
website design ebooks	2.52	2700	3.46
web designing ebook	18.06	7400	3.3
web design e books	2.94	3480	2.43
free web design ebook	13.86	8360	1.98
web design e book	6.72	6340	1.67
website design ebook	10.08	8230	1.49
web design ebook download	10.08	8510	1.39
web design handbook	18.06	19800	0.46
business ebook	835.38	144000	0.4
web design ebooks	18.06	24200	0.31
web design ebook	74.76	50900	0.29
web development ebook	39.9	95800	0.04
web design tutorials	374.22	379000	0.03
web design books	167.16	549000	0.01

FIGURE 5-2 These search terms reveal no attractive search markets.

It might be worth competing for a few of these terms, but I would also look elsewhere for more, easier traffic. These search terms are Step 3 terms (people searching for the same type of solution as we offer). The lower awareness steps often have much bigger markets. The question is, what are they looking for?

Ask, Where Is the Market?

The market bulges around Steps 1 and 2 (as with most of the sites in this list, and probably yours too). The Step 1 market wants to make better web sites, but does not know where to start. The Step 2 group is already aware of existing solutions, such as books, courses, and online tutorials.

Think Laterally to Uncover Alternative Needs

If people are not searching for the most obvious phrase, what are they looking for? Figure 5-3 shows more keyword analysis, this time for phrases associated with learning web design. In this example, terms with competition of under ten thousand can deliver far more traffic than the "web design ebook" market. "Learn web design" stands out, because it is relevant to the offering, has potential traffic of 374, yet only 4,690 competing pages.

	SEO Traffic (Broad)	Title Comp	SEOT/TC2
online web design course	49.56	345	4163.83
learn web design	374.22	4690	170.13
web design classes	204.54	4030	125.94
web design courses	559.44	9570	61.08
learn web design online	13.86	3640	10.46
web design training	306.6	18200	9.26
web design training course	18.06	10700	1.58
web design course	456.96	64500	1.1
website design training	74.76	42100	0.42

FIGURE 5-3 Far more people are searching for ways to help them learn web design.

Some basic keyword research combined with a bit of lateral thinking can help you target potentially far more profitable segments. In this case, I would explore a range of related terms, such as "learn to be a web designer" and "how to make better web sites." The time is very well spent. Someone searching for an online web design course could certainly be persuaded to buy a low-cost ebook.

Some of these terms are Step 1, such as "learn web design." Others are Step 2, like "web design training course." Both types of visitors will need to be persuaded that this particular solution could meet their needs. This will be easier to achieve with different landing pages targeted to each group.

▶ The Step 1 visitors could be told that the best way to learn how to make effective web sites is through worked examples and case studies.

▶ The Step 2 visitors need to be steered away from their initial goal. A visitor coming to my "web design course" page could be met with a message saying that most courses are both expensive and of limited value because they are not taught by professional practitioners.

▶ For each group, I would find the best way to introduce the ebook as a must-have solution, and explain all the value they will get (taking them to Step 3 then 4), then tell them the book will give them value they cannot get elsewhere and reinforce the claims with real testimonials (Step 5, building the belief that they *need* this solution).

Bridge Natural Health

Bridge Natural Health provides a wide range of therapies at its center in Derby, England. The center delivers a wide range of treatments, including conventional and alternative therapies, every one of which can be applied to a number of conditions or complaints. This is a classic example of where the narrow approach is insufficient, and how the multiplicity method can help a site achieve explosive growth.

Problem: Marketing a Diverse Range of Solutions

Clearly, if the site focuses on the common denominator—"natural health," "remedies," "treatments," and so on—it will only address people looking for the generic term, which has to be a tiny minority of the number of people out there who have a real problem and are looking for a real solution. People searching on "natural health" may not even be in the market at all; they could be researching the area in general!

Where Is the Bulge in the Market?

Again, we find a rich seam at Steps 1 and 2: people who know they have a problem, and either do not know how to get it treated (Step 1), or do not know the best way to get it treated (Step 2).

There may also be a significant market at Step 0: people who are living with a physical or emotional condition and for whom it is not a complaint but an accepted fact of life. It may be possible to reach out to this market by publishing stories in the local press of people who have found they can sleep better or live more comfortably after years of living with some condition.

Semantic Patterns

The more developed markets are at Step 1 and 2, so I would always start there. They have a present complaint, so it is far easier to sell a solution.

In situations of this type, it is common to see a page that lists all the problems that a single solution may address; for example, a page on hypnotherapy with a long bulleted list of the commonly treated conditions. On the plus side, the page will at least feature in the results "hypnotherapy for sleep disorders," because it mentions both terms on the page. However, if its relevance is spread across dozens of conditions, the page will not be very competitive for any of the terms. Plus, it will make for very dry reading, unlikely to convert any but the most determined or desperate visitor.

When you have multiple solutions and multiple problems together, the answer is, of course, to turn to multiplicity. Yes, you need a page about hypnotherapy. But you need a page about "hypnotherapy for sleep disorders," as well as a page about "hypnotherapy for stopping smoking." These pages do not need to be very long; they are addressing Step 3 visitors, who know their problem and have expressed an interest in a specific type of solution. So their job is to say, "Yes, you are in the right place. Here is just the solution you're looking for. It gets very good results, it's in your area, it's affordable, and here's how to book."

When I work through this kind of challenge with a client's site, I would use the semantic matrix method I introduced in Chapter 4 with a matrix of the form:

(Problems?) × (Solutions?) × (Location)

This indicates that the client could create landing pages that either address a either particular problem, or discuss a solution or treatment, or both. And, because the market for treatments is local, they should all mention the geographic locality. Every city has a hypnotherapist, an osteopath, and an acupuncturist, so no one is likely to travel very far for treatment. There is no point attracting traffic from outside the geographic range.

This would generate a wide range of landing pages, including:

▶ Acupuncture Derby (a Step 2 page, which would also mention the symptoms that can be treated with the solution)

▶ Back pain Derby (a Step 1 page, which would also mention all the solutions the center can offer to address the problem)

▶ Acupuncture for back pain Derby (also a Step 2 page, which is linked to from both the previous pages)

Although keyword research shows that very few specific searches include the local place name, I would ensure that all relevant locations within the likely range are present on every page, to match future long-tail local searches.

If Bridge Natural Health finds that the majority of its clients for certain issues or treatments fall into certain gender and age brackets, Facebook advertising would let it target different custom-written ads directly at the core demographic for that complaint-treatment combination. It can also target the ads at a precise geographic area.

Muazo

Muazo.co.uk is an e-commerce site that sells a relatively small range of high-value designer items for men, including wallets, headphones, and sunglasses. The site aims to be the exclusive supplier in the UK. As you can see on the original home page shown in Figure 5-4, the site is primarily visual. This means it has little text content that search engines can use to match pages to prospects' searches.

Problem: Short Lifespan Products

The life cycle of the products Muazo offers is limited. As a first-mover vendor, there is always a risk of the products getting picked up by other sites, and the exclusivity is lost. Lines are frequently replaced after a few months. From an SEO perspective, this raises a significant problem. A page dedicated to a particular line of products will eventually disappear, so the value of in-bound links will be greatly reduced.

FIGURE 5-4 The Muazo site is style-led but is short on content for search engines.

Muazo needed a content strategy that could help the site build incremental value for search engines, and which could also attract more customers to buy the current products.

Where Is the Market on the Awareness Ladder?

The existing market is entirely Step 3 to Step 4: people who know the specific brand they want to buy. Because the products are quite exclusive, the site can attract people who are actively searching for somewhere to buy them. However, by definition, the markets for these exclusive items are also quite small.

There is often a lot of business to be found at Step 2 and Step 1. So I will always ask what the up-stream markets could be looking for.

Strategy: Permanent Landing Pages

I considered what people who have a problem for which one of Muazo's exclusive products may be looking for. What is their *immediate need*?

I investigated a range of possible search terms, including the more generic "birthday gifts for guys" (a Step 1 phrase, looking for initial ideas), and terms including "sunglasses" and "headphones" (which are more like Step 3).

Figure 5-5 shows my keyword analysis for the "gifts for guys" and "headphones, wallets, and sunglasses" segments, using the same method as before. There are several attractive terms, offering useful traffic with relatively low competition.

	SEO Traffic (Broad)	Title Comp	SEOT/TC2			SEO Traffic (Broad)	Title Comp	SEOT/TC2
birthday gifts for guys	49.56	2480	80.58		unusual eyewear	0.84	52	3106.51
unique gift for boyfriend	13.86	1380	72.78		interesting wallets	1.68	111	1363.53
birthday gifts for brother	12.18	1460	57.14		unusual wallets	6.72	227	1304.12
unique gifts for guys	13.86	1710	47.4		coolest wallets	6.72	310	699.27
birthday gift for boyfriend	136.5	6040	37.42		funky eyewear	6.72	470	304.21
unique gift for man	22.26	2590	33.18		coolest eyewear	0.84	170	290.66
best gift for boyfriend	49.56	3870	33.09		unusual headphones	0.84	201	207.92
cool gifts for him	12.18	2000	30.45		coolest shades	3.78	483	162.03
unique presents for men	5.46	1350	29.96		funky headphones	26.04	1650	95.65
best gifts for him	1021.86	19200	27.72		coolest headphones	13.86	1250	88.7
best gift for man	39.9	4060	24.21		unusual sunglasses	6.72	1080	57.61
birthday gifts for dad	111.72	7680	18.94		interesting sunglasses	1.68	548	55.94
birthday gift for man	60.9	5860	17.73		unusual shades	13.86	1620	52.81
unusual gifts for him	18.06	3460	15.09		funky shades	39.9	2850	49.12
cool gifts for dad	18.06	4190	10.29		funky wallet	39.9	3220	38.48
birthday presents for him	39.9	6590	9.19		cool wallets	167.16	7000	34.11
unusual gifts for men	111.72	11200	8.91		coolest sunglasses	26.04	3070	27.63
unique gifts for dad	22.26	6410	5.42		stylish headphones	60.9	7170	11.85
birthday gifts for men	559.44	43300	2.98		stylish wallets	12.18	3420	10.41
best gifts for men	204.54	28300	2.55		cool headphones	167.16	14300	8.17
best gifts for dad	26.04	13600	1.41		unique wallets	49.56	7850	8.04
unique gifts for him	74.76	39800	0.47		stylish shades	6.72	3130	6.86
birthday gifts for him	204.54	66000	0.47		funky sunglasses	111.72	13400	6.22
unique gifts for men	167.16	62400	0.43		unique headphones	13.86	6410	3.37
cool gifts for men	39.9	56700	0.12		birthday gift's	0.84	1640	3.12

FIGURE 5-5 Investigating search markets lower down the Awareness Ladder produced valuable target terms.

My theory was that we should create a set of permanent landing pages on the Muazo site, one for each targeted theme, which would in turn link through to the current offerings within the scope of the theme. I selected "best birthday gifts for guys," "funky headphones," and "unique wallets" as my titles for an initial set of test pages.

I created these pages with editorial content that addressed the immediate need and interest of the respective visitor, and furnished them with descriptive text, images, and links to the current lines, as shown in Figure 5-6.

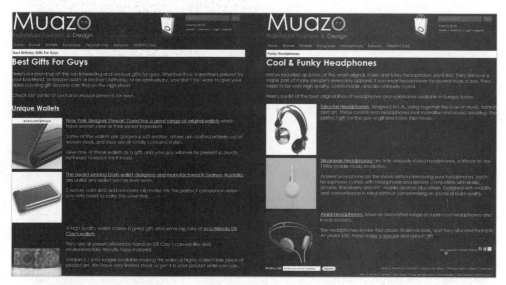

FIGURE 5-6 Simple editorial-style landing pages for Muazo.co.uk

I then spent just a few hours on some preliminary link-building. The important factor is that links to these permanent pages can *persist indefinitely*, plus the page the visitor lands on should always be able to fulfill the promise of the link. Muazo will always be able to offer advice on the best gift for the guy in your life, even if it changes its product line-up completely.

After a couple of months, we started to see some interesting results from the experiment. Even with minimal link-building activity, 10% of the site's traffic now arrives via one of the four static pages I created.

The "funky headphones" page is the second busiest landing page on the site, after the home page, responsible for over 5% of all visits (which underlines the importance of good keyword research). At the time of writing, this page has a #6 ranking on Google.co.uk. It was the landing page for 58 visits from organic search, only one less search visitor than the site's home page got.

By adding a further 35 pages, each targeting a different phrase, Muazo's gravitational pull would increase to the point where it should more than double its initial traffic.

And the value of these persistent pages could continue to build indefinitely into the future.

Imagic2015

Christophe Mely has one of the rarest jobs in France. He is an "écrivain public"—literally a scribe. Several hundred years ago, when most of the population was illiterate, if you needed to send a written message, you would visit someone like Christophe. Today, he offers a range of professional writing and administration services.

Problem: Selling Your Services When No One Knows You Exist

Christophe's previous web site had a page that listed his services, which range from writing legal letters to love letters and typing services. As we know, combining multiple subjects on one page does not do a good job of topping the search engines in any of them. Again, the way forward lies in multiplicity.

The problem for this modern-day scribe is that he is one of the last few of his kind. Most people in France won't know what the term means, and it certainly won't be the first thing that pops into their mind when they hit Google.fr. (Christophe has had a web site online for a few years, but is not aware that it has generated even one lead!)

Where Is the Market?

We can discount Step 3 upwards altogether for Christophe, because practically nobody knows his profession still exists. His markets will mostly be stuck at Steps 0 and 1. They don't know of any available solutions to help them with their current challenge, so they are probably turning to the Web to seek guidance.

> **NOTE** *Always look first at the highest step on the Awareness Ladder where you know there is a market, and which you don't currently address.*

Starting at Step 1, then, what questions are present in the minds of enough people for it to be worth marketing to them as a distinct group? Because the site will be in French, in this case, I did not carry out keyword research. Instead, I interviewed

Christophe about what people actually ask him for. What are they trying to achieve, and what help do they need in order to achieve it?

Apply a Semantic Matrix

Here is another example where semantic matrix should come in useful. The pattern in this case would seem to be:

(Help with...) × (Type of document)

In the "Help with..." category, I would include:

- ▶ "How to write..."
- ▶ "Correct way to..."
- ▶ "Format for..."
- ▶ "Tips for writing..."

Christophe knows the types of documents he is called upon to write, so all we had to do was create a set of landing pages that matched as wide a range of the queries as possible.

Because the "how to" items have similar meanings, to create a page for each may result in several very similar pages. This is not necessarily a problem provided the market for that search term is big enough (as shown by keyword research), and you have the resources to write unique content. Provided the competition is not too high, it may be sufficient to include all the combinations on a page dedicated to the document type, in other words, to include "how to write a love letter," plus "tips for writing love letters" and so on on the same page.

> **NOTE** *Google does not appreciate duplicate content. It will tend to ignore newer versions it finds, and list only the "original."*

Fortunately, our man is precisely the right person to create this content. He knows his subjects inside out, and he can type like a demon. Because they are directed at Step 1 audiences, the pages that Christophe creates should all follow a similar pattern:

- ▶ Stress the importance of the correct form or manner of the document in question.
- ▶ Mention the potential impact of doing it wrong (creating pressure).

▶ Describe what a good example of the document should do, mention what it should include, and give some examples or general advice. This will both reinforce the need to do it right and also prove the author's expertise in the area.

▶ If the content creates the impression that there are further nuances to the art of writing a successful document of this type, it will emphasize the need to get specific professional help.

▶ Introduce Christophe, the friendly guy who is helping teach you about this area, and say that he helps people do this kind of thing successfully. This brings the visitor to Step 3.

▶ The page should then include (or link to) Step 4 content, which explains the reasons why it really pays to hire the professional.

▶ Finally, a call to action (Step 5) invites the visitor to get in touch with Christophe to discuss how he can help.

Me2Solar

Me2Solar is a new brand of portable solar chargers that can recharge portable electronic devices. They come in various sizes suitable for a range of uses.

The smaller models are suitable for business travelers, who want to be able to recharge their cell phones, satellite navigation systems, and PDAs while traveling, as well as families going on vacation, who can recharge their phones, GPS devices , and portable games consoles, without having to carry a number of adapters and heavy chargers.

Larger models are designed for adventurers and explorers, who can charge satellite phones and other vital equipment.

The web site projects the brand's qualities of modern technology combined with smart design and ease of use, as shown in Figure 5-7.

Using Content Strategy to Differentiate Benefits

Similar products are available on the market, but Me2Solar's products have advantages over competitors' offerings, being very lightweight, flexible, and durable. This means its prices are slightly higher, so it needs to emphasize its benefits over the competition.

FIGURE 5-7 Our design for Me2Solar's product pages reflect the high quality and high-tech properties of the brand.

Where Is the Awareness Bulge?

There will be a significant market at Step 0: people who accept the way things are, unaware that there exist products that could make their lives easier.

At Step 1 are those who are aware of the inconvenience of having to carry power chargers and adapters, or the risk of being left without power. This is likely to be a good-sized market.

Keyword research shows there is also a good-sized market at Step 2, as shown in Figure 5-8. These are adventurers and technology-savvy users who are already aware of this new technology, and are looking for the right model, particularly for cell phone charging.

	SEO Traffic (Broad)	Title Comp	SEOT/TC2
solar powered mobile phone charger	12.18	143	5956.28
solar powered cell phone charger	22.26	243	3769.75
solar cell phone chargers	26.04	330	2391.18
solar powered phone charger	60.9	519	2260.91
emergency mobile phone charger	74.76	578	2237.76
solar powered mobile charger	10.08	278	1304.28
solar power cell phone	26.04	658	601.44
portable solar panel charger	10.08	461	474.31
portable cell phone charger	91.14	1670	326.8
solar power cell phone charger	6.72	504	264.55
solar cell phone charger	204.54	3480	168.9
solar power phone charger	22.26	1240	144.77
sunsei 150	7.98	816	119.85
emergency cell phone charger	136.5	3510	110.79
solar electric fence	136.5	3810	94.03
portable solar cells	5.46	873	71.64
foldable solar panels	6.72	982	69.69
portable solar power charger	12.18	1440	58.74
voltaic solar panels	13.86	1630	52.17
portable solar generator	91.14	4700	41.26
flexible solar panels	111.72	5420	38.03
foldable solar panel	49.56	3640	37.4
solar mobile phone charger	91.14	5030	36.02
portable solar generators	22.26	2680	30.99
portable solar panels	136.5	7010	27.78
small solar panel	111.72	7470	20.02
flexible solar panel	111.72	7470	20.02
solar phone chargers	74.76	6890	15.75
solar car charger	204.54	12600	12.88
mini solar panel	33.18	5450	11.17
solar powered chargers	60.9	8270	8.9
portable solar panel	136.5	13000	8.08

FIGURE 5-8 Solar charging for cell phones is a very attractive search market.

How to Market to the Various Groups

For the Step 2 market, the objective is simply to present the appropriate Me2Solar product, and to provide information that allows the prospect to compare the product with alternatives, positioning the benefits and value for money.

Group tests are a simple way to show head-to-head comparisons. You can publish your own comparisons of the features of your product and the competition's offerings. These tests are a good way to feature competitors' brand names with comparison keywords, such as "better," "best," and "most reliable" on a page that also offers visitors valuable insight.

NOTE *It can also be good PR to submit your offerings to relevant blog and magazine sites for purposes of tests, particularly where you have a competitive advantage and the product is novel and newsworthy.*

At Step 1, does your research indicate that people are searching on particular problems? If so, target those problems directly. I would start by looking for phrases that indicate looking for a solution, such as "How can I?" "How to..." or "Best way to..." and either create landing pages for these terms (if the market and competition are stronger), or perhaps add Q&A content to existing pages that literally mention a number of these exact phrases.

For Step 0, you have to go out to the market. Your task is to let people know that something is possible that they are not aware is possible. If it is not in the general consciousness, you can often make your announcement into news.

Competitions are a time-honored way to get your offering noticed by an unaware market. Offering a free product to a publication (online or offline) as a competition prize is a win all around:

- ▶ The publication gets to show something that will attract their readers' attention.
- ▶ The readers get news about something that they can visualize using.
- ▶ You get exposure.
- ▶ You should also be able to capture the contact details of every respondent, giving you an instant mailing list of prospects who were probably previously unaware of your product and *have just jumped from Step 0 right up to Step 3 or 4.*

Ville & Company

Ville & Company is a small consulting firm based in London, which has a special focus on public sector clients. Its market is dominated by a small number of large consultancies, so it should not attempt to compete on the same terms as the big players. Ville has an extremely strong offering for its target market, being more experienced, more personal, more flexible, and more affordable than the large competitors.

Its home page (see Figure 5-9) emphasizes its positioning, focusing on real people, to distinguish the company from large, faceless consulting firms.

Problem: Competing without Going Head-On

The market's mind-set is conditioned by the status quo. Until they are aware of the existence of firms like Ville & Co., prospects are likely to assume that they only have a choice of "the big five." In this case, they are unlikely to be searching for "more affordable alternative to Brand X." How do you reach out to people who are not looking for what you offer?

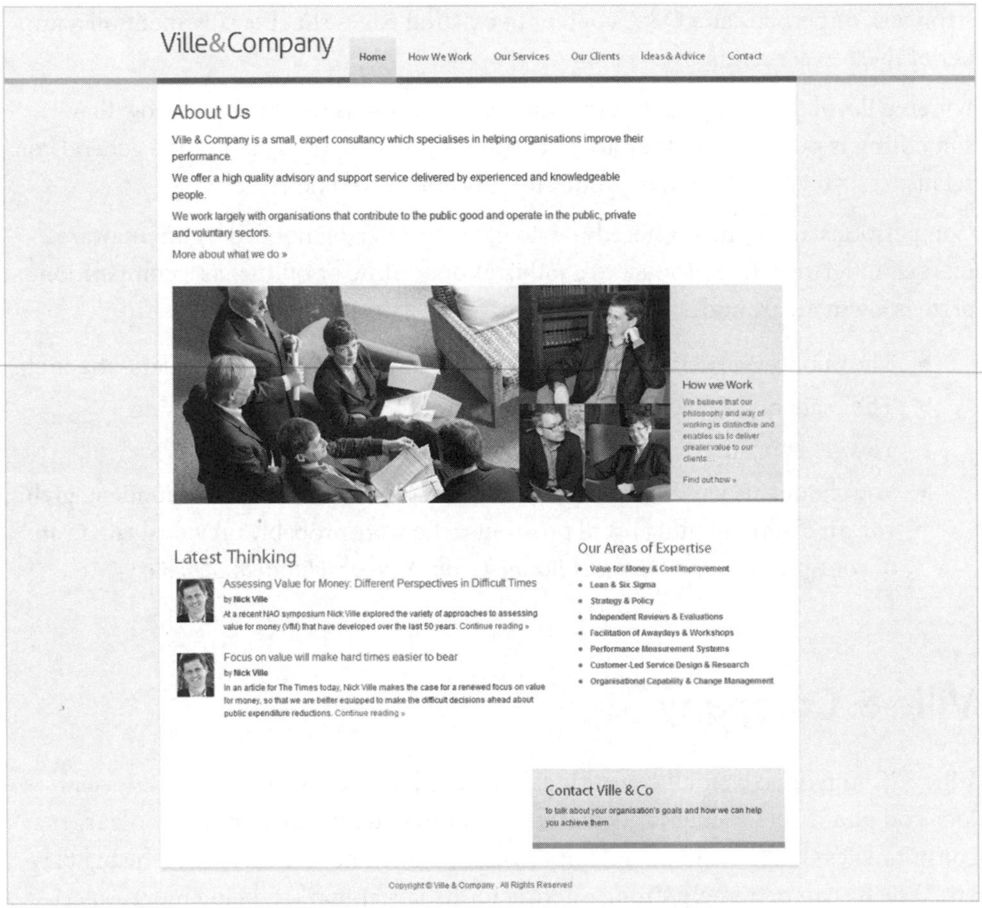

FIGURE 5-9 Ville & Company's web site is all about people.

Where Is the Market?

If we accept the context of inquiry as "right consulting firm to hire," the market could be at Step 2. For any given problem, prospects are all aware of the massive consulting firms, but not aware of Ville & Co.'s particular offering.

However, if we broaden the scope to "a strategic or organizational challenge," and remove the context of "consulting firm required," the market shifts. Simply by discounting the competition as viable solutions in the prospects' minds, they move from Step 2 to Step 1: aware of the problem but *no* likely solutions.

A Game-Changing Strategy

In any no-win game situation, the ideal solution is to *change the game*. In this case, we should ignore the direct comparison with the competition, and change the question. If prospects are not actively looking for alternatives to the big players, what are they looking for?

They are looking for help with a wide range of problems, which may originate with policy, compliance, or with management difficulties.

With a domain this broad, it seems absurd to undertake keyword research. Even if you did find the historical search data show a handful of people searching on a particular topic, it would not be worth tailoring content strategy to target those individual search phrases. For a consulting firm, which works with high-level organizational intelligence, any output must be of a high value, which takes time and energy. A different approach is required.

Going back to the client's *positioning*, how do they intend to distinguish themselves from the competition in the prospect's mind? They are more flexible, more approachable, and more human. The ideal content strategy should resonate with those brand values. And, because it is not possible to address the full breadth of the problem domain, they need to turn the problem on its side and look for a *qualitative differentiator*.

My suggested strategy is to focus on the issues that are *new*, whatever is about to emerge as the next big challenge for Ville & Company's market. As part of its on-going customer care, Ville's consultants should always be listening for what issues are *about to become important*.

They should quickly get to work on a briefing paper that is targeted at the senior executives, permanent secretaries, and government ministers that make up their market. The paper should give these individuals useful advance warning of what is about to come over the horizon.

The paper should be distributed as early as possible through any appropriate channels. Ville & Co.'s target market is actually quite a small community, focused in an area of only a few square miles of London.

Providing valuable context-sensitive information in this way delivers several advantages:

- ▶ It delivers real value, which gets attention.
- ▶ It implicitly gives evidence of the expertise of the authors, positioning them as experts.
- ▶ It builds trust. Anyone who has so much knowledge and expertise that they can afford to give such valuable strategic intelligence away must have huge reserves.
- ▶ It reinforces all the brand values: personal, flexible, fast-moving, high integrity, and so on.
- ▶ All of which keeps the Ville & Company brand present in the mind of the target prospect, without having to sell at all.

Effectively, Ville is creating Step 0 content, which notifies people about problems they don't even have yet, and propelling the prospect right through the steps up to Step 4: aware of the benefits available. In doing this, Ville is raising the prospect's awareness of their offerings and benefits, which means that when a future problem emerges, the prospect may already be at Step 4 (in the context of "Ville as the solution").

When the next strategic headache comes along, the hope is that these individuals will think "Ville" before they think "big-ticket consulting firm." All without selling, and by creating a relatively small amount of content (which will, of course, be published on the company web site).

> **NOTE** *Get in first. If you can be the first to publish on a particular topic online, you can achieve an unassailable position. The very first article, if it is insightful, newsworthy, and valuable, will start a conversation. Subsequent articles and blog posts will reference the original article, as will later posts. So, as soon as people start searching on the term in any numbers, your initial post will be at number one and will always be seen as authoritative. It will get more traffic, which gets it more links, closing out any competition.*

Bolwell RV

Bolwell is an Australian company that started out making sports cars in the 1970s. It has gone on to develop solutions in fiberglass and composite materials for a range of products, from truck bodies to aerospace.

Its newest venture is a high-tech caravan (as they are known in Australia), which fundamentally reinvents the idea of how caravans are built and how they work. Its "Edge RV" is more aerodynamic, tougher, stronger, and cleverer than other products on the market, being constructed of bonded composites like carbon fiber, without the use of screws and rivets.

Twin Challenges: New Brand and New Direction

Bolwell is faced with two distinct problems in its online marketing. First, nobody is searching for its brand name, because it is new to the sector. Second, its product is so revolutionary that it does not fit the questions people are asking the search engines today.

By definition, there cannot be a significant market looking for something if that thing is truly new. If they were, the existing manufacturers would have picked up on the opportunity by now (if they had the technology).

A Brand New Market

The market for the Edge RV is at Step 0 in one sense. They are familiar with other caravan designs, and accept that the current state of the art is the way it is. So, in a "which caravan shall I buy?" context, they may be at Step 2. But taking the context of the completely new solution the Edge offers, the market is totally fresh. Acceptance of the current offerings on the market means there is little by way of a problem.

Keyword analysis validates this perspective. As Figure 5-10 shows, there is a good range of appealing keywords (limited to the local search market). But most of the terms refer to existing alternative designs or competitors. People are searching for what they already know is out there.

Approach for a Step 0 Market

Another hurdle that Bolwell's campaign will need to face is the fact that it has a brand new domain name. Although it seems that the market is relatively uncompetitive, many of its competitors' sites are around ten years old and are likely to have a large number of inbound links, which gives them a position that is difficult to attack.

One valid tactic in this type of situation is to go for the competitors' brand names and alternative caravan styles, and I recommended that the site do this. Working to a tight launch deadline, the initial marketing site will go live with an FAQ page. The

FAQ content can focus on comparing the Edge's effectiveness and suitability against alternative recreation solutions already on the market.

	SEO Traffic (Broad)	Title Comp	SEOT/TC2
caravan trader australia	2.52	22	52066.12
caravansforsale	6.72	44	34710.74
avan caravans	60.9	227	11818.59
roadstar caravans	39.9	189	11169.9
caravans millard	60.9	241	10485.36
jayco swan	306.6	592	8748.4
tray top campers	12.18	128	7434.08
fifth wheelers	49.56	267	6951.98
jayco expanda	306.6	672	6789.43
5th wheel caravans	5.46	96	5924.48
pop top caravan	1518.72	1660	5511.39
5th wheelers	74.76	379	5204.64
caravans pop top	683.34	1190	4825.51
caravans viscount	74.76	407	4513.16
caravans regal	18.06	228	3474.15
jayco camper trailers	39.9	369	2930.35
caravans jayco	683.34	1620	2603.8
caravans coromal	136.5	795	2159.72
off road caravan	204.54	1120	1630.58
penguin jayco	49.56	556	1603.18
roadstar caravan	26.04	426	1434.9
caravans forsale	4.62	185	1349.89
jayco heritage	39.9	586	1161.92
jayco vans	22.26	454	1079.97
campervan sales	39.9	682	857.84
jayco caravan	559.44	2560	853.64
coromal caravan	91.14	1050	826.67
slide on caravan	33.18	721	638.27

FIGURE 5-10 Keyword research results around "caravan Australia."

One of our favored techniques for capturing new search-friendly content is to include a "Did we answer your question?" form on content pages, as shown in Figure 5-11. If visitors do not find what they are looking for, they can enter their question, which can then be published in the Q&A, preferably on the same page. This technique generates excellent content because it captures real people's questions in their own language.

However, the page will never compete on a keyword against a caravan or motorhome retailer who has a page that's ten years old and filled with brand name after brand name. So this tactic will not win the game. And when you can't win the game, you change the rules! I proposed a three-pronged strategy.

USING OFF-SITE ADVERTISING

Plain old-fashioned banner ads have had bad press since more targeted methods have come along. Because banner ads give you a crude blanket approach, the *CPM* (cost per thousand impressions) prices have dropped significantly from their peak in the late 1990s.

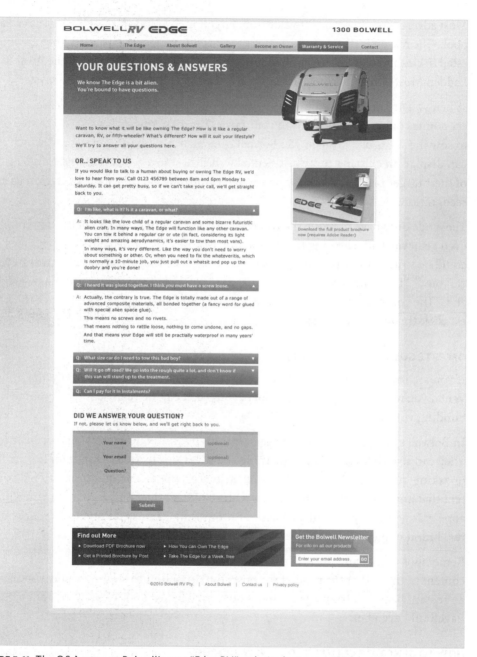

FIGURE 5-11 The Q&A page on Bolwell's new "Edge RV" web site features a "Did we answer your question?" form for capturing visitors' immediate concerns.

Most advertisers can get better value from targeting their ads through AdWords or Facebook. The reason is that most advertisers are playing at Step 2 and above. They are interested in closing sales, so they go for the hottest leads, which are higher up the Awareness Ladder. Most don't know how to work with Step 1, and Step 0 is a complete mystery.

When you are marketing a totally new solution at Step 0, as in Bolwell's case, the economics of banner ads turns in your favor. The only job you have to do at Step 0 is to sow the seeds of a problem. So Bolwell can create a range of banner ads, which it can display on existing caravan-oriented web sites at low cost, right under the noses of their target market. With a wide enough campaign, their brand can start to gain recognition.

These ads only have to pique the reader's interest, enough to get a click. They could even get away with showing the Edge's futuristic design. Other classic approaches could be to announce the new benefits, such as "The most aerodynamic caravan you can buy," "Tow with a regular 4-cylinder car," or "Voted as most exciting new product at…" The company can test a range of appeals and figure out which produce the highest click-through rates.

OFF-SITE GUERRILLA MARKETING

If you are investing in link-building activity, it pays to kill two birds with one stone. When you're marketing a new product at Step 0, it can be really easy to combine link-building with PR.

In Bolwell's case, it has a good range of forums dedicated to recreational caravanning. They can search for people complaining about various features (or lack of features), or asking questions about suitability of various products, and add promotional content that announces the revolutionary feature of the Edge. This forum content should appear as genuinely helpful, not salesy. Enthusiasm is fine, as is posting under your real brand name, as long as you post with integrity.

Remember that forum posts can be many years old, and it is easy to add your own content to the end of the page. If the post contains a link to your own site, you have an instant backlink from a page that is both established and relevant. If it has a good PageRank, even better.

HOW TO GENERATE CONTENT FOR A NEW PRODUCT

As previously mentioned, testimonials and FAQs can provide rich content for the long tail, as well as helping target specific problem or "how to" phrases. The Edge site will use a single FAQ page at launch, which should probably propagate across other pages as the body of content grows.

Testimonials also provide valuable third-party validation, which is particularly useful at Step 4, when you want to convince someone to believe in the advantages of your solution. But, with a brand new product, Bolwell has no list of previous customers that it can mine for web site content. Where can it source testimonial-type content?

What I advised they do is set up a video booth at the product's launch event (which is at a large trade show). People will get their first glimpse of this space-age caravan, and will be able to see its unique design and ingenious storage solutions.

At that moment of excitement, the manufacturer should whisk the prospect in front of a video camera and get an authentic reaction to seeing the product in the flesh. Asking a few short questions, such as "Do you own a caravan now?" "What model is it?" and "What do you think of the new Edge?" would also be beneficial.

Bolwell can then post these short clips to YouTube (www.youtube.com/), and ensure they are tagged with the new brand, as well as with any other brand names or relevant keywords mentioned in the clip.

NOTE *Video content is far easier to consume than text content. A series of short clips about a new product can fuel a strong emotional response. At the time of writing, YouTube is the #2 most searched search engine in the world, after Google, but has a tiny fraction of the database. Add to this the fact that Google has started posting YouTube video results on the first page of its regular results, and it makes an extremely powerful marketing channel (that is currently underused).*

EasySpeedy

EasySpeedy provides high-quality unmanaged hosting services at its secure datacenter in Copenhagen, Denmark. Its major differentiator is that it can let customers combine *any combination of* dedicated servers and cloud servers on a fast, unencrypted private network. Figure 5-12 shows our home page design, which clearly pushes the flexibility of the service and the "myPrivateNetwork" sub-brand.

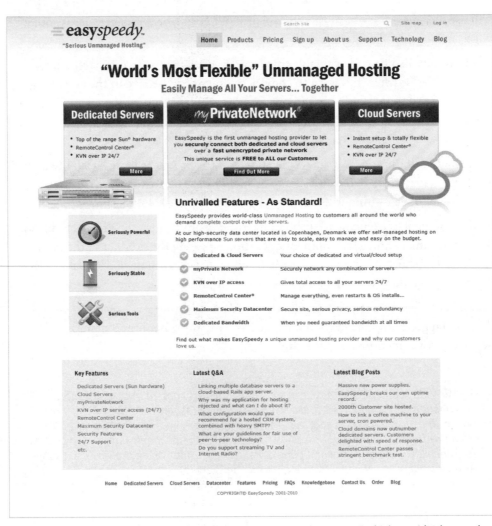

FIGURE 5-12 EasySpeedy's home page design features a "super footer nav," which provides keyword-rich site-wide links to some of the site's landing pages.

Differentiating in a Crowded Market

Hosting is a very busy marketplace, so it is critical to differentiate, both when you are fishing for traffic, and also to reinforce your benefits once they arrive. EasySpeedy has a clear distinguishing feature in that it offers unmanaged hosting only, so that needs to be foremost in its content strategy.

The keyword research, shown in Figure 5-13, reveals a wide range of viable terms, most with competition in the thousands. Most customers know exactly what they are looking for, which means the market bulges at Step 2. The task at Step 2 is to introduce your service and to move on quickly to differentiate your benefits.

Nobody is looking for EasySpeedy's particular strength, so the market for combining cloud with dedicated servers is probably at Steps 0 and 1. Some people who may benefit from it may not know it is possible (Step 0), and other may just be aware of the need, but don't know how to solve the need (Step 1).

	SEO Traffic (Broad)	Title Comp	SEOT/TC2
dedicated unmetered bandwidth	136.5	1850	398.83
private network host	2.94	585	85.91
cloud hosting providers	10.08	1090	84.84
guaranteed bandwidth	74.76	3060	79.84
european colo	0.84	443	42.8
linux dedicated server hosting	111.72	5260	40.38
iscsi hosting	0.84	465	38.85
host multiple servers	4.62	1110	37.5
dedicated unlimited bandwidth	60.9	4640	28.29
europe colo	0.84	679	18.22
dedicated server hosting unlimited bandwidth	1.26	846	17.6
dedicated private network	1.68	1010	16.47
unmanaged dedicated server	10.08	2710	13.73
secure colocation	12.18	3330	10.98
dedicated server bandwidth	74.76	8270	10.93
unmanaged server hosting	4.62	2300	8.73
unmanaged dedicated servers	3.78	2090	8.65
cloud-based storage	7.98	3150	8.04
sun server hosting	2.1	1620	8
best iscsi	33.18	6830	7.11
best cloud hosting	4.62	2650	6.58
iscsi host	26.04	7390	4.77
cloud hosting provider	2.1	2170	4.46
secure dedicated server	13.86	5700	4.27
dedicated hosting europe	5.46	4020	3.38
european data center	10.08	6140	2.67
best dedicated servers	26.04	10400	2.41
cloud hosting company	1.26	2370	2.24
online storage space	136.5	25700	2.07
europe data centre	6.72	5750	2.03
unlimited bandwidth hosting	374.22	51300	1.42
europe data center	13.86	9970	1.39
european data centre	6.72	7570	1.17
unlimited bandwidth	835.38	84700	1.16
security data centre	12.18	10800	1.04
cloud servers	91.14	29800	1.03
cloud hosting solution	0.84	2870	1.02
unmanaged web hosting	0.84	2970	0.95
secure dedicated hosting	2.94	5880	0.85
cloud computing company	26.04	23300	0.48
best dedicated hosting	91.14	45500	0.44
best linux web hosting	10.08	15400	0.43
private network hosting	0.84	4450	0.42
dedicated hosting	5081.58	382000	0.35
cloud host	49.56	38300	0.34
unmanaged hosting	18.06	23500	0.33

FIGURE 5-13 EasySpeedy's keyword research shows the majority of Step 2 terms.

A Combination Approach

EasySpeedy should combine both Step 2 and Step 0 approaches, in a similar way to Bolwell with its revolutionary product. It is building a range of good Step 2 pages, offering plenty of long-tail content, based around the results of the keyword research. In addition, I would suggest a Step 0 campaign, using the same techniques proposed for Bolwell: banner advertising and guerrilla link-building.

Because it already has customers in more than a hundred different countries, it may pay to feature a list of its preferred target countries on all pages, to gain an advantage in the "unmanaged hosting (country)" market.

The second step of the marketing strategy is to hit every visitor with the brand values. They should get the immediate impression that this is an extremely efficient, modern, and professional company. Visitors who engage with the brand will have high expectations of the service, and will be prepared to pay the appropriate prices. Visitors who are shopping on price alone may qualify themselves out at this point, which benefits the company.

> **NOTE** *It is better to distinguish your position in the market positively on every page. Differentiation cuts two ways. For every unsuitable customer you discourage, you will encourage another, more suitable customer.*

Applying the Awareness Ladder to Your Site

The worked examples in this chapter have illustrated a range of different approaches, each one based on the same simple steps:

▶ Describe the present situation and the marketing challenge.

▶ Use common sense and keyword research to identify where the market is concentrated. Ask whether there may be more than one market.

▶ Explore what content strategy will attract the right people, at the right point in their awareness, such that the site can engage their attention and lead them up the Awareness Ladder toward closure.

You have seen a toolkit of tactics for reaching out to markets at different levels of awareness, and I have started to explore what landing pages need to do in order to engage visitors and keep them moving forward.

Although most web sites start around Step 3 on the Awareness Ladder, there are nearly always large and potentially profitable markets searching at Steps 2, 1, and sometimes even at Step 0. Each step requires a different approach. You should ask, "What is the level of awareness of people at this step? What are they looking for right now? How can we fulfill that need and capture their attention?"

One size never fits all. Some early-stage markets may be profitably reached through banner ads. For others, AdWords or Facebook advertising may be more profitable. In some scenarios, a wide range of landing pages on your site will help you target search traffic immediately. In others, you should focus your efforts on off-site tactics, using forums, blog comments, and YouTube videos.

When you execute a good content strategy, you will have done half the job. In addition to attracting more visitors in more markets, you will have created landing pages that seem to meet their present concern. Part II of this book addresses the specific techniques you need to apply to catch visitors' attention and to retain that attention all the way up the Awareness Ladder to complete your goals.

PART II

Designing for Conversion

CHAPTER 6

Making Your Site Sell

In Part I, I showed you how to use multiplicity to increase the marketing scope of any web site, first by flipping your products into multiple propositions for different markets, then by reaching deeper into those markets using the Awareness Ladder model.

These methods help you identify your target markets and create an ever-expandable range of funnels arranged in a concentric structure for targeting every market and drawing them into your site.

You will now have far greater insight into what every market wants at each step of awareness. Your next task is to engage every prospect and to keep them engaged with your site. That is what you learn in Part II—design for optimizing conversion.

In this chapter, I show you how to analyze your funnels to identify where you are losing visitors, and introduce the new approach for optimizing your site.

The following chapters take you through a complete step-by-step method for crafting compelling web pages that keep all visitors moving forward to completing their goals, which is the way to achieve your goals.

> **NOTE** *This chapter assumes that you already have Google Analytics running on your site. Other analytics and web server stats packages may offer similar data and tools, so if you don't have access to Google Analytics you will still be able to apply the core principles effectively.*

The New Approach to Design for Conversion

As we know, the old approach to web design is based on guesswork. You create a web page based on your intuition and see how well it works. If it does not seem to perform well, you might consider changing the design. There is no guarantee the redesign will deliver better results than the old design, because no one's first best guess is likely to be optimal. You could find that your redesign performs worse than the design it replaced, but because the changes were made wholesale you won't even know why. That's what life is like with the old model.

The new approach for designing web pages for optimal conversion draws on the discipline of direct marketing. Direct marketing applies the *scientific method* to the problem of working with human behavior. Accepting that people are ultimately unpredictable, the direct marketer's approach is to *test* the effectiveness of any message by measuring the way that people actually behave, to generate statistical results, and then to respond based on the facts.

> **NOTE** *In web site optimization, just as in science, nothing is ever held to be the final truth. When they find a method that works well, marketers will not say it is the best possible method. They are always open to discovering a better way. So optimization is an ongoing process of continual improvement.*

You Can't Improve What You Don't Measure

Without measuring how something works, you can't know whether you have improved it, so measuring the effectiveness of each step in a sequence is the prerequisite to optimizing any process.

The most basic goal of web page optimization is *to keep people on your site*. Visualize your site as a system of pipes. Visitors enter through funnels at various points, and proceed through the system. If they make it all the way through the system, they will reach a goal at the end.

Your web site will leak visitors at various points. Optimization is all about spotting where the leaks are, and fixing them to keep more visitors inside the system, so that more of them reach their goals at the end.

So to improve the efficiency of your site, you need to know where you lose the people you lose. If you don't know where the holes are, you don't know what needs fixing or improving. What's more, if you don't know what your conversion rates are today, you can't even know if you *do* manage to improve them. Only once you have quantified something can you have something to measure success against.

Bounce Rate

One of the first metrics you'll notice on many of your Analytics reports is *bounce rate*. This is the percentage of visitors who arrive and leave the site from the same page. Bounce rate can be a handy indicator of poor performance.

One reason for a high bounce rate may be that your page is attracting the wrong traffic: The search engine result suggests your page offers a solution to certain queries, but perhaps the content does not live up to the expectation. A well-crafted content strategy should minimize this effect.

If the page is attracting the right visitors, a high bounce rate could indicate the page is failing to engage them, which is a more serious concern. Look out for high bounce rates on your landing pages.

Note that bounce rate does not always signify a failure. Context plays a significant role. One example of good bounce rate could be on an FAQ page that successfully helps visitors solve a problem, perhaps preventing a support call. It may also be that visitors are leaving your site to go somewhere you want them to go. It is this type of question you need to ask when analyzing your funnel.

To give a real-world example, I published an article on a technical CSS topic that attracts significant traffic (more than 1,800 search visits monthly). That article has a very high bounce rate at over 90%. But the average time spent on the page is almost 5 minutes, which means visitors are engaging with the article. Because that particular content is not likely to fulfill our agency's major goals of generating new customer leads, I have placed Amazon affiliate content at the bottom of the page, encouraging visitors to browse CSS textbooks on Amazon.com, thereby causing them to leave the site (and increasing the bounce rate), but also contributing toward a minor goal of generating affiliate income.

Exit Rate

A more helpful metric than bounce rate is a page's *exit rate*. This represents the percentage of page visitors who leave a site from a particular page. Though still a crude metric, exit rate provides a more accurate indicator of a traffic leak.

Spotting leaks through high exit rates can help you identify where a page just isn't doing its job. Consider a high exit rate as an indicator that a page has failed to achieve one of two essential functions: Either the visitors simply do not know what to do next, or the page has failed to convince them it is worth proceeding.

I suggest using relative exit rate as the primary metric when modeling your site's current funnel, because it can indicate a fundamental failure either to engage visitors or to keep their interest. Minimizing a key page's exit rate is a good indicator that the page is at least encouraging more people to proceed through the site.

Again, exit rate is not always a failure. You would expect a high percentage of visitors to leave from a "Thank you for your order," "Thank you for contacting us," or "You have logged out" page.

The process for starting to optimize your web site has three simple steps:

1. Modeling your site's funnels
2. Analyzing your funnels
3. Optimizing your funnels

I will walk you through each step in sequence.

Step One: Modeling Your Site's Funnels

Before you make any changes to your web site, it is absolutely essential to get a clear picture of the present situation. Consider you are your web site's surgeon. A surgeon won't operate on a patient without first having all the facts at hand. Operating on the wrong area could make the overall situation worse. Knowing the facts will help you diagnose the situation and show you where to make the first incision.

The process of optimizing your site's conversion begins with visualizing its funnels. Every possible path from a landing page right through to a goal completion is a funnel. The funnel's conversion rate is the percentage of visitors entering the funnel who go on to complete the goal.

A funnel works by successfully driving visitors forward, which should mean to the next awareness step. If the visitor quits the process, that represents a leak in the funnel. The optimization process is about spotting and fixing leaks.

Identifying Your Goals

To measure your conversion rates you have to know *what success means* for your web site.

Your web site is essentially a series of messages, which you intend will eventually lead all visitors to complete some goal. The goal will vary, depending on the market and its level of awareness. However, it should always involve some *commitment action* on the part of the visitor, such as:

▶ To purchase

▶ To sign up

▶ To share information

▶ To contribute

▶ To watch a demonstration video

▶ To find help

NOTE *To measure conversion, you have to have a goal—a result you can measure.*

If you don't think you need to convert anyone to do anything, consider what opportunities you may be missing. Whatever the objectives of your business may be, there are many ways your web site can support them.

You may not actively sell from your web site, but could (or should) it generate leads or contacts? You may earn income through advertising. Your site could distribute sales material or provide cost-efficient customer support. An e-mail list is a particularly valuable resource for any site, so start one today (even if you don't know what to do with it yet).

NOTE *If your goal is to promote a message, Google Analytics will also help you track a minimum amount of time spent on the site or number of pages viewed in a visit as goals.*

For example, one of our clients has an e-commerce site. One of the site's goals is to collect marketing data. Visitors who may not want to shop online can easily get directions to his physical store by entering their postal code. This code is captured and used to measure the effectiveness of print advertising campaigns in different regions.

NOTE *Write down one or more measurable goals. These will usually equate to arriving on a certain page, such as a purchase confirmation or "thanks for contacting us" page.*

Ensure your goals have some real business value, such as sales, lead generation, or building your marketing list. Avoid vague goals that have no direct value. Only invest your time in tracking goals that are useful to your business objectives, such as actually submitting a form, downloading a white paper, or purchasing a product.

Configuring Goals in Google Analytics

Before you use Google Analytics to model and monitor your funnels, you should first set up goals within Analytics. Do this by clicking the "Edit" link for your web site profile in the main Analytics menu (see Figure 6-1).

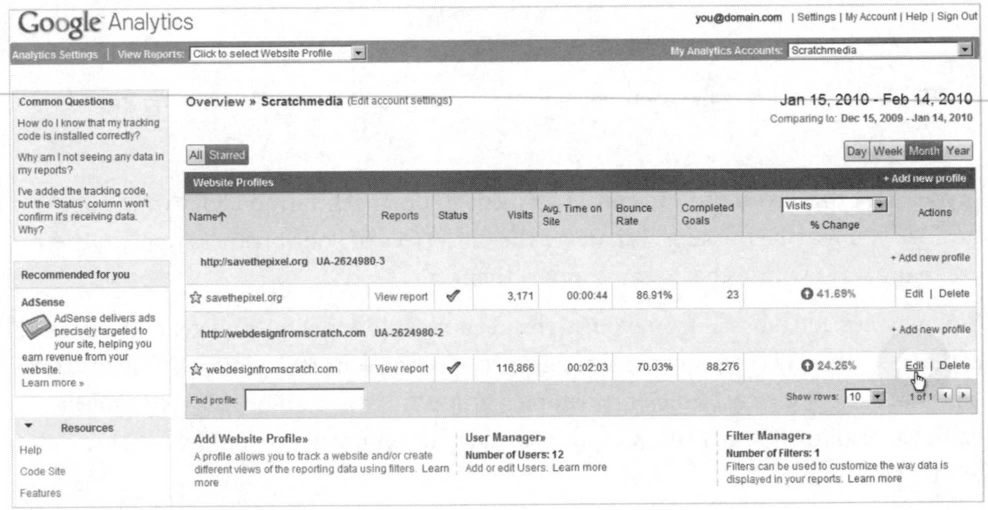

FIGURE 6-1 Access goal set-up by clicking the "Edit" link on an Analytics profile.

The Profile Settings page lets you edit your main options to configure Analytics for each web site. The second block is for displaying and creating goals, which are divided into four sets. To start defining a new goal, select + Add Goal in the first available set (see Figure 6-2).

I recommend using different *goal groups* for different types of goals, because some Analytics reports will only show statistics summarized for a whole group. So if you have one goal for selling a product and another for generating leads or newsletter sign-ups, set these up in separate groups.

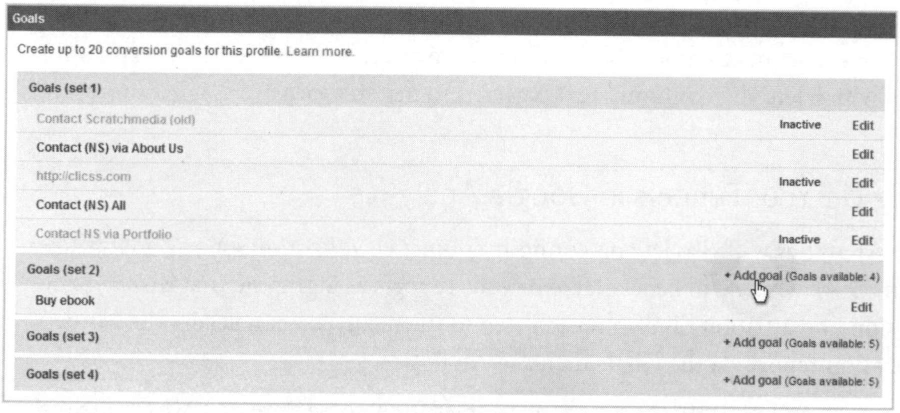

FIGURE 6-2 Adding a new goal in a goal group in Google Analytics

Figure 6-3 shows one way the add/edit goal form can appear. The options can change dynamically depending on the type of goal you set up. Google provides clear help throughout Analytics, so I won't repeat all the basics.

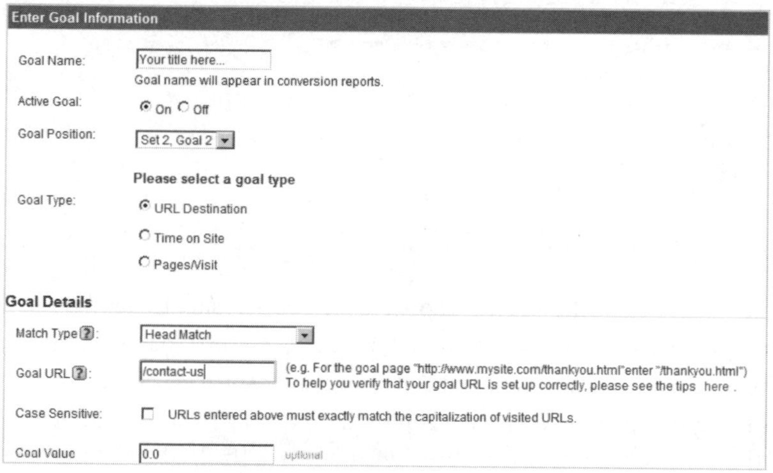

FIGURE 6-3 The form for defining a goal

In Figure 6-3, I am using the default goal type of "URL Destination," which means the goal will be achieved when a visitor arrives on a page that matches a certain name.

I have selected the "Head Match" match type, which means I want the goal to be counted when someone arrives on a page address that starts a certain way (for example, /contact-us.php, /contact-us.php?from=menu, as well as /contact-us2.php).

If I had selected "Exact Match," the goal would only be achieved when the visitor lands on an exact page name. The third more advanced type is "Regular Expression Match," which lets you configure text patterns to match against.

Setting Up Your Funnels in Google Analytics

Google Analytics will also let you configure *funnel visualization* for any goal (shown in Figure 6-4), which will be available in your reports as a graphic that displays the conversion and attrition rate from each step to the next. You can access the funnel visualization report via the Goals menu in Analytics.

You can optionally specify the first page in the funnel to be required, which means only visits that include that start page and result in the goal page being reached will show in the funnel visualization.

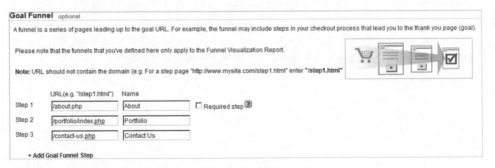

FIGURE 6-4 Configuring a Goal Funnel in Google Analytics

Figure 6-5 shows the Analytics traffic sources report for my ebook site. Instead of looking at the overall site (with the Site Usage tab), I have clicked the Goal Set 1 tab, which shows me the percentage of visitors from different traffic sources who completed a certain goal (buying an ebook). This tells me that referrals from my main site convert 25% more than traffic from Google. Direct visitors have the highest conversion rate, probably because they visited the site previously, and have come back to make a purchase.

I recommend defining all your site's goals within Google Analytics, as well as all the main funnels to those goals. Before long, you will be able to look at the funnel visualization reports in Analytics and start to analyze where the weak spots are in your funnels. In the meantime, simply look at the exit rates for key pages as an indicator of where people are leaving the site.

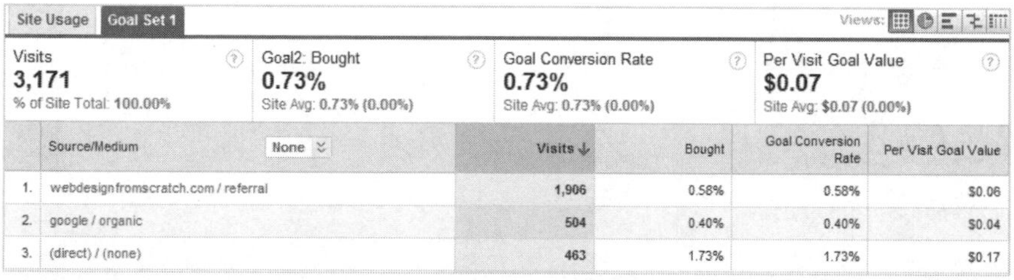

	Source/Medium	Visits	Bought	Goal Conversion Rate	Per Visit Goal Value
1.	webdesignfromscratch.com / referral	1,906	0.58%	0.58%	$0.06
2.	google / organic	504	0.40%	0.40%	$0.04
3.	(direct) / (none)	463	1.73%	1.73%	$0.17

FIGURE 6-5 Viewing a Google Analytics report in the context of a goal

Step Two: Analyzing Your Funnels

The next task is to map out the actual flow of traffic through your main pages to your main goals, looking at three categories of visitor behavior:

- Proceeding to the next intended step
- Going somewhere else on your site
- Quitting the site

The purpose of this exercise is simply to visualize where your site is leaking the most visitors. It makes sense to start your optimization process with fixing the biggest leaks, before you can move on to progressive refinements.

Measuring Your Conversion Rate

Once you have identified one or more goals, you will be able to measure your starting conversion rate (CR). If you have configured a goal in Google Analytics, you will also be able to view the CR for that goal graphically (as shown in Figure 6-6), including changes in conversion rate over time.

> **NOTE** *If you have not set up goals in Analytics, you can still figure out your conversion rates for each goal simply by dividing the number of times each goal was reached in a particular period by the number of relevant visits to your web site in that period.*

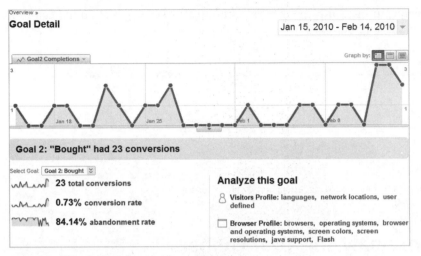

FIGURE 6-6 The Analytics report for a single goal

Knowing your conversion rate may be interesting, but it does not usually give you *actionable information*. If your conversion rate goes up or down, you need to know why, and at what steps the leaks are occurring. The overall conversion rate of a funnel is a high-level indication of its effectiveness, but in order to optimize, you need to break the process down into more detail, which is where funnels come in.

Attrition Rate

At every step through a funnel, some of the visitors who entered the funnel will leak away. The number of visitors who successfully move forward can only diminish with each step. It can never go up.

The conversion rate of any funnel is a product of the cumulative *attrition rate* at each step along the path from an entry point to a measurable goal. Your objective is to deliver as many as possible to that goal, by minimizing the attrition rate at each step.

Figure 6-7 shows a simplified view of a funnel. 100% of visitors enter the funnel at the top. 68% of those drop off at the first step, then a further 47% are lost at the second step, and finally there is a 41% attrition at the final step. The result is that only 10% of the original visitors make it all the way to the goal.

Once you can visualize your conversion funnels like the example in Figure 6-7, you can start to identify the steps that demonstrate the greatest opportunity for improvement.

In this case, the first step (with the greatest attrition rate of 68%) would seem to offer the most potential for improvement, but all three steps merit attention.

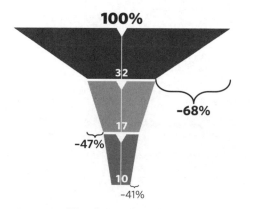

FIGURE 6-7 Visualizing a funnel in terms of attrition rate

Visualizing Your Funnels in Google Analytics

The *funnel visualization* view in Google Analytics makes it quite straightforward to see the click-through rate from step to step, as Figure 6-8 shows. Analytics lets you define the steps in your site's funnel, and will give you a diagram showing how many visitors you convert or lose at each step.

Once you have set up your goals and given them some time to run, you will be able to view many of the reports in Analytics within the context of your goals, as well as analyze in more detail the paths people take to achieve the goal.

The attrition rates in the funnel in Figure 6-8 are 89%, 63%, and 97%, respectively. Each score needs to be interpreted in the context of the page in question. From this site's home page, common sense tells me that a click-through rate of 11% to the About page is not bad. I would be more concerned about the later steps.

The horizontal colored bars at each step show the proportion of people who proceed to the next step or do not proceed. Of those that do not proceed, some may go somewhere else on the site, and some may leave the site altogether. The lists shown on the right-hand side of each step indicate where those who do not proceed go instead. You should be most concerned about the exit rate.

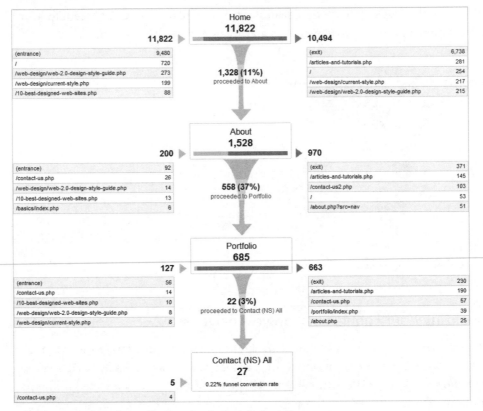

FIGURE 6-8 The funnel visualization view in Google Analytics

The Law of Multiples

Imagine the path through your web site, from home page to goal, is a 300-mile train line. If the track is strong, flat, and clear for 299 miles, then heads across a bridge that has a section missing, how many trains are going to reach their destination?

It doesn't matter how well maintained the rest of the track is, how many trains begin the journey, or the value of goods they carry. If a bit of track is missing your success rate will be zero. Fix that section of track and the improvement in success rate will be astronomical.

The Law of Diminishing Returns dictates that the closer you get to optimal, the harder it gets to make further improvements.

The Law of Multiples tells us that the effects of the conversion rate of individual steps are cumulative, that is, any impact you have on any step along the path will apply to the whole conversion rate. Double the conversions at any step, and overall conversion will also double.

Because it is practically impossible to double a click-through rate of 50%, you can much more easily double a click-through rate of only 2%. Either one would double the final conversion rate, which is why we *focus first on the easier wins.*

As soon as you model your funnel, you will see exactly where to start focusing your optimization efforts. Unless you know the attrition rate from each step to the next, you could waste resources on steps that perform better.

Goal Value, CPV, and EPV

There is no target conversion rate at this point. The first target you should be interested in is *profitability*. To measure profitability, it helps to know your *Cost per Visitor (CPV)* and *Earnings per Visitor (EPV)*.

If your web site's EPV is more than its CPV, you should be in profit. In other words, the value your site delivers for your business is greater than the cost of running the site and attracting traffic. (Later, your objective will be to increase profitability—the margin by which your EPV exceeds CPV.)

Only you will be able to provide these numbers. It is relatively easy to measure profit for an e-commerce site, but a web site's indirect value is more subjective. For example, if your site generates sales leads for your business, you may want to estimate the average profit earned from each lead, and assign that value to a lead-generation goal. If your site gathers a list of e-mail address, can you estimate the lifetime value of each name on that list?

Consider the business value generated by each goal. Analytics lets you assign real or nominal values to any goal. Many e-commerce services will pass back an actual value that will tell Analytics the sale value of each transaction. (For more info, search Google for "How do I track e-commerce transactions?") You can also give any goal an arbitrary value on the configuration screen (see Figure 6-3). Setting goal values lets you view the traffic sources and paths through your site that are most profitable, which will also help you target areas to optimize first.

If you know the real cost of the time and services spent on building and maintaining your site, you may be able to put a figure on your CPV by dividing that cost spread over time by the total number of visitors. A simple way to reduce your CPV and to increase your EPV-to-CPV ratio is to drive more traffic to the site. However, bear in mind that while accurately targeted traffic is likely to increase your average EPV, more of the wrong traffic could reduce EPV, so raw visitor numbers are not always meaningful.

> **NOTE** *If a likely goal from your site is for visitors to pick up the phone and call you, you need a way to keep track of phone calls generated by the web site. A great way to do this is to use a telephone script that includes the question "How did you hear about us?" Also consider doing this for any face-to-face leads.*

When you have modeled your web site's goals and funnels, you will soon be able to see each funnel's performance in Google Analytics. Look first for pages with high exit rates or low click-through rates. These should indicate where you can achieve the most significant improvements.

Step Three: Optimizing Conversions through the Funnel

In the "first best guess" approach to web design, we built web pages from our own internal perspective, which we hoped would attract traffic and help people find what they were looking for.

The new approach takes a far more direct and analytical approach. When you work with multiple funnels, you can spot how visitors are progressing with greater precision, and take specific steps to optimize every step in each funnel to maximize conversions.

Here is the simple and straightforward process for optimizing any funnel:

1. Identify leaks.
2. Generate alternative ideas.
3. Test to see what worked.
4. Repeat.

The first step is straightforward. Just look for the worst leaks in your most important funnels.

The second and third steps work together. You need to apply all your best knowledge and ideas to the problem. Creativity alone will not give you solid progress. You must test each change you make so that you know whether it had a positive or negative impact.

▶ Chapters 7, 8, and 9 take you through a comprehensive system for generating ideas for how to make your pages work better.

▶ Chapter 10 applies all the principles to every step on the Awareness Ladder.

▶ Chapter 11 introduces the methods you can use to test your ideas and to know definitively what works best.

Finally, optimization delivers best results when you do it as an *iterative process*. When you switch from the "first best guess" approach to a culture of optimization, whenever a change is made and tested, you get to see—and then choose to keep—only the things that are proven to work better. Every cycle builds on previous successes, creating a culture of continual improvement.

Optimization Combines Creativity and Analysis

Analysis lets you measure performance with quantifiable results. It will tell you if design option A converts better than design option B. Without these numbers, you can't be sure of selecting the best-performing option. When you test different options iteratively, your numbers will ensure you only select the best-performing option, guaranteeing forward progress is achieved.

However, testing and measuring can only describe what *is*—the *past performance* of A and B. Simply measuring performance can't tell you *why* A is better than B, nor can it reveal what might work better.

Consider that the process of optimizing your design is similar to the process a scientist follows when trying to figure out how things work. A scientist will start with an idea or hypothesis, then construct an experiment to test that idea. The experiment should deliver empirical evidence, which may indicate whether the idea is valid or invalid. That result may require a new hypothesis to be formed, or even lead the scientist to question the theories upon which the hypothesis was based.

The scientific method has made possible huge advances in technology, despite the fact that it rarely gives a definitive answer. Because any theory is only as valid as the evidence that supports it, and the process is never complete, scientists always remain open to the possibility that their current working theory may be proven wrong.

Apply exactly the same discipline to increasing the conversion rate of your web site. Testing will give you measurable results, but no final answers. To find an option that improves on your current best option requires insight into why one approach works better than another, and the ability to visualize an even better solution. The numbers may help point in the right direction, but they can't take you there.

In marketing and design, just as in science, previous theories exist that describe how things should work. It is foolish to ignore the lessons of the past that teach us how people tend to respond in different situations, and how to persuade them to be willing to take the action you want. Efficient optimization requires not only being familiar with this body of knowledge, but also having the insight to apply that knowledge to each new problem with sensitivity. Like a scientist, you need to be able to generate new ideas—hopefully even brilliant flashes of inspiration—and that is the domain of creativity.

So what do we do if neither analysis nor creativity can give us the answers we want?

The solution lies in unifying both methods into a single process, in which creative possibilities are explored and then validated through analysis. I'll describe how this approach plays to the strengths of both mindsets and also provides a rewarding experience for all stakeholders.

The Limits of Creativity

Though, in theory, creative endeavor is boundless, the process needs to be channeled in order to be efficient. It is not possible to test an infinite number of creative possibilities without an infinite budget. The optimal design solution is out there, but it can only be discovered through a disciplined, methodical approach.

The challenge you face when optimizing your web site is how to harness the strengths of the creative process in the pursuit of continual improvement. If not every idea can be put to the test, you have to use heuristics (rules-of-thumb) from received wisdom to help direct your creative energy.

Originality is a dangerous frontier land. At once, it is the place where great original advances can be discovered, but it is also full of opportunities to fail. The saying, "The pioneers take the arrows, the settlers take the land," applies perfectly to the quest for the optimal web site.

Biology provides the perfect analogy to guide our discipline. Life constantly generates mutations, most of which fail. Occasionally, a new solution emerges that is more successful than previous solutions, and which can become established in its environment. This evolution works extremely well over a very long timeline (millions of new tests), and your resources will certainly not stretch that far.

Use Conventions

A design solution that has become established in its environment is called a convention, and conventions provide the ideal starting point for optimization, offering the best probability of success. They work because they have worked before, and because they are familiar. You don't have to think how to use a log-in panel that requests "user name" and "password," because you have seen and used thousands of similar panels before.

The familiar is often unconsciously perceived as safe and easy; the unfamiliar as risky or difficult. Is it possible that there is a more effective solution than the user name/ password log-in box? Certainly there is, but to find it you may risk trying many poorly performing alternatives.

The rule I always apply is to use conventions wherever the design problem is familiar (such as where to place a logo or the "log out" link) and where a conventional solution already exists. That leaves more creative energy to apply to the truly unique problems that every design challenge presents, which include the big questions of audience and proposition that actually most greatly impact success.

So apply creative thought from start to finish to every aspect of your web design, take advantage of conventions that have been proven to work, but rely finally on the results of your own tests, because every web site's design challenge is unique.

Test Your Best

Combine your creativity, insight, common sense, intuition, and experience to each new problem. But only try ideas that you have reason to think will work, avoiding random guesses. I would never advise testing any old dumb idea; you'll probably waste time and money. For the best results, always strive to create a better solution, applying all the resources at your disposal (with just a dash of the unpredictable).

Of course, you should never assume that your own best idea is any good at all. You must always test, but test things you have reason to think will be effective.

In our team, we've coined the term "CICO" (which stands for "crap in, crap out") to describe the effect of testing poor ideas. Especially when you start running tests on your site, it's tempting to test a weak option for the thrill of seeing a result.

When doing tests, your objective is to improve on the original (control) solution. There's barely any value in showing an idea that doesn't perform as well as what you had before. It will most likely provide a negative learning experience, which may point in the direction of a better solution, but hasn't carried you any nearer to that solution.

At the same time, don't be afraid to experiment. Because of the way split-testing works, you will always be able to observe performance, and respond quickly by killing off poorly performing options and moving forward what works. Provided you are not practicing CICO, any detrimental effects will be short-lived but the gains you can make will stay with you.

Attention and Momentum

Attention is the currency of your web site. When new visitors arrive, they have a certain amount of attention. They use that attention to scan the landing page, *looking for one thing*. If they find that one thing, it generates more attention. If they do not find the one thing, their attention may run out. If the visitors get to the point that they believe they are more likely to find what they want by going back to the search results than by persevering with your web site, you have lost them.

The exact flavor of the one thing depends on the visitors' current goal. Do they want to find the product they're looking for, to get the answer to a question, or to be entertained? (If you have built your web site around the new multiplicity model, you should have a pretty good idea, because you know which funnel they arrived on.)

Whatever the visitor's precise goal may be, the one thing is always to answer one simple question: "Am I in the right place?"

That's it. Answering that one tiny question is the only thing your web page needs to do. The more quickly and decisively you can answer the question, the more attention your pages will generate, and the more people you will keep interested so that they continue to move up the Awareness Ladder.

The challenge, of course, is *how* to answer the question most effectively. That's what the rest of the book is about.

Every Page Is an Advertisement

I would like you to view every page on your site as an advertisement. What is it an ad for? For *the next step*, whatever that is.

Consider that it is the job of every page you publish simply to get people to move to the next step. To do that, you must first get their attention, in the same way that an advertisement must get the attention of a passerby, television viewer, or newspaper reader, so that it can deliver its message.

Once you have their attention, you must help them find the answer to their question, "Am I in the right place?" When they find the clue that they are going to get what they want, their attention is reinvigorated, and they take the next step forward. Provided you can keep them moving forward step-by-step, you can eventually help them achieve their goal (and your goal).

> **NOTE** *Some people say you have seven seconds to persuade people to keep reading. I don't know if that's true for your site, but it is shown that plenty of visitors leave without even scrolling, which means many pages fail at the first hurdle. They don't manage to get visitors' attention even to get them to start interacting.*

Reese's Pieces

Reese's Pieces is a type of candy made by the U.S. brand Hershey. In the movie *E.T.— the Extra Terrestrial*, the central character Elliot used a trail of the candy to lure E.T. from the shed in the yard all the way to his bedroom.

The key point is that getting an alien out of a shed all the way into the house and up the stairs is a difficult task. What Elliot did brilliantly was to break the big action for E.T. into a sequence of much smaller actions. All the alien needed to do was to move a few inches and it would get another small reward. Each commitment was small, and offered a clear reward, but together they constituted a huge achievement for the boy.

This approach can help you deliver big goals through your web site, simply by breaking a large commitment into smaller, easier steps. Each page just needs to engage the visitors and help them find the next step along the path to what they want. Then repeat on the next page. By achieving these simple steps, you will minimize leaks from your site, and have an alien in your bedroom before you know it! (Acknowledgment to Ben Jesson of Conversion Rate Experts, who I first heard tell this analogy.)

When you have identified a structure for addressing the needs of more segments, the challenge is to get as many visitors as possible to proceed up the ladder.

The Three Elements of Conversion

For a page to get visitors to proceed to the next step, it must let them know they are in the right place. To do that, three things need to happen.

These are the three critical elements of conversion:

▶ Get their Attention.
▶ Keep them Engaged.
▶ Call them to Action.

All three elements must be present. You cannot get someone to engage with a page unless you quickly capture their attention first. Then, you need to communicate your message to get them to the point that they want to take the next step, which is your call to action.

Get Their Attention

As the Awareness Ladder shows, there is little value in presenting a proposition if people are not ready to appreciate what is on offer. Any proposition must directly match the *immediate need* of prospects at that level of awareness.

If Joe speaks to people who are not aware that any treatments for baldness exist and advertises "Get 50% off Joe's Miracle Hair-Gro!," he will not catch the attention of many folks there, because they have never heard of his product and have no idea how it can benefit them.

If he addresses them with "New Treatments Available for Baldness," he will catch the eye of people who are ready to take that step in awareness.

Joe's job at that point is *not* to get those people to buy straightaway! That would be unrealistic—and unsuccessful. Remember, every prospect has to pass at some point from Step 0 to Step 5 on the Awareness Ladder, and through every step along the way in sequence.

All Joe has to do is to get folks to take the next step up the ladder. Because the step is small, Joe knows he does not have to sell. He can simply offer what's available at the next step, and let the next step do its job.

What gets attention is a clear proposition that speaks directly to the viewer on an emotional level. A good proposition has the following properties:

- ▶ **Specific**—Speaks to the present concerns or desires of each specific market
- ▶ **You-oriented**—All about the viewer, not about us
- ▶ **Clear benefit**—"What's in it for me?"
- ▶ **Immediate gain**—Offer me a solution to what I want *now*.

Each stage of your visitors' journey starts with an appealing proposition that seems to speak to them and to offer something they want. The next chapter is packed with examples and ideas for transforming your propositions into attention magnets.

Keep Them Engaged

Now that you have someone's attention, you need to get them to proceed toward their next goal. The appeal alone may not be enough. What else do they need to know in order to be convinced to complete the journey (or this stage of the journey)?

Here, you are deep in the magnificent realm of advertising copywriting, among great libraries of knowledge learned from thousands of split tests in newspaper, mail-order, radio, and television advertisements.

There has been so much learning in this area that marketers long ago agreed on some fundamental laws. These laws work over and over in all media, online as well as off-line. If you are hoping to deliver optimal results online you must fully understand what these laws are, and how they work, so that you can *test* their effectiveness in your own campaigns.

The laws of content writing boil down to basic common sense. Unless you keep providing more reasons to proceed, people will lose *momentum* and may give up before they reach the next goal.

Basically, keeping momentum is a question of ensuring people keep discovering stuff that interests them. Techniques for building and maintaining momentum fall into two groups:

- ▶ *Affirming the positive signs* that people need to see
- ▶ *Resolving their concerns*—fears, doubts, and objections

What do people expect to see that will confirm they are heading in the right direction to get what they want?

- ▶ They must identify with the proposition as it unfolds, and feel it really applies to them.
- ▶ They must also continue to get the right impression of the brand, building a sense of trust.
- ▶ They must see confirmation that their specific requirements are met.
- ▶ They must see signs that satisfy their doubts and concerns.
- ▶ They must be kept aware that their goal is in sight without being knocked off track.

All these aspects provide momentum, which we need to build in order to keep people moving forward through the steps to the final goal.

Chapter 8 explores in detail dozens of techniques for building momentum.

Call Them to Action

Without action *now* you have no action *ever*. It is in human nature to put off action to a later time. We cannot afford that. There is only the present moment. If your web site does not convince someone to convert right now, it is unlikely to get them to convert next time.

This is the final commitment you require of your visitors. If they do not have enough momentum to complete the final step, they will fail. If they have built up enough momentum, the final stage should have a good conversion rate.

It is always possible to invite people to take the action you want them to take, provided you follow a few basic principles:

- ▶ The call to action must *exist*, and be clear and bold. If you don't ask, you won't get.

▶ The *timing* must be right. You may be a great catch, but if you walk into the bar and propose marriage to the first woman you see, you will not succeed, because she does not know enough about you to make an informed choice. You can only call to action from the top of the Awareness Ladder.

▶ You need to have provided enough positive signs and resolved enough negative concerns for the action to appear *reasonable*. If there are still "what ifs" in the prospect's mind, those might give reasons not to act.

▶ There must be enough *momentum*. The prospect must feel confident enough in the offering that it makes sense to take the action offered.

▶ Finally, any call to action must provide enough urgency to induce action *now*.

Chapter 9 presents all the techniques you need to create powerful calls to action.

CHAPTER 7

Get Their Attention

The sole purpose of your web site is to deliver complete propositions to your target visitors. The form of any proposition is, "This is how what we do addresses your need." A proposition is the bridge between what they want and what you do. It should be present from the first glance, and should get stronger as the visitor continues to engage.

If you have defined a landing matrix and created web pages for each step on the Awareness Ladder in each target market, you have a massive advantage, because you have already identified both your visitors' *need* and *level of awareness*.

From whatever point they enter any funnel, your web site must carry them forward, step by step, all the way through to the goal you want them to reach. Depending on the page, the next step may be a goal conversion, or a step up the Awareness Ladder.

The first thing any page must do is quickly get across the message, "Yes, you are in the right place." Everyone, whether they have just arrived from search engine results, followed a link from another site, or proceeded from a previous page on your site, needs to see evidence that they are going to find what they are looking for. This gives you *attention currency* to help carry the visitor forward to the next step.

When you have designed your site in the concentric model, you already know the awareness step of each individual page, which gives you a great advantage. You will have a very good idea of what your visitors are *already aware of* upon arrival and *what they are looking for right now*. That helps you show them exactly what they need to see to know they're on track. If you already have a matrix of landing pages targeted to specific search terms, you may even know the precise language they used to find you, so it's great to use that language.

To have any chance at converting visitors to a goal, you must first convince them that they are likely to get what they want from your web site. Unless they are compelled to look further, no message will succeed.

This chapter gives you a complete toolkit of techniques for grabbing a visitor's attention and answering that golden question, so that you maximize the attention you need in order to deliver your proposition.

Optimization Discipline

You will notice that I have not started to address the functional techniques of optimization, how to test one approach against another. The reason is that, before you start to optimize, you should start from your very best first guess, using the very best intelligence available. There is no point testing how badly your existing pages perform today; your analytics should tell you that.

Sure, it can be quite exciting to see rapid gains, but if you *know* you can do better, you should use "better" as your starting point. I invite you to work through the next four chapters thoroughly, and apply as many of their lessons as possible, before you start running optimization experiments.

Walk the Road

Ken McCarthy tells marketers to get out of their cars and "walk the road" from the customer's perspective. You are familiar with your products. You may be bored with seeing the same messages every day. But until you slow down and follow the process from start to finish—as your customers will experience it—you can fail to notice critical details.

When you notice a step where people are failing to proceed, ask:

▶ What do they need that is not there? (A *hole* in the road.)

▶ What's there that should not be? (A *rock* in the road.)

As you read through the following chapters, compare the guidance with what your site does today, compile a hit-list of improvements, and then apply the changes in broad strokes to your web site.

Repair First, Then Optimize

Start by looking out for the most obvious rocks and holes. When you start making changes, each fix should produce immediate tangible improvements. I would not really call this *optimization*, any more than fixing a broken car engine can be called *tuning*.

Later, once the road is in good enough repair that most people *can* complete a journey, look at making the journey more appealing and compelling. As each improvement takes your site a step nearer optimal performance, the Law of Diminishing Returns comes into play, and you may notice that advances get both slower and smaller. That can be a good sign that you are in the business of optimization.

Failure to grab attention is often one of the quickest and easiest holes to fill. If people are simply failing to interact with a page, failure to get attention is the first thing to look at. Look for high exit rates combined with low time spent on pages as a sign that a page is falling at the first hurdle. If a page does not engage visitors, it cannot convert them to the next step.

Draw on Outside Influences

When you find a proposition that really appeals on the right level, do not be too proud to copy its format or general appeal (although not its exact words—you need to craft your own language to address each market segment's precise needs).

> *"Until you've got a better answer, you copy."*
>
> HELMUT KRONE (ADVERTISING ART DIRECTOR WITH DDB)

Knowing when to re-use proven effective patterns is one of the key skills of good marketers. Do not think that your proposition needs to be totally unique.

This principle applies to everything in marketing and design. When there is an existing model that works well, use it, unless you know a better way. Do not waste energy trying to reinvent conventional solutions. Save your creativity for the important work of understanding your market and their needs in depth, and to assess the best alternatives to test.

When Attention Comes Second

Not all pages necessarily need a strong attention-grabber. For many regular pages, all that is needed is to confirm you're in the right place. If you click "Contact us" you expect "Contact us." Click "King Size Memory Foam Mattress" and you expect instant confirmation you're in the right place.

In these instances, the main heading should simply make the visitor think "Yes, here I am." To get visitors to engage with the page, you may use secondary devices to catch their attention by highlighting key messages that do not belong in the most noticeable headline:

- ▶ Add minor headings or a subhead (an additional, often longer, headline that follows the main headline).
- ▶ Consider "pull-quotes" (callouts).
- ▶ Highlight keywords in the body text using bold text or background colors.

WARNING *Don't make everything bold. I made all the body text in an article bold as a test, and the average time-on-page went down 15.8%, which suggested more people gave up reading.*

Getting Attention: The Power of Appeal

When someone searches the Web for a solution to their needs, they don't care about your company, your products, or their features. The only thing that matters is finding a solution to their own immediate need—"How is what you offer going to solve my problem?" So any message you show will be interpreted through the filter of "what's in it for me?"

In advertising, an ad's dominant message of "here's what you want, right here" is called its *appeal*. You don't want visitors to have to figure out why it may be worth their while to continue looking at a page. A message that is totally focused on telling prospects exactly what's in it for them will bypass the need for any filtering and speak directly to their self-interest. The appeal should be immediately evident in the features you notice first on the page—starting with its headline.

It is an unquestionable fact that the primary factor in successfully addressing any market is finding the right appeal. Twentieth-century marketers found that appeal is the single factor that has the greatest impact on the conversion rate of any promotion. John Caples reported one ad selling *nineteen times* the amount of another similar ad, the *only major difference* being the choice of appeal used.

> *"To discover the correct appeal is often difficult. There may be many wrong appeals and only one right one. If my advertising agent had a year in which to prepare a campaign for my product, I should be perfectly satisfied if he spent eleven months in search of the right appeal, and only month—or one week, for that matter—preparing the actual advertisements."*
>
> JOHN CAPLES, TESTED ADVERTISING METHODS

The history of test-driven direct marketing and advertising provides a body of knowledge on what features motivate people to buy. I will take you through the most important rules, and provide examples from my own web designs and optimization experiments.

Headlines Rule

One feature that I need to mention up front is the page's *headline*. Tests show that the first thing people look for on web pages is *text* that confirms where they are. Pictures can have multiple meanings, whereas text is more specific.

So every web page should have one piece of text that stands out above all other text, making sure it gets read first. This headline should do two things:

▶ It should confirm where you are (that is, in the right place).

▶ It should grab your interest and give you a *reason to look further*.

The legacy of advertising copywriting provides a wealth of evidence on what types of headlines grab attention and compel people to read on. Several approaches have been proven to work and have become general laws. Such patterns apply to generating instant appeal in any medium.

> **NOTE** *Many great books break down the art of headline writing, such as* Breakthrough Advertising *by Eugene Schwartz (Boardroom Classics, 1984),* Tested Advertising Methods *by John Caples (Prentice Hall, 1998), and* Scientific Advertising *by Claude Hopkins (Advertising Publications, 1966). I'll relay some of the advice that I have found most useful in my own design and marketing.*

THE PURPOSE OF A HEADLINE

Headlines need to do only one thing, which is to get the prospect to engage with the next content on the page. Do not set out to tell the whole story in your headlines. A headline can never complete the whole step. They are the first course, designed to get your juices flowing.

If you tell too much, you may give the readers the impression that they do not need to read on, either because you have already answered their question, or because you have given them a reason to disqualify the page. So your headlines should do enough to get someone to read the next piece of content.

HINT AT VALUE TO FOLLOW

If a headline gives away too much information, it may both create interest and fulfill that interest, without compelling the visitor to engage with the rest of the content.

Similarly, don't expect your initial message to *convince*. All it needs to do is *engage*. Trying to achieve too much too early could be counter-productive.

A good rule of thumb for headlines is if your reader will think, "I can skim-read that, and come away with something useful." Examples include:

▶ "How to Attract The Perfect Partner"

▶ "5 Proven Ways To Succeed at Interviews"

▶ "How I Saved $4000 Tax—Legally"

AVOID CLEVERNESS

It is very tempting to try to stimulate interest by being cryptic or intriguing. Avoid this temptation. Keeping it simple, bold, and direct will appeal to the most people.

"A great offer will do better than any amount of creative ideas."

DRAYTON BIRD

Intrigue can be an effective tool, but it is difficult to judge. An intriguing headline must suggest value to the reader, such as:

▶ "One Thing I Wish I Knew Before I Bought A New Car"

▶ "5 Money-Saving Tips Your Parents Didn't Tell You"

▶ "How I Doubled My Salary With One Phone Call"

▶ "Tax Secrets the IRS Doesn't Want You To Know"

Even when you do stimulate interest, ensure you target the visitor's self-interest, not your own. The safest way to get attention is usually to go straight for the visitor's self-interest with a direct promise:

▶ "Make Up To $300 Extra Per Week From Home—Risk-Free"

▶ "10 Simple Tips That Could Double the Traffic to Your Web Site"

▶ "The Best Hair-Loss Treatments Revealed"

I look for three major factors in crafting an appeal. This chapter addresses each of these factors and shows you when and how to use them to best effect:

▶ **Relevance**—This page should be appropriate to my present situation.

▶ **Self-interest**—It should offer me a quick solution to my immediate need.

▶ **Emotion**—It should engage with me on an emotional level.

Look for one or two things that you believe will grab attention, and consider whether they can be formed into an interesting headline that contains some relevance, self-interest, and emotion. You just need to do enough to get attention and start to build interest.

Researching Powerful Propositions

Before defining your proposition, a quick research exercise is to carry out a Google search for your keywords and look at the top pay-per-click results —results that advertisers are paying to include alongside the natural, organic results, and which are identified with the text "Sponsored link." Look for what makes a compelling appeal.

I did Google searches for "reduce tax bill," "discount silver jewelry," and "weight loss." The PPC results are shown in Figure 7-1. Because the top results are likely to come from the top-bidding ads, these are more likely to be profitable, which means they must generate clicks. Examine the appeals in these nine randomly selected ads. Notice how many work on an emotional level, appeal to self-interest, promise quick results, and prompt urgent action.

Sponsored Links	Sponsored Links	Sponsored Links
Time's Running Out The govt is closing the legal options to save on taxes. Act now!	**We buy your Old Silver** Sell your **Silver Jewelry** & Get Cash Fast. Request a Free Pack Now!	**Special K® Personal Plan** Get Free, Tailored Meal Plans From Kellogg's Special K®. Sign Up Today
Paying too much tax? Instant access to a range of tax saving schemes - 100% guarantee	**Silver Jewelry** at SWAG **Silver Jewelry** buy today online! Free Delivery & 60 Day Refunds	**LaserSlim SmartLipo** Lose excess body fat in 1 hour! As seen on TV - Free consultation
Tax Reduction Advice on taxes and finance Find **Tax** Reduction	**Wholesale silver pendants** Over 91,000 beads and bead supplies Same-day shipping. 100% Guarantee.	**10 Best Weight Loss Pills** "2010's Best **Weight Loss** Pills" Free Shipping & 100% Risk-Free!

FIGURE 7-1 Survey paid ad results for hints on what appeals sell.

Make Your Appeals Relevant

If an appeal is going to get your attention, it has to be relevant to you. The more relevant it seems to be, the more easily you will connect with it. So look for an appeal that is *just broad enough* to include the audience of this page, but no broader.

> **NOTE** *An appeal that is too broad is like a Swiss Army knife. It has a knife, but not a good one, so it is not of interest to people who need a good knife. It has a saw, a magnifying glass, and a pair of scissors, but these are all less useful than a dedicated tool. You will not get good results by offering the same generic proposition to a range of visitors who need specific things.*

Figure 7-2 shows the original headline of an e-commerce site together with my rewritten headline. The original text did not contain any direct benefits to the shopper. The rewrite added two benefits of buying towels from this supplier: good quality and low prices. The result was an *instant 9.25% increase in sales*. This is a useful start, because it is fairly relevant and says what's in it for you, although it does not evoke emotion.

FIGURE 7-2 Simply altering the main heading increased sales from this e-commerce site's home page by more than 9% (http://towelsdirect.co.uk).

The headline in Figure 7-2 gives quite a generic appeal. This may be appropriate for a home page, which deals with the site's highest-level offering, low-cost towels. All landing pages should seek to be as specific as they can be, while still including the whole relevant audience. A diverse landing page strategy makes it far easier to be specific, which means less work and better results.

Target a Specific Market

For the towels site, the market is at Step 2. They know what they want: to save money buying towels and linens. The next step is to introduce this particular supplier or product, and its benefits. I would have a page dedicated to each target market (hotels, salons, nursing homes, and so on) that emphasizes each offering, such as "Cheap Quality Towels for Hairdressers," and another for "Buy Bulk Linens for Nursing Homes Online." Keyword research will provide the best keywords.

These landing pages can also go on to emphasize the supplier's track record *with the particular market segment*. "We are the trusted supplier to over 300 salons" is far more powerful for a salon owner than a statement that does not speak to them so directly.

A headline announcing "Business Owners—Tips for Reducing Your Tax Bill" would appeal more directly to a business owner than just "Tips for Reducing Your Tax Bill." The click-through rate may be lower, but the cost per click could also be lower and the conversion rate higher, making the campaign more cost-effective.

MULTIPLICITY BRINGS PAY-PER CLICK SAVINGS

The benefits of multiplicity are magnified when you are buying your traffic through pay-per-click advertising using AdWords, Facebook, or any of the other networks. If you plan to drive traffic through pay-per-click advertising, focusing pages at specific profiles also helps you capitalize by matching more specific ad content to specific landing pages.

For example, if your proposition sells equipment for fly fishing, you will get much better results with ads targeted to "fly fishing tackle" than simply "fishing tackle." Any clicks you get will be from people who want *exactly* what you have to offer. If your proposition is too broad, you will get clicks from prospects you cannot serve. The click costs money, and there is no sale.

If you address your content at specific roles, Facebook's pay-per-click ads can be very powerful , being highly targetable to people's profiles. Because individuals provide personal information to Facebook, you can write ad text to target users in certain positions. For example, showing "What Finance Directors Should Know About New Tax Law" only to people with that job title will get you much better click-through rates than focusing just on the offering.

SLICING AND DICING YOUR OFFERINGS

It is possible to take this principle much further, *deliberately slicing* your offerings thinner in order to address even finer segments.

If I am looking for a supplier of used fly fishing tackle in Rochdale, and I see an ad promoting "Rochdale's Biggest Supplier of Used Fly Fishing Tackle Supplies," I am very likely to click the ad, because I believe it's local to me. And if the page I land on has the same title, I will instantly know I am in the right place, and I am likely to browse further.

Even if the store supplies all kinds of fishing tackle over a large geographical area, it could achieve much better return on investment through segmenting its audience in this way, so that the ads and landing pages seem to be addressed directly to more distinct groups of visitors.

NOTE *Consider what factors you can use to slice your offerings to speak more directly to your prospects. Go beyond the logical groupings that are immediately obvious to you, and consider the external perspective. What could the people who need what you offer conceivably be searching for today?*

It is proven that focusing your appeal on a specific market segment generates a feeling of belonging. If your target market is overworked teachers, address your appeal to them directly. A headline like "Overwhelmed in the Classroom?" will connect instantly with that specific market and exclude less relevant segments.

One of the most effective ways to get someone's attention is to address them personally. You have to look no further than direct mail that lands in your mailbox. When something has your name on it, you are likely to pay attention.

> **NOTE** *The most effective ads are those that say the equivalent of "Hey you! Yes, you sir, in the green shirt!"*

Any communication that seems to have been written just for you will merit further investigation, because it appeals to your subject of primary interest—you!

For example, I could describe this book as *"Packed with tips on increasing conversion rates of web sites,"* which is all very well. It's an accurate enough description, but it's not going to grab attention.

But if I know more about you, I can focus my message more on you and your interests, by saying perhaps *"I'll show you how you can turn more of your web site visitors into paying customers."* Does that work better? (Do you see how many of the words in that second sentence begin with the letter "y"?)

We are all human beings, seeking connection and meaning through relationships. When a brand or a message speaks directly to you, or seems to reflect where you are, you are likely to identify with it as yours.

Check out your bathroom cabinet or kitchen cupboard for products that speak directly to a customer in a clearly defined segment. If you see "Specially formulated for people with curly hair," it seems to make a promise that it will perform better than another less-focused product. (It doesn't, of course, make that promise.)

When there are many competitors in a market, the simple linguistic act of distinguishing your offering from the rest can be enough to give people the one positive reason they need to choose yours.

In just a quick look around my house I found the following physical products:

▶ A hair product called "Brilliant Brunette"—which would probably clean blond hair just fine.

▶ A toothpaste just for 4–6 year olds—which would also work for 3-year olds or bigger kids.

▶ "Family size" orange juice—which is no more appropriate for a family than it is for someone who just drinks a lot of orange juice.

The only reason the orange juice is marketed as "Family size" is to make it appeal more to someone buying for a family (which is the majority of the market) than the next carton that doesn't make that connection. It is no more suitable than the next product. There is no intrinsic family-appropriate-ness about the juice. It's just plain old orange juice. But it is made to seem more appropriate just by the use of language that isolates a market segment.

> **NOTE** *It has been proven that print ads can double their conversion rates through the simple technique of mentioning the host publication. If an ad runs in the* Daily Bugle, *adding a corner flash that says "Exclusive to Daily Bugle readers!" will connect readers with the ad because it applies to them (obviously). Even someone who does not identify himself as a* Daily Bugle *reader must surely be reading the* Bugle *at that moment, so will not be put off by the exclusive claim.*

In Figure 7-3, I rewrote the main heading text on this software marketing site. The original said "ZEFYR—ONLINE ACCOUNTING SOFTWARE." The alternative heading removed the caps and changed the text to "Complete Online Accounting Package for Small Businesses."

This small change converted 15.4% more visitors to subscribe. Why? I think the main reason is because small-business owners identify that the product is *for them*.

FIGURE 7-3 More accurate targeting on a main heading increased the conversion rate by 15.4%.

YOU-ORIENTED LANGUAGE

Another obvious but overlooked technique is simply to talk to the visitor as "you," instead of talking about yourself all the time. (Who do they care about?)

Figure 7-4 shows the results of rewriting the introductory text on our agency's home page. The new copy is much more about "you." Notice how it also stresses benefits over what we do.

The two factors tend to go hand-in-hand. Writing you-oriented copy requires stepping into the visitor's point of view, where features appear as benefits.

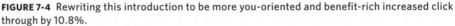

FIGURE 7-4 Rewriting this introduction to be more you-oriented and benefit-rich increased click through by 10.8%.

Match the Promise of the Link

One of the early warning signs of low conversion rates is question marks floating above visitors' heads. A great way to create question marks in people's minds is when a page does not match the *promise* of the link they clicked. You can't do much about links from other people's pages, but ensure that any links from your own pages are fulfilled when the next page loads.

If I click a link that offers "Ten Easy Tips for Losing Weight," I expect to be able to see immediate evidence of the tips as soon as I arrive on the next page. If I click "Contact us," I expect something that is clearly a contact page, not something clever and cryptic.

If I get something else I might assume the site is broken. When a page shows me just what I expect to find, there is no mental friction and all my attention is available to get the page's unique message.

Figure 7-5 shows the top section of a page design for a site that sells ranch land across the USA. Each state would have its own landing page. When you arrive on the page, you expect the page to announce exactly what's there for you. Many pages could benefit from a simple, obvious "You are here" statement.

FIGURE 7-5 My home page design for a site that... well, I'll let you work it out.

Distinguish Your Offering

Clearly demonstrating your *unique value proposition (UVP)* can be a great way to grab visitors' attention. Your UVP is a description that summarizes what sets your offering apart from alternatives.

It should *positively* differentiate you from the competition. A good way to distinguish positive differentiation is to ask whether a competitor may conceivably say the *opposite*. If no one would take the opposite position, you are not positively differentiating.

For example, if one of your values is "exclusive," this can be a positive value, because someone else may claim "popular." If one of your values is "cheap," someone else may have "high-value." Being a small-scale boutique producer is opposite to being a large-scale producer, and both are valid.

However, if you promote the value of "high quality," this is not a positive differentiator, because no competitor would claim "low quality." Do not claim reliability as a core value, because no one would claim to be unreliable. It is pointless to claim "desirable" because no competitor would identify with "undesirable."

If you can identify a strong UVP, make it instantly getable to every visitor. The most common way to do this is to use it for your *strap line* or slogan. My redesign for Atom (see Figure 7-6) uses the strap line "Simple online CRM and job management for Building Contractors." "Simple" is a positive differentiator because competitors may promote the power or comprehensiveness of their functionality.

Note how the target market is mentioned specifically in the strap line. Instead of "Home," the first item on the navigation menu says exactly what the product is and who it's for. And the page's headline shouts out the proposition.

FIGURE 7-6 The strap line, headline, subhead, and main navigation all help to distinguish the target audience.

Try these tips to help you focus on identifying a great unique value proposition:

▶ Look at your current competitors. Write words that describe what is distinct about them. For each word, write down the equivalent for your business.

▶ What can you say about your offerings that your competitors can't say?

▶ What do your prospects not yet know about you that might give them confidence in you?

▶ In what ways do you delight your existing customers? What nice things do they say about you? What gives them pleasant surprises? Do you promote these things today?

▶ Where do you provide exceptional service for customers (and neglect to talk about it)?

Use as many of these distinguishing features to differentiate your proposition from the crowd, and also to differentiate your prospects by their needs and expectations.

Write for the Undecided Prospect

Anyone who comes to any web page fits into one of three categories:

- ▶ Those who are determined to proceed to the next step, if it is possible
- ▶ Those who are not going to proceed, whatever happens
- ▶ Those who *may* proceed to the next step

When thinking about relevance, assume that *everyone* who visits every page is in the latter category—the "maybe" group, and write just for them.

Creating content only for the "maybes" is not going to have any negative impact on the "yes" or "no" groups, and it provides the key to optimize your conversions.

The "yes" group is going to click through to the next page anyway, so you do not need to create content for them. The "no" group is not going to proceed. They may just be coming to find a specific bit of information, collecting pictures, or researching prices for someone else. Whatever the reason, they are not in the market to be converted to the next step, so you should not write for them either.

Going back to Joe and his Miracle Hair-Gro, instead of saying "Buy my product—it really works!" he can refer to his landing matrix and craft a message specifically for a particular market (middle-aged men who are starting to go bald) and a particular level of awareness (know of his product, but do not trust its effectiveness). Joe might write, "How Miracle Hair-Gro Stopped Me Looking Old Before My Time."

Self-Interest

The second critical factor in creating appeals to capture attention is to make it appeal directly to the prospect's self-interest. We are all motivated to act in our own best interest. Telling visitors exactly what's in it for them is the number one way to get their attention.

NOTE *There is a school of thought that every choice we make is based on what we think will increase our own personal happiness. Actions that at first appear selfless, like giving money to a stranger, are done in order to get a feeling of satisfaction. It is possible to see payoffs even in apparently self-destructive choices.*

Remember to focus the language of your appeal on "you" (the visitor), not on "us." No one cares about your point of view, unless it benefits them directly, so get into theirs. Make it your goal to delight your customers by giving them just what *they* want to hear. You can't convert prospects by putting your needs before theirs. Only the belief that they are going to solve their needs, problems, and desires can trigger action.

Your prospects' needs are simple. Avoid the temptation to over-complicate or be clever. Your job is not to impress yourself, just give your market what they want.

"That which is written to please the writer rarely pleases the reader."

SAMUEL JOHNSON

Here are a few examples of targeting a headline on what's in it for the reader. See how they make the proposition immediately interesting and relevant to the audience:

- ▶ "Understanding Camera Metering" to "How To Master Camera Metering"
- ▶ "Why ProductX?" to "How ProductX Will Help You Work Faster"
- ▶ "Why StyleY is Cool" to "If you code AJAX, StyleY will change your life"
- ▶ "1000s of Free Fonts" to "Download 10,000 Fonts With 1 Click"
- ▶ "26 Great New Web Apps" to "26 Must-Have Web Apps You Never Heard About"

Visitors are looking to you to give them something to get their interest, in order to be encouraged to read on. Remember that your target visitors (that is, the undecided ones) do *want* to be in the right place, and they are open to being interested. All your page needs to do is to provide enough interest to persuade them there is value on offer.

Because we look for noticeable text to confirm where we are, and that text is usually the focal point of the page (which should be the beginning of the page's unique content) this section also focuses on techniques for writing interesting headlines.

"What's in It for Me?"

No one cares about what you do. All they care about is how it will benefit them. If you find any of your marketing messaging describes what you do, read it through the eyes of a potential customer, and ask "What's in it for me?" If there is no *benefit* to the customer, flip it so there is, or get rid of it.

For example, in Figure 7-7, we simply changed a few small elements to the page on SkinnerInc.com that explains to potential sellers how they can sell through Skinner to be more relevant to the seller, and *instantly generated a 213% increase* in downloads of the evaluation form.

▶ We changed the heading "Selling at Auction" to "Consigning to Auction is Easy with Skinner." Easy is a benefit, and the change of focus helps make the process feel less remote.

▶ We switched the two photos showing people's backs to a single photo showing an expert doing an evaluation, which feels more accessible and human.

▶ We changed the lower heading from "Determining Auction Estimates and the Appropriate Auction(s) for Your Property" to "How we Evaluate your Property," which is easier to understand.

▶ Finally, we added an extra call to action button for "Get a Free Evaluation Today."

The combined effect of these small changes is to help the reader believe that it is easy to go down the offered route.

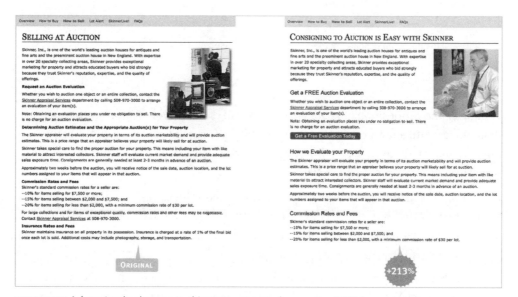

FIGURE 7-7 A few simple changes to this page generated a massive 213% increase in conversions.

Promise to Solve a Problem

What specific need does your offering propose to solve? Addressing that need directly and offering the promise of a solution will speak to the prospect's immediate concern and trigger an emotional response.

If the benefit is saving time, focus your whole appeal around that. If the need is to save money, reduce stress, cure an ailment, avoid fines, or reduce risks, let your entire message resonate clearly on the specific solution. The headline in Figure 7-8 tells the visitor exactly what they can do on this site, and promises a specific result.

FIGURE 7-8 This home page headline makes a strong promise.

Benefits

Whatever the proposition, it is benefits, not features, that hook visitors' attention. Benefits fall into a few broad categories, including financial gain, saving time, increasing personal attractiveness, having fun, improving self-esteem, or being able to do something you couldn't achieve before.

It is critical to encourage visitors to take action today. This is easier when you give them a benefit that is *quick and easy*. The promise of getting what I want today is more likely to get me to act now than some future benefit.

Count the number of benefits in my design for Surfulater.com in Figure 7-9. The page opens with a strong you-oriented, immediate, and benefit-laden headline: "Capture and Find the Content You Need… instantly!" It follows with a sequence of minor headings that address specific benefits. "Save Anything Instantly," "Retrieve Instantly," "Edit & Annotate Freely," "Easy to Manage," and "Share it Around" are all punchy benefits that could catch the attention of a prospect with a specific need in mind, leading to the call to action, "Try it Now FREE," to which the reasonable response should be, "Why not!"

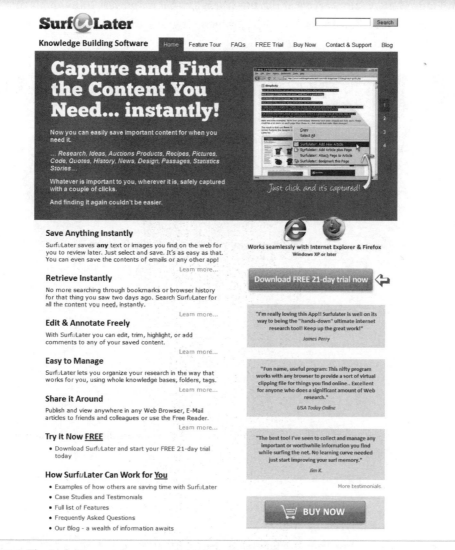

FIGURE 7-9 The Surfulater.com home page is loaded with benefits.

Benefits Appeal, Not Features

As I explained in Chapter 3, if your messages present only features, try flipping them to benefits. Go the extra mile to connect "what it does" to "what it does *for you*." Instead of listing benefits, evoke them emotionally by helping your visitors visualize how much easier their life *will be*. How will the benefit impact the life of the reader?

In Figure 7-10, visitors arrive at the site, a service that empowers individuals to cut their own debt, with a single clear problem. It grabs attention immediately by strongly asserting, "Yes you can!"

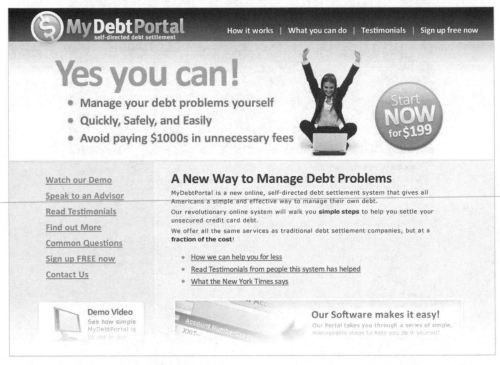

FIGURE 7-10 My design for a self-service debt management site answers the immediate personal question with powerful and direct appeal.

More examples of flipping features to benefits in headlines:

▶ Same-day delivery (feature) becomes a benefit: "You can relax, knowing your goods will arrive by 5pm."

▶ Server up-time (feature) becomes a benefit: "While you focus on your customers, we'll be working to ensure your server is online 24/7."

▶ Long battery life (feature) becomes "Don't worry if you have to jump on a last-minute flight. Our laptop battery will take you from London to New York—and back again."

▶ Great customer service (which is still a feature) becomes a personal benefit: "Our award-winning on-board team will ensure you arrive relaxed and ready for the day ahead."

▶ Low prices (feature) become "With the $500 you'll save by buying from us, you could take the family away on a surprise vacation."

▶ Double-taped seams (feature) become "Whether you're sailing offshore, trekking to base camp, or watching your child's soccer match, our double-taped seams ensure you stay warm and dry all day."

Put Benefits Before Features

Notice how many items in the preceding list start with the benefit, and *then* associate the feature. It is the benefit that grabs my attention by connecting emotionally with my imagination. The feature should follow, creating a connection in my mind that the benefit is a consequence of the feature.

This simple connection helps create desire for the product on offer. If a web user is comparing a few alternatives, she will assign more value to the one that offers her a personal vision, that the benefit will somehow enhance her life. Other products may have the exact same features, but unless they are served to her as emotive benefits, they will not seem as compelling.

My home page design for an online bed store, as shown in Figure 7-11, leads with a reassuring promise "You can sleep well." The headline is a simple, direct benefit, which has two meanings, suggesting you will get a good night's sleep on our comfortable beds, and also that you can rest easy because you can trust this vendor. There are no features in the headline, because the site has a wide range of products on offer. But this high-level benefit neatly applies to everything they sell.

AddAction is a low-cost but high-quality hosting provider, competing in a tough market. In my preparatory interview, we explored what its existing clients love about the service.

FIGURE 7-11 Features never sold anything. This headline tells the customer the direct benefit to her, before explaining how it may be achieved through one of their range of products.

The company had recently received the following message from a happy customer: "I submitted my ticket and 9 minutes later the issue was resolved. The best support ever!" To me, that kind of passion is pure marketing gold, so I made it the focal point of their new home page design, as shown in Figure 7-12.

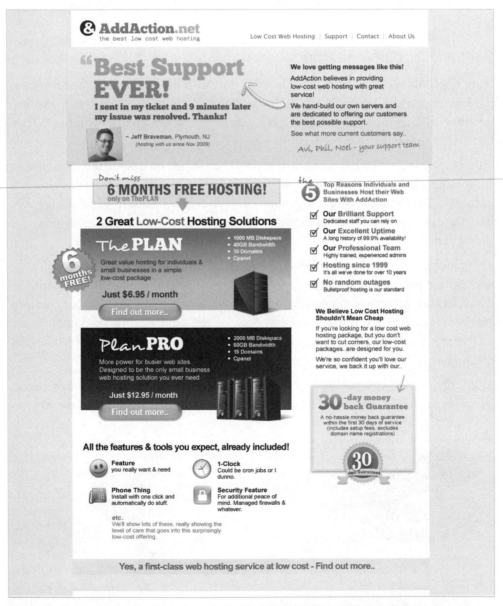

FIGURE 7-12 Instead of competing on features in this packed hosting sector, this home page design suggests important benefits (support) that connect more directly with the visitor.

When It's OK to Lead with Features

Sometimes it might be appropriate for a high-level page (such as a home page or section page) to mention features. For example, if your keyword research suggests that there is a significant market looking for "exhibition experts," you may lead with that descriptive feature, provided you then go on to highlight your benefits, as in Figure 7-13.

FIGURE 7-13 Apply common sense. If you have a market that's looking for features, by all means lead with matching text on landing pages.

Emotion

"People choose to buy based on emotion and then justify with logic" is one of the fundamental laws of sales. The buying decision is usually *already made emotionally* before logic comes into consideration, whether we are aware of it or not.

> **NOTE** *Rational thought and emotion occur in different parts of the brain. Emotional responses actually happen faster than thought, so psychologists tell us that emotion influences more of our choices than we imagine.*

It is tempting to rely on facts, but information is not the key to prompting action. Always look for emotional reasons that would compel a visitor to proceed. You can give all the reasons you like for why something makes sense, but unless people connect emotionally with the idea, they will not take action. Emotions, like love, fear, attraction, and hope trigger action in ways that ideas alone cannot.

Features are in the realm of logic, but benefits touch us personally and are in the realm of emotion. We actually make buying choices based on emotions, then justify our choice with reason. So it is benefits that cause us to choose to act. Without benefits to connect with we are unlikely to engage with a proposition. We may then also need more solid information to reinforce our choice.

For example, instead of a generic proposition like "Flowers delivered," see how the following appeals qualify their target market, solve a problem, and offer the buyer tangible benefits:

- ▶ Give Your Girlfriend the Perfect Valentine's Gift—Under $30
- ▶ How To Let Her Know "I Love You"
- ▶ Funeral Wreaths Delivered In 24 Hours—Guaranteed
- ▶ Last Minute Treat? These Gorgeous Summer Bouquets Delivered Nationwide Next Day
- ▶ Nothing Says "I'm Sorry" Like This Bouquet
- ▶ A Splash of Color to Brighten Any Day

Demonstrating emotions like enthusiasm, passion, and commitment will evoke similar responses in your reader. Don't shy away from letting your own emotion show in your web site copy. Your customers are human, and they respond like humans, which means they are dominated by their emotions.

Figure 7-14 shows a large headline I created for the home page of a life coach. The text "Live your life fully. Enjoy true success. Love every minute" works entirely in the emotional realm. Who would not accept the offer of these benefits? Because the services and benefits a life coach can offer can be so broad, this introduction sets out to make a bold claim that inspires and creates enthusiasm at a high level. If prospects connect with the emotions on display and are inspired, they will look further.

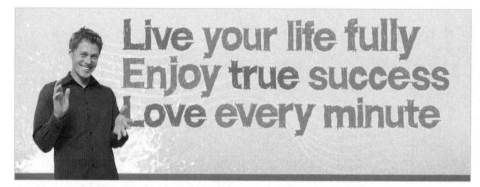

FIGURE 7-14 These promises speak directly to the emotional results on offer.

NOTE *Simply adding quote marks to a headline often increases believability and conversions, because it suggests the statement is coming from a real person.*

Figure 7-15 shows the content on our agency's contact page before and after a rewrite. The page used to invite the visitor to get in touch, in a businesslike but aloof tone. When we made it all about "you" (with seven mentions compared to two previously), and added a photo of our London sales office, conversions leaped by 94.7%.

Show the End Result

An easy shortcut to emotional connection is to show visitors a picture of the goal they want to reach. We are motivated by the promise of an easier or more enjoyable life, and it is this vision that keeps us moving forward. Showing the goal reached helps keep the visitors' eyes on the prize, which can soften the cost of whatever they have to do to reach it.

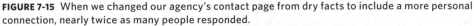

FIGURE 7-15 When we changed our agency's contact page from dry facts to include a more personal connection, nearly twice as many people responded.

For example, visitors to the BankLoans.com home page, shown in Figure 7-16, are looking for the possibility of buying their home. My redesign connects with the visitors' end goal by showing the image of a person moving to a new home with a smile on her face. This image connects with their personal desire and gives a strong signal that they are in the right place to get what they want.

Fear

Fear can be a strong motivating emotion, but it is most effective when you can make the pain of the fear immediately present, and offer instant relief.

- ▶ "Are You Giving Away $$$ Every Month?"
- ▶ "Hurry! Get Yours Before They're All Gone!"
- ▶ "Protect Your Family From Deadly EMF Radiation Today"
- ▶ "Why Men Never Call Back—And What You Can Do About It"

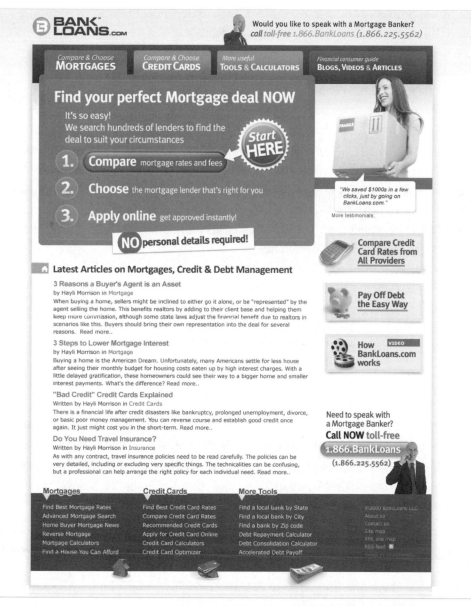

FIGURE 7-16 Showing the end result, moving home with a smile. Note how the emotion in the image works in partnership with the main headline, which offers specific and immediate benefits.

As advertising on tobacco products has shown, the fear of a possible future negative event is not a strong motivator. Human nature is more inclined to act on something for immediate benefit or relief than some potential risk. The exception to this is where the future problems would impact others, such as dependent family, so insurance advertising uses the fear approach to good effect.

Reversing the Promise

It is hard to make a clever headline that generates good results. When you are working against the clock with limited attention currency, you generally do not want to risk making people think too much. However, one approach that can work to get people to read on is to *tell them why the offer may not be relevant to them*!

For example, when writing copy to promote a course in more effective life management, I came up with the headline in Figure 7-17: "If You're Getting Everything You Want from Life, Don't Read This!" Such appeals may stimulate a sense of exclusion, which we naturally want to overcome.

> If You're Getting Everything You Want from Life, Don't Read This!
> (If you're ready for more, read on...)

FIGURE 7-17 Most people would admit they are not getting absolutely everything they want from life, so this teasing reverse inclusion will exclude few prospects.

Credibility

Whatever emotions you stimulate in your appeal, you should sail as close as you can to the wind, but keep your appeal *credible enough* to merit further investigation.

Ken McCarthy says that we all have two built-in filters, which the marketer must avoid tripping. One is the "So what?" filter and the other is the "Nonsense!" filter. Make sure that every statement you make will get through both of these filters.

A common way to trip the "So what?" filter is to ask a rhetorical question. Rhetorical questions are questions that do not require an answer. Questions will only get people to read if they require an answer. A frequent mistake I encounter is the "Why Should You Use Us?" headline. This tends to be answered with, "I don't know. It's your web site. You should be telling me."

Two tips for keeping on the right side of people's "Nonsense!" filter are to back up any claims you make with facts and evidence, and to acknowledge possible doubts in the reader's mind (for example, "Like you, I was doubtful that a service that seemed so cheap could deliver the quality I was used to, so I asked a bunch of questions...").

Designing for Attention

You need to ensure your attention-grabbing content is the first thing people notice. If you draw someone's attention to something, be sure you want them to read it.

When thinking about what your web page needs to communicate, you should now have a good idea of which values or concepts should be prominent. A few basic principles for graphic design will help you to get the attention you need, cleanly and efficiently:

▶ Getability
▶ Noticeability
▶ Navigation
▶ Imagery
▶ Look and feel

Getability

If visitors can find the signs to answer the golden question ("Am I in the right place?") in the first few seconds, they are likely to decide that moving forward offers better odds than moving backward, which means you have their attention. If they do not find those clues, retreating may seem the better option, and your attention-seeking has failed.

I call the quality of how easy it is to "get" a page's purpose *getability*.

The page's first job is to say "Yes—you are probably in the right place." When a page has good getability, visitors will say "I get it, and I know what to do next," without really needing to think. The signs they need will jump straight out. This means those key clues need to be the first things they notice.

What visitors need to see to know they're in the right place depends on the context. Consider where they are on the Awareness Ladder, what they are trying to achieve, and how they may have arrived at the page.

In just a thin slice of time, your site has to come across as the right kind of site, with the right subject matter and tone. (Of course "right" might mean cheap or expensive, professional or amateur, depending on the values you want to communicate.)

All you need to do for high getability is to present plain, obvious communication. Any cryptic, conflicting, or misleading messages will cause mental friction, reduce getability, and damage your conversion rates.

One of the most effective ways to increase getability is to strip away things that are not required. Identify the features that can help answer "Am I in the right place?" and try removing anything that does not. The result has to be more attention available for the content that matters, which can only increase your chance of getting someone's attention. The pure simplicity of the Google search page, with one primary function that dominates attention, could be one of the main factors in its success.

You can simplify any aspect of content or design, including layout. Figure 7-18 shows a test we ran on a previous version of the "Save the Pixel" sales page. Simply removing the left-hand column, with its navigation options, newsletter sign-up box, and extra info, *increased sales by 20.5%*. Because there are fewer things for visitors to look at, they are more likely to engage with the core message.

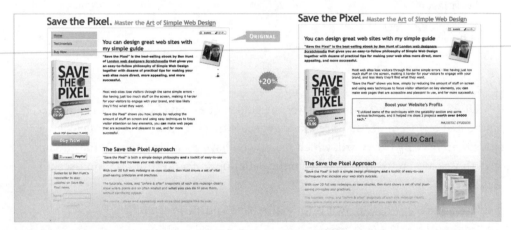

FIGURE 7-18 Removing the side column on the old "Save the Pixel" sales page delivered a 20.5% increase in sales by focusing on the proposition.

Figure 7-19 shows a view from Gurushot.com, a web-based application we designed and built, which shows visitors wisdom quotes in response to their queries. The site's design excludes any elements that are unnecessary for delivering the desired experience, allowing users to focus directly on the content.

Noticeability

Getability depends on another factor, which is the relative *noticeability* of the various elements presented. Every element has its own level of noticeability—how strongly it pulls the eye and calls attention to itself.

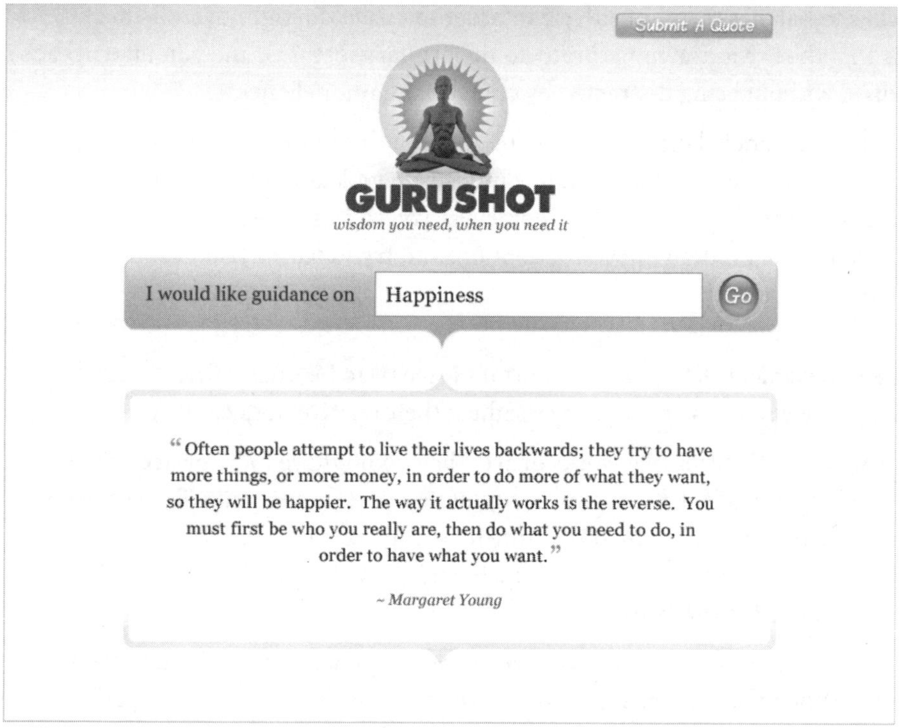

FIGURE 7-19 Gurushot.com has a minimalist design that focuses attention on the relevant content.

I identify eight design factors that can affect noticeability:

- ▶ Size
- ▶ Contrast
- ▶ Boldness
- ▶ Color
- ▶ Position
- ▶ Space
- ▶ 3-D Effects
- ▶ Movement

The important thing to remember is that these factors all work together in the same space. You can use any combination of them to change the relative noticeability of visual elements.

The trick is to balance them sensitively in order to create the right overall effect, which is that the eye is drawn naturally to the primary features, and can take in each one in turn, without being distracted by competing minor elements.

How to find the right balance is outside the scope of this book. It requires sensitivity and experience. The fundamental technique is to look at the page as though you are seeing it for the first time, and to spot where your eye is drawn. If it is the wrong place, consider what is drawing your attention, and try to fix the balance.

SIZE

The bigger an element is, the more important it seems to be. Increasing the relative sizes of visual elements is an easy way to adjust their relative noticeability.

Don't treat your web pages like works of art. They do not have to be perfectly balanced. The longer you look at an entire page design, the farther you will drift from the way it is actually used—which is scanned quickly for clues. Try to make a page entirely consistent and balanced and you will end up with something that lacks the critical edge it needs to grab attention.

Many pages can afford to increase the size of the initial headline and other primary messaging. When you remove unnecessary visual clutter, you have more space available, so you can enlarge the primary signals, as shown in my design for EventRight, shown in Figure 7-20. The eye can only settle on elements that have content value: the identity, navigation, copy, and content imagery.

CONTRAST

Tonal contrast is a very important factor. The sharper an element's contrast (the balance between light and dark) with its surroundings, the more it stands out. I will offer some important tips on using contrast in your page designs.

Try squinting at the page through almost-closed eyes, so that the screen blurs. Can you spot some areas of contrasting tones (usually dark-on-white)? If not, you may not have anything that has enough contrast to draw the eye. Many designers have a natural tendency to reduce contrast of a design the longer they stare at it. Try to add some content that is both important and higher-contrasting (which can be large text, or imagery).

Figure 7-21 shows the EventRight design with a blur effect applied, which reveals strong contrast around the logo (top-left) the main call to action (top-right), the dark navigation strip, the photograph at the bottom right, and the black-on-white heading at the top of the content area. The heading in the header strip does not show up so well, because it is white against a mid-tone background, so it may be more effective either to use black text or to darken the background.

FIGURE 7-20 Using fewer visual elements lets you make the most important ones larger and more noticeable.

FIGURE 7-21 Use the squint test to check how many different areas of strongly contrasting tones your page has.

If you see more than about ten areas of contrast, you could end up with a page that is drawing the eye in too many different directions, which means that it will not be able to focus on any one area.

Edges of strongly contrasting tones draw the eye. If you find it's hard to read a web page, check the contrast between the main content area and the page background. If there is high contrast, this will constantly pull your attention away from the content. I prefer to use white for the main content area and light tones for backgrounds, creating a low-contrast boundary.

BOLDNESS

Boldness is a feature that emphasizes tonal contrast. Stronger, heavier lines create clearer tonal boundaries, which draw the eye. Boldness is most often associated with text. Use either large type size, and/or a bolder typeface for your main headings. Lightweight text will be less noticeable. You may also apply bold weight to specific words in content, if you want them to jump out.

COLOR

Color works in a similar way to contrast, in that it can create distinction between elements. Pages should have a basic color scheme (which may be subtle and consistent, or brash and cheap, depending on the brand).

The two basic principles are:

▶ Use the same colors to tie together areas.
▶ Use contrasting colors (usually from the opposite side of the color wheel) to draw attention to specific features.

For example, if your main page hue is cold and blue, you may use orange or red as a highlight (or "spot") color, which would stand out. If the design is based on a warm color scheme, you might use blue or green for contrast.

I recommend keeping the background colors of pages soft. Also, if you use too many different colors on the same page, it becomes difficult to make anything stand out, and the reader may feel overwhelmed.

POSITION

Clearly, your main message should be near the top of your page. Specifically, it should be at the top of your content area. This assumes that the regular page "furniture" (including logo and permanent navigation) are easily distinguishable, which means the visitor can group them and ignore them to move straight to the main heading and imagery.

Do not put so much at the top of the page that the primary content risks ending up "below the fold" (that is, the visitor will need to scroll to see it)!

Follow conventions when positioning elements on screen. Eye tracking research shows that some areas of the page, such as the top-right corner, tend to be seen as lower priority than others. Other areas, like the top-left of the main content area, are more often focused on.

When you first look at a page, where is your eye drawn? It is likely to be an element that combines several of the noticeability factors.

Use those noticeability factors to draw attention to the page's unique main content, starting with the headline. If attention is drawn to a feature that is not *unique to the page*, or to content that does not help get visitors' attention, there is a great opportunity to improve click through.

SPACE

Putting space around any element makes it more noticeable. It is easier to recognize the shape (silhouette) of an object if it is not crowded by other elements.

I advise removing boxes and lines wherever possible, because this creates more space on your page, meaning that everything can be slightly easier to read, and allows you to use more extra space around your most important elements.

I also like to use increased line height in body text, and also to add extra vertical space between columns, as I find this increases readability.

Figure 7-22 shows a section from an e-commerce page I redesigned recently. Note how each element has enough white space around it to make it easy to read. Don't be tempted to cram content close together—unless you do not want it to be read!

3-D EFFECTS

Some graphical effects create the illusion of 3-D space. These include gradients, drop shadows, and reflections. When you give an element space or shape in this way, it literally stands out from the page.

We are naturally drawn to things that are shiny or seem to have shape. There are a few general rules to using 3-D effects. Because, most of the time, they use light shading to create the effect, it is advisable to keep the source of the light consistent. If light seems to come from many directions at once, it can break the illusion.

I would also advise against using too many effects. You do not want to draw attention to too many elements, so reserve 3-D effects for particular content. Use it minimally on elements that are present on every page, because you do not want to make these too noticeable.

HP C7250 Ink
PhotoSmart C7250 Ink Cartridges

HP C7250 ink cartridges and supplies. Guaranteed quality, discount-pricing, and same-day shipping! Compatible with the following model(s): C7250

HP C7250 Ink, PhotoSmart C7250 Ink Cartridges

☑ **Compatible HP PhotoSmart C7250 Ink**

SAVE with our compatible ink cartridges, color and page yield guaranteed to meet or exceed OEM brand ink cartridges.

Buy only what you need and obtain quantity discount pricing. All quantity discount items are added together to calculate your pricing tier, including quantity discount items already in your shopping cart. Learn more about our quantity discount pricing.

Item		You pay just	Add
★	Remanufactured HP Ink Cartridge, Cyan, 400 page yield. Replaces HP part number: HP 02 Cyan, C8771WN,C8771WN#140.	Buy 1 $6.00 each Buy 4-7 $5.50 each Buy 8-11 $5.00 each Buy 12+ $4.50 each	1 ⇒ 🛒
★	Remanufactured HP Ink Cartridge, Cyan, 400 page yield. Replaces HP part number: HP 02 Cyan, C8771WN,C8771WN#140.	Buy 1 $6.00 each Buy 4-7 $5.50 each Buy 8-11 $5.00 each Buy 12+ $4.50 each	1 ⇒ 🛒
★	Remanufactured HP Ink Cartridge, Cyan, 400 page yield. Replaces HP part number: HP 02 Cyan, C8771WN,C8771WN#140.	Buy 1 $6.00 each Buy 4-7 $5.50 each Buy 8-11 $5.00 each Buy 12+ $4.50 each	1 ⇒ 🛒
★	Remanufactured HP Ink Cartridge, Cyan, 400 page yield. Replaces HP part number: HP 02 Cyan, C8771WN,C8771WN#140.	Buy 1 $6.00 each Buy 4-7 $5.50 each Buy 8-11 $5.00 each Buy 12+ $4.50 each	1 ⇒ 🛒
★	Remanufactured HP Ink Cartridge, Cyan, 400 page yield. Replaces HP part number: HP 02 Cyan, C8771WN,C8771WN#140.	Buy 1 $6.00 each Buy 4-7 $5.50 each Buy 8-11 $5.00 each Buy 12+ $4.50 each	1 ⇒ 🛒
★	Remanufactured HP Ink Cartridge, Cyan, 400 page yield. Replaces HP part number: HP 02 Cyan, C8771WN,C8771WN#140.	Buy 1 $6.00 each Buy 4-7 $5.50 each Buy 8-11 $5.00 each Buy 12+ $4.50 each	1 ⇒ 🛒

★ **Save More with Discount Pricing on ANY starred items!**
Add 1 more of <u>any</u> starred item to get an instant discount on all

⊕ Add to Cart

FIGURE 7-22 Although this page section includes a lot of content, I ensured all the important information has some space around it for good readability.

Figure 7-23 shows my design for Synctus.com, which makes a clever device that synchronizes files on special hard drives between multiple locations via the Internet. The design creates the illusion of a large shape that seems to be on a flat virtual plane, creating a 3-D suggestion of a diagram showing how data moves between multiple back-up storage devices.

Note how the headline "Synch files between offices… Quickly, Securely, Easily" distinguishes the market for the product. The only people who would ever need this solution will be those with responsibility for IT for organizations that have multiple offices. So the headline immediately qualifies that market *in*, disqualifies the rest, and also includes three differentiating features.

FIGURE 7-23 The Synctus site uses the illusion of 3-D space to draw attention to the product and main content.

MOVEMENT

Things that move grab our attention. It is an unavoidable biological fact. We are tuned to spot movement, which could be prey or a threat. Some of the most annoying online ads use this fact and apply animation to catch your eye.

There is a more subtle type of dynamism that you can use, which is the suggestion of movement. Diagonal lines and shapes are more dynamic than square angles, so use them to draw the eye (but be careful not to lead the eye off the page).

TESTING AND FIXING NOTICEABILITY

Figure 7-24 shows the results of a fascinating test. I initially redesigned the header strip of towelsdirect.co.uk to focus more on benefits to the customer. (To run the test, I used Google Website Optimizer, which is covered fully in Chapter 11.)

Here are the changes I tested:

▶ I increased the noticeability of the logo, phone number, and the three key features.
▶ I crafted a new strap line (the title that goes with the logo to explain the offering).
▶ I added a badge graphic claiming "#1 Choice."

The result was a significant *drop* in conversion rate of 45.4%!

FIGURE 7-24 Three headers on towelsdirect.co.uk, showing a huge turnaround in conversion rates from a few seemingly minor changes.

I had to ask what might have caused such a negative impact. I wondered whether the badge and the other features were drawing attention *away* from the content, so I tried the third strip, where I removed the badge and reduced the size and contrast of the text. This produced a *46.5% increase* in conversion rate over the original strip!

What could explain the switch?

▶ Perhaps the "#1 Choice" badge lacked credibility.
▶ Maybe the heading was too cluttered and visually distracting.

▶ Or, it could be that the most noticeable items were not what people needed to see to get their attention.

The lesson to draw from this example is that all the content and design factors interact in complex and subtle ways. We should use all the skills and knowledge at our disposal to make our very best guess designs, but we must always test.

> **WARNING** *Increasing the noticeability of an unhelpful element can have a negative impact on success. If you have made something more noticeable or readable and conversion drops, look more closely at what draws attention. How could it be unhelpful?*

Navigation

Your site's permanent navigation does three jobs:

▶ Tells you where you are

▶ Tells you where else you can go

▶ Gives you a means to get there

All three factors are important for getability. A new site's navigation structure works like signage in a store, giving visitors a good idea both of where they are and what is available, which gives them clues as to what kind of site they're on. So ensure your top navigation is clear, descriptive, and useful. Even if visitors do not see the next step forward on the page, hopefully your clear navigation will offer them somewhere else to look without leaving the site.

Notice how the simple navigation in Figure 7-25 makes it totally clear where you are now, including an arrow that points to the content, as well as where you can go next. A strong headline communicates the proposition, and the simple layout leads the eye through the message to two clear next steps.

Imagery

Although graphics do not *generally* impact conversion as much as text content, the first imagery you notice when arriving on a new page is important for getability.

Ensure that the first images people notice directly communicate the subject matter of the page.

Western Interpreting Network

| About Win.tv | VRS | VRI |
| Video interpreting services | FREE Video Relay Service | Video Remote Interpreting |

Video Interpreting Services Aid Communication between Deaf or Hard-of-hearing & Hearing People

Win.tv provides **video interpreting services** to help **deaf** and hard-of-hearing people communicate freely with hearing people using **video conferencing** technology.

We offer two great **remote interpreting services**:

> **Win.tv VRS** - which connects a hearing and deaf/hard-of-hearing person through a dedicated interpreter, allowing both parties to communicate more easily - FREE.

> **Win.tv Video Remote Interpreting** - puts a professional Americal Sign Language interpreter on site through a video link, giving you ultimate flexibility and speed, cutting costs and helping protect the environment.

Win.tv is entirely owned and operated by deaf people. Because we use this service every day, we can guarantee all our translators are full trained to the highest standards.

Watch a Demo

Does Videophone Counseling Work?

0:00 / 3:13

Existing Users Say..

"I can say that without doubt Win.tv has made my life better!"

Noel Ironleg, CA

"After using several systems, this is hands-down the best."

Penelope Bluetooth, TX

"Would definitely recommend Win.tv to anyone with a deaf relative in the US"

Amish Patel, India

Our Video Interpreting Services

WIN.tv VRS

FREE

Win.tv Video Relay Service

Deaf or hard-of-hearing users can make calls to hearing recipients.

Call a deaf or hard-of-hearing person from a regular phone.

Communicate freely using professional dedicated ASL interpreters by video link.

FREE to use, for calls orginating from, or placed to, US numbers.

Learn more

WIN.tv PRO VRI

Video Remote Interpreting

Win.tv's VRI gives you your own fully qualified ASL interpreter present through video link.

Maximum flexibility and speed

Massive savings compared to on-site visits.

Lower risk - you have the back-up of a whole team on hand, with no transport links to miss.

Reduces travel pollution.

Learn more

Coypright & footer links...

FIGURE 7-25 My design for the home page of Win.tv features simple navigation that makes it obvious where you are and where you can go.

For example, if your site has a photo of a car on it, what does that say? You could sell cars, insurance, driving lessons, valet services, or car polish! If you sell insurance, make sure the imagery supports your intended message. If you sell driving lessons, clearly show driving lessons, and people will get they're in the right place.

> **NOTE** *Tests run by the Ogilvy agency several decades ago proved that when people are presented with an advertisement that features an image of some item, they are likely to assume the item has something to do with the ad. So if you sell computer software solutions, don't show a bridge. If you sell loans, don't show an empty park bench (both real examples from sites I have redesigned).*

One thing you do know about everyone who comes to your site is that they are people. People are most interested in two things: themselves and other people. As social animals, we get a lot of information from others' faces, so our brains are tuned to pay attention to faces.

Showing a human face is an easy way to increase the attention-pulling power of a page. If that face is smiling and looking at the camera, it gets even more attention.

Figure 7-26 shows two versions of the main product shot from a client's sales page (bibletimeline.net). The original picture had shown the chart's format, but did not give an idea of either the size of the product or the details it provides.

For our initial test, we added a close-up of a small area of detail, showing more of the information that is available on the chart. We also added width and height measurements showing its scale. We expected an increase in conversion rate, based on the principle that people like detail. However, there was no improvement at all.

FIGURE 7-26 Adding a smiling person boosted conversions by 38%.

In the second experiment, we overlaid a photo of a young woman pointing to the chart and smiling to the camera. This put the chart into a human context. People could immediately get the scale of the chart, and could picture themselves using it attached to a wall. Adding the woman resulted in a massive 38.8% increase in click through to the purchase page.

Look and Feel

Although key content should clearly communicate where you are and try to capture attention, it is not advisable to ignore the *softer* elements of a page's message. These are the subconscious signs of the *quality* of the site, and might be communicated through branding, color scheme, typefaces, or content imagery.

If the page doesn't look right, or if you make a visitor think, "Er, am I in the right place here?" you are off to a bad start.

When done well, these values should come through in the general look and feel. The page should just look and feel right.

If you are selling expensive hand-made shoes, the site should have muted colors, close-up photographs of the artisan's skill, and an elegant old-world feel, giving a feel of timeless quality that embodies attention to detail.

However, if you are selling cut-price shoes, perhaps a cheap-looking site is more appropriate. A page that uses primary colors, star flashes, and bold headlines in full caps would suggest the page has been put together in a hurry by a retailer who is too busy selling shoes to take time to craft his web page. It may also suggest that little has been spent, reinforcing the sense that the shoes are being sold as cheaply as possible. (Some sites spend a lot of money to get this look just right.)

Figure 7-27 shows two of my early designs for a large UK tile retailer, tile.co.uk. The design on the left is bigger, brighter, and bolder, which suggests a more aggressively priced offering. The design on the right appears more up-market, with its muted color scheme and softer features. The choice of approach came down to how the client wished to position the brand.

There is no right answer to what the right look and feel is. (It is a great candidate for broad-strokes testing, using A/B split tests.) The guidance will come from the qualities you need to project in order to qualify the page as "the right place."

Although these look and feel factors may not grab attention as such, their job is to match the visitor's expectations, so the site *qualifies* for further investigation.

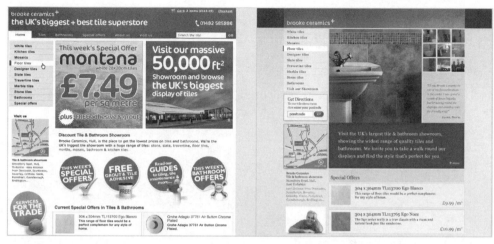

FIGURE 7-27 Two alternative approaches for tile.co.uk—but which is the right one?

Does your logo project the right qualities and values? Is the personality right? Do the colors and fonts project the feel a visitor would expect? Is the layout familiar?

Resist the temptation to make your site different from the crowd, if doing so would make it harder to *get* what kind of site it is.

Getability Tests

Use these quick tests to check how getable your page designs are:

- ▶ Try ignoring all the words on the page. Do imagery and graphics give the right first impression that you're in the right kind of place?
- ▶ Take just the first three things that you see when you view the page (without scrolling). Do they convey enough to give you confidence to keep looking? If after taking in the first three things, there's no incentive to keep reading, stop and introduce a good one.
- ▶ Remove all body text and just look at headings. Does the page work when just reading the headings? You can't assume that any visitor will read all your content, so ensure the content that stands out most conveys your message.

If you have applied the tips in this chapter, you should be confident you can get more attention. This gives you some currency to continue communicating your proposition. Next, you need to use the attention to keep your visitor engaged and build interest in the next step.

CHAPTER 8

Keep Them Engaged

Each of your web pages is an advertisement for the next step forward. The only way to achieve your ultimate goals is to get your visitors to the top of the Awareness Ladder. From whatever point they enter, your purpose is to get their attention and then to get them moving onward and upward. For that to happen, you have to keep your visitors engaged.

This chapter looks at techniques you can apply to maximize engagement on your web pages to move more visitors up the ladder toward conversion.

Assume every visitor is an undecided prospect who is open to taking the next action. You have already achieved the first crucial step by getting her attention. Once you have her attention, you must keep her interest so that you can communicate your message. The longer you keep her engaged, the more thoroughly you can get your message across.

When you have communicated your message as well as you can, your visitors should be willing to take the next action you present. What needs to happen for them to be ready to do so? An engaging web page should do four key things:

- ▶ Affirm the *positive signs* visitors are looking for.
- ▶ Resolve their *concerns* and *build trust*.
- ▶ Build *interest*.
- ▶ Make it *easy* to keep engaging.

Your visitors need positive reasons to take any action. They need to trust that it will produce the result they expect. They must be interested in the promised outcome. And the whole process needs to feel easy.

Affirm the Positive Signs

No one will take any action without sufficient reason to do so. What gives us the motivation to move forward is the positive vision of a life that is better, easier, or less painful. If you can get your prospects to imagine the benefits of a proposition in their lives, you have done most of the work, because that vision will create powerful emotional responses that make it easier to take action.

Whenever we interact with a web site, we are motivated by some goal. Now that a web page has gotten our attention, we suspect we're in the right place to get what we want. But we are not yet convinced enough to take action. We need to see more reasons first, signs that confirm we are moving in the right direction, getting closer to our goal. I call these signs *affirming positives*.

As we proceed, the scent trail gets stronger. Interest, anticipation, and desire build. Finally, we are convinced enough to commit to the next step. Examples of questions that require affirming positives include:

- Will it work?
- Does it meet my needs?
- Will it fit?
- Does it have a proven track record in my industry?
- Do other companies use this?
- Is this the best price?
- Do they serve my area?
- Is there a support package?
- Can I afford to run it?
- Will it work with my setup?
- Is it suitable for domestic use?
- Will you deliver?

Whatever positive signs we need, they must all be answered with a "Yes!" When our affirming positives are checked off, we are ready to proceed toward conversion. Missing affirming positives are holes in your road—things that should be there but are not. A hole in the road could stop visitors in their tracks.

Remember to use these methods to ensure you provide enough affirming positives:

- Consider the *present concerns* of each market segment and what signs they may be looking for that tell them they're in the right place.
- Be *thorough*. Provide comprehensive information to serve the needs of every personality type (but don't force me to wade through it all).

▶ Stick to the *facts*. Show details, backed up with numbers where relevant.

▶ Provide *evidence*. Stories are far more credible than empty claims.

The problem is, we each need different reasons. This raises the challenge of how to present all the affirming positives required to address all your target visitors' needs.

When you use the multiplicity approach, and distinguish your funnels by market and their specific need, you should have insight into what signs each market may be looking for. This should help you filter the content required to keep each type of prospect engaged.

Long or Short Copy?

In a medium like mail order advertising, long copy sells. The long-standing motto in direct mail is "The more you tell, the more you sell." This has been proven time and again.

I would say the same principle applies to marketing on the Web. But some important differences exist.

The reason why long copy sells in print is that it lets the copywriter put forward many angles, each of which could appeal to different types of people. Different people may be looking for different qualities in the proposition. The more reasons the copywriter includes, the more likely he or she is to connect with what each of us is looking for.

> *"Whatever claim you use to get attention, the advertisement should tell a story reasonably complete. When you once get a person's attention, then is the time to accomplish all you ever hope with him. Bring all your good arguments to bear. Cover every phase of your subject. One fact appeals to some, one to another. Omit any one and a certain percentage will lose the fact which might convince."*
>
> CLAUDE C. HOPKINS, SCIENTIFIC ADVERTISING

Some web marketers apply the long-copy approach directly to sales pages, and create *squeeze pages* that are 10 screens long, bombarding the reader with every angle, every fact, testimonials, and multiple calls to action. The reason they do that is because it has been proven to work.

Do not assume that the long sales format is the only solution for any of your web pages. These long pages typically sell only one thing. Your web site may need to represent the breadth of what you offer, which means it needs navigation. People may expect to see links to your contact page, your home page, or your privacy policy.

Your web site is not a standalone single-shot message, like a sales letter or mail order ad. It can be a *conversation*, or many concurrent conversations that can adapt intelligently to different visitors' needs.

As well as funneling visitors toward the center of your concentric web site model, you can also offer them the option to move sideways, to find more detailed information on a subject, or even to switch to an alternative appeal.

Engaging Different Personality Types

Different people think and interact in very different ways. Not least when it comes making a commitment such as buying.

In our company we use a very simple and effective personality profiling tool called DISC. DISC categorizes people's behavior using four factors: Dominance, Influence, Steadiness, and Conscientiousness. Each of us exhibits some mix of these flavors. In many cases, one factor is stronger than the others and shows up more in our behavior.

I find understanding DISC an extremely useful tool for visualizing how to market to everyone. Each DISC characteristic has its particular buying style. Each buying style has a corresponding most effective selling style. If you are going to reach the maximum market, you need to sell to every type. To do that, it is vital to understand what each type values most.

▶ The Dominance characteristic values competency, results, and action.

▶ The Influence characteristic values action, enthusiasm, and relationships.

▶ The Steadiness characteristic values relationships, sincerity, and dependability.

▶ The Conscientiousness characteristic values dependability, quality, and competency.

Applying the DISC profiles to the way people buy shows up some interesting patterns. To get commitment from one of the types, it is necessary to give them the things they value most. Everyone has some mix of the following tendencies:

▶ When selling to strong-I personality types, they want to feel a personal interest, to see action, but the key is to show enthusiasm. Without that, they are unlikely to feel connected enough with the proposition. Strong-I prospects are more influenced by compelling positive messages.

▶ With strong-S types, understanding and sympathy are key to generating the trust they need to commit. This is not always a quick process, and they are likely to take more time to come to a decision. They are likely to need repeated positive messages that reassure their need for personal connection.

▶ Strong-C types need to get all the facts in order to know they are making the right choice. They need more details and evidence about the quality and performance of what they are investing in. This can also take longer than with other types. They often need to see the most detailed information, and value facts and evidence over emotion.

▶ Strong-D people are outgoing and action-oriented, like I types, and also interested in competency like C-types. They want action and the promise of results. Like strong-I types, they want positive, confidence-inspiring messages, but will respond better to bold, action-oriented language than emotive personal language.

HOW TO COMMUNICATE TO DIFFERENT TYPES

In general, strong-D and strong-I personality types require *less information*. If they get excited about the possibilities, they are likely to commit. Strong-S and strong-C types need *more information* in order to trust the proposition.

None of these approaches is any better, worse, or more or less effective. The key point is that some personalities need more information, whereas others can be converted with less. This is why long copy has *traditionally* outperformed short copy. It makes it easier to give everyone enough information.

The same goes for your web site. Saying too little is riskier than saying too much. You should present all the arguments, reasons, and facts. You should also consider content that speaks to the needs of each personality type:

▶ **Dominance**—State that you have all the expertise required to deliver results, that you are committed and ready to deliver now. Remember to defer to their authority.

▶ **Influence**—Show passion and enthusiasm. Let them know you are really keen to work with them, listen to what they need, and get them excited about the possibilities available.

> ▶ **Steadiness**—Take the time to show they can trust you. You care about your customers, really listen to their needs, and make sure you provide a reliable service.

> ▶ **Conscientiousness**—Provide all the facts and details they require. Do not skimp on the evidence. Give them whitepapers, charts, case studies, and give them the opportunity to ask you more questions.

COVER ALL THE BASES

To give every visitor everything they need, you need to cover all the bases. Make all the information easily available, but don't require everyone to read it.

Lots of facts without a human connection will be unappealing to I and S types. Too much personal connection will turn off D and C types, as will failing to prove your credentials.

If you rush C and S types, they may not be ready to commit. However, forcing I and D types to wade through lots of information may lose their interest.

I would avoid the temptation to make assumptions about a whole market, such as thinking that most accountants will be high-conscientious types. We all have our natural tendencies, which we may adjust in order to do our jobs. Your accountant market will have representatives from all personality types, so always be thorough and provide everyone with content they can connect with.

Everyone is looking for different affirming positives. Every phrase on your page could be a hook for a different type of visitor. Using a variety of factors in your copy is like putting several different types of bait on many lines. Use one type of bait and you'll only catch one type of fish. Use the full range, and you will maximize your chances.

How to Say Less and More

Ideally, you want a way to show different content to each personality type. Fortunately, the Web medium means you can. Some people skim-read all the headlines in a newspaper, whereas others read the stories that interest them word for word. That works on web pages too. But because web sites are interactive, even more options are available:

> ▶ You can give people the high-level story together with links to "break out" and get more information if they need it.

▶ Because web page space is cheaper than paper, you can also present multiple calls to action. You may include a link to the next step after your introductory claims (for more impulsive visitors), and additional links further down for those who will want to read more.

▶ Visitors can launch pop-up windows or layers to get a bit more information about something.

▶ You can use funky UI tools like JQuery to provide a range of information on the same page using tabbed controls, iframes, or slide-out "concertinas."

▶ Instead of requiring a single page to do the whole job, you can also give links to pages that are customized for different types. Each page can have a unique appeal, such as:

   ▸ "Full details on how we'll save you money year on year. Compare our 5-year performance to the market." (C)

   ▸ "We take extra care to customize the perfect savings package for you and your loved ones." (S)

   ▸ "What will you do with the $1000s you save?" (I)

   ▸ "Guaranteed savings plans by our experts." (D)

Though, generally, showing more information works, it doesn't work for everyone. You may run a test that proves that extensive evidence works better than touchy-feely people factors, but that does not validate or invalidate either approach. Both may be right—for different people.

Long copy may work for more people than short copy, but that does not mean that one version will work best for everyone. A combination of approaches may be better still.

On the Web, you can write for *all* your visitors, addressing everything they value most. Use all the approaches at the same time. Make detailed information available for people who need it, but don't make anyone *have* to read it.

The same goes when you ask for information from your visitors. On our agency's web site, we use a simple feedback form for new prospects to get in touch. Some write five words, and others want to send us over 1000. Neither is better or worse. Some people are more comfortable writing lots of information (C), whereas others would prefer to communicate by phone (S and I). Others may just say, "I need this— can you do it?" (D).

So if you request information via forms, accommodate everyone. Let the more impulsive people provide just a little info, and let more thorough types add more if they wish.

In the early days of web design, most people used to say, "People don't read on the Web—so keep your word count down." In fact, that is not true. The fact is, although *most* people *usually* don't read, just skim, *everyone* does read *some* of the time.

When you're looking to find "Am I in the right place?" or trying to find the link that will give you what you want, you'll skim. But once you've found what you want, especially if you need to take it all in and understand it clearly, I bet you'll want to read. If we write everything only for skim-reading, we may fail to convince people who need the details.

Claude Hopkins stresses that advertising is sales, and your ad (or web page) is a salesperson. You should expect it to justify its performance like any other salesperson. As you would not think of limiting a salesperson to a certain number of words in a conversation with a prospect, do not think you need to do that with your online message.

Content Over Style

Getting the information across is critical. You have caught their attention, and now that attention is running out. The clock is ticking, so you must keep your visitors engaged. A great way to waste attention is to write poetic language designed only to stimulate emotional feelings and that fails to communicate anything relevant.

There is nothing wrong with using descriptive or beautiful text — where it specifically supports your objective of communicating positive benefits. Taking a couple of lines to describe "the solid thump of the door closing, the smell of the leather, and the tingle down your neck as you fire the ignition" can really help to stimulate the imagination and build desire.

Unless the copy communicates real value and supports the proposition, remove it. As my friend the copywriter Phil Brisk is fond of telling designers, "Don't decorate—communicate!"

> *"If there is any doubt in your mind as to whether to use style copy or selling copy, remember that advertisers who trace the sales results from their ads use selling copy."*
>
> JOHN CAPLES, TESTED ADVERTISING METHODS

Provide Details

"Backing Up Your Claim With Statistics Boosts Conversion by 67.8%"

OK, I made that stat up, but how did you respond? The fact is, numbers and stats are proven to boost credibility, because they suggest both attention to detail and integrity.

If you have statistics that support your proposition, use them. Look at all the *performance indicators* at your disposal, and consider which of them might appeal as in Figure 8-1. (Your competitors may be able to boast the same or better numbers, but only if they think to do so.)

Be specific. If your widget improves performance by 51.9%, saying "51.9%" is far more believable than "over 50%."

FIGURE 8-1 My design for a real estate site's home page lists the numbers of properties on the system.

> **NOTE** *A new client of ours, a large hosting company, is so good that they get on average just one support ticket a day. You can bet I'm going to be using that in their marketing.*
>
> *Another client provides an online trading platform that gives access to more investment funds than any of their competitors. Publishing these facts, backed up with numbers, is an efficient way to create a very positive impression and keep visitors engaged.*

Show Evidence

If you want to make a point, don't just tell me—show me! And cover as many angles as possible to leave me in no doubt.

If you make the best pizza in town, don't just *tell* me you make the best pizza in town. Why? Because I won't believe you. Anyone can say "Best pizza in town." If you want me to believe your pizzas are the best in town, you have to use *evidence*. Here are some great examples of evidence from different angles:

- ▶ I'll believe you when you tell me that all your dough is made fresh on the premises.
- ▶ I'll believe that you import your cheese and pepperoni from Naples.
- ▶ I'll believe you delivered 26,309 pizzas last year.
- ▶ I'll believe you received "Best Take-Out" Award from the local newspaper every year for the last 4 years.
- ▶ I'll believe letters from customers who have left the area and just can't find another pizza as tasty in their new town.
- ▶ I'll believe a picture of a customer receiving a case of wine after visiting every week for 10 years.
- ▶ I'll believe a story about Donny, who has been making pizzas for a decade, and the time and care he takes to get the tomato sauce just right.
- ▶ I'll believe you when you say I may have to wait up to 40 minutes for my order, because you can't rush a good pizza.
- ▶ I'll believe the 12 reasons why your pizzas cost twice as much as the place at the other end of the street.
- ▶ I'll believe a quote from a customer who says "I have to say I wasn't sure a $20 pizza could possibly be worth the money. Now my husband and I drive into town at least once a month for our treat."

Next time you find yourself stating a claim, think what evidence you can use to tell the story for you.

Resolve Concerns and Build Trust

Providing all the affirming positive signs is not enough to convince a visitor to take action. They may have doubts, concerns, or objections in their minds that need to be resolved before they are prepared to move forward. Every concern is a potential rock in the path; something that shouldn't be there but is. Remove the concerns, and the path to conversion will be clear.

Such concerns will usually start with a "What if...?" Use those words as triggers to help you identify possible concerns.

- ▶ "What if I buy it and it doesn't fit?"
- ▶ "What if I find it cheaper elsewhere?"
- ▶ "What if I don't like the result?"
- ▶ "What if I don't understand how to use it?"
- ▶ "What if I want to cancel after the first month?"
- ▶ "What if I need more help?"

Again, one size does not fit all. Consider all possible objections for different types of personality. Create content to resolve each one, and test what works best where. Figure 8-2 shows the intro panel from one of my designs. The large headline text is most noticeable, and quickly communicates a differentiator, which in this case is a promise designed to ease doubts.

FIGURE 8-2 This site's intro leads with a headline promise aimed at resolving common concerns. The copy continues the theme of the proposition.

Always put information at the point people need it. If they'll likely be asking a question at a certain point, don't make your visitor dig into FAQs to get an answer (or, worse, have to contact you, because many will give up instead).

Some common mechanisms for resolving concerns include promises and guarantees, third-party validation, and customer testimonials. Use as many as you can at the point they are needed.

A great example is Zappos.com. Every product page features the following *trust devices*:

▶ Prominent 365-day return policy

▶ Free shipping both ways

▶ 24/7 customer service phone number

▶ A testimonial from a happy customer

▶ Links to privacy and returns policies

▶ Safe shopping guarantees

▶ Secure shopping guarantee

▶ Link to customer service center

▶ Three customer service awards

Promises

Before submitting their information, people may expect to see a *privacy policy* in place, so make sure the link is placed prominently near the point where you ask for personal information. A lot of sites now show more personal messages, like "We hate spam too. We will never give your details out to anyone."

If you're selling goods online, it may help to display evidence of your *returns policy*.

Any personal promise can help resolve fears and doubts. Simply saying, "If you are not happy—for any reason—call Tina and Joe at 555-1234 and they will do everything possible to help" can cover a broad range of doubts.

In fact, just showing a phone number can really boost confidence. It tells visitors you have real people that they can really talk to if they have any problems.

Figure 8-3 is an example of two different trust mechanisms. The top one is a privacy guarantee, and is followed by evidence of mass media recognition.

FIGURE 8-3 This example features both a privacy guarantee, and evidence of mass media recognition.

Guarantees

What guarantees can you offer your prospects? Making guarantees is a great way to increase conversion rates. The payoff is usually far greater than the risks. In fact, the bolder the guarantee, the more trust it inspires.

Offering an immediate and complete no-quibble refund makes it far more likely that people will commit to buy, and actually less likely that they will experience problems later (thanks to that trust).

Think of it this way. If you can double your sales by offering a total guarantee, and 10% of those additional customers take you up and request a refund (which is very high—under 1% is more likely), will you be better or worse off?

Figure 8-4 shows the guarantee from the AddAction home page. The introductory text and the hand-drawn arrow feel very human, reinforcing the personal brand values.

FIGURE 8-4 A bold guarantee from AddAction, presented with personality that helps gain trust

Third-Party Validation

Make full use of any factors that may help qualify your site as trustworthy in the eyes of a prospect. Any social proof in the form of third-party validation or awards can help build interest and trust.

If you have an e-commerce site, in addition to ensuring your site uses a valid SSL certificate, find out what validation *trustmarks* your site or shopping cart may be qualified to display. People expect to see a padlock icon, or some other kind of security certification image, before handing over payment details.

Consider signing up to any third-party services that can enable you to show guarantees (like VeriSign, McAfee, TrustGuard, ScanAlert, or PayPal Secure Payment—there are many more). These show that your site has met the required standards to ensure visitors' security. The presence of a familiar logo will help increase trust.

Be prepared to test different placements of these symbols. I would usually try putting the logos at the top of the page (for instant "safe place" getability), near any payment calls to action, *as well as* throughout the checkout process, to keep the sense of safety present.

Figure 8-5 shows part of a checkout form I designed for a client with an e-commerce site. It has a comprehensive set of trustmarks, including payment options, security approval, money-back guarantee, and shipping.

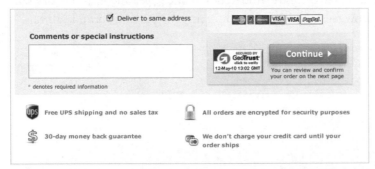

FIGURE 8-5 The bottom of one of my payment forms includes a wide range of trustmarks.

If you have won any awards or gained industry recognition, make the full PR use of the fact, even if you may take it for granted. Figure 8-6 shows a site I designed many years ago for a local ice cream maker, which makes no secret of their proudest achievement.

FIGURE 8-6 This home page makes a single bold statement. With collateral like that, what more do you need to know?

Testimonials can be pure gold for communicating details so they are believable. Use the following tips to create killer testimonials.

ASK!

Don't wait for people to send you feedback. (One of the clearest lessons we have learned from our optimization work is, "If you don't ask, you don't get.")

Contact all your previous customers and ask them:

- ▶ "What were you looking for in (whatever)?"
- ▶ "Why did you choose to use us?"

▶ "What were your concerns?"

▶ "What was your experience?"

▶ "What would you say to someone in the same situation as you?"

▶ "Would you recommend us to a friend? Why (or why not)?"

KEEP IT REAL

These open-ended questions will encourage people to be open and frank and generate sincere-sounding quotes. Overwhelmingly positive gushing testimonials lack credibility.

Any testimonial that covers the angles from the preceding questions will match a prospect's thought patterns and will seem transparent and trustworthy.

> *"I really needed X, and I was recommended to try* Product A. *I was initially dubious about whether it would work for me, but I was intrigued. It arrived by courier the next day, and I was up and running immediately. It has definitely helped save me time and effort. I would not hesitate to recommend* Product A *to my friends and family."*
>
> JOHN DOE, 8TH GRADE SCHOOLTEACHER, KY

Testimonials do not need to be polished or elegant. The more they sound like a real person talking, the easier real people will connect. When you read the testimonial I created for a web site home page in Figure 8-7, although it has all the right words in it, it just doesn't sound like a real person said it, so it is not credible.

Why I Use LumensDirect

Josh Gold, Designer ▶

"When I'm designing a new bar experience, I need to trust the quality of all the components I specify 100%.

At LumensDirect I can source the latest and most stylish models of low-energy lighting solutions from around the world in one place.

Because every product is sourced direct from the manufacturers, the favorable pricing helps me keep my costs down."

FIGURE 8-7 I wrote this testimonial, and you can tell.

PLACE TESTIMONIALS FOR MAXIMUM EFFECT

Use testimonials in the most powerful places. The last thing I would recommend is to file them away in a page under a link called "Testimonials." Doesn't that sound dry? Can you remember the last time you clicked a link that said "Testimonials"? No one wants to read pages of quotes.

Here's where testimonials really work. Use them *within* your content—*as* your content—to reinforce specific positive points, or to counter specific objections.

> ▶ On your Shipping page, include a testimonial about how quick the thing arrived.

> ▶ Near the point of payment (and throughout the checkout process), show testimonials that reinforce the choice to proceed. This is all about resolving fears. Quotes that say how great the service was, how they would definitely use you again, and what a pleasure it was dealing with your company, will all help keep a slightly undecided visitor moving forward.

> ▶ If you are describing benefits or features of your offering, use customer quotes and stories to show evidence of each benefit, as shown in Figure 8-8.

FIGURE 8-8 This testimonial sits adjacent to a call to action, reinforces the reason to take the call to action, and even has a big fat arrow that points to the button to click.

AUDIO AND VIDEO TESTIMONIALS

People connect and respond to people. Capturing a testimonial in text is useful, but it is not as believable as actually hearing or seeing the person.

Recording customer's voices—or even getting videos—can be extremely effective. Many services online (including www.yourrecordingline.com and www.audioacrobat .com) will let customers dial in by phone and leave a testimonial, which is then converted to MP3 format for you to include on your site.

You can record video testimonials using tools like QuickCam (www.agriya.com/ products-quickcam) and SiteClip (www.seetheface.com/siteclip) for publishing on your site.

It is also possible to record video chats (using Skype or iChat) using screen-capture software like Camtasia (`www.techsmith.com/camtasia.asp`) for Windows or iShowU for Mac (`store.shinywhitebox.com/index.html`).

Whatever medium you use, try to get a real, authentic-sounding quote. Don't be tempted to edit the content to make it sound more slick. You must also explicitly get the permission of the customer to publish his or her quote on your site.

Style Tips for Building Trust

One thing you know about all your visitors is that they are people. It is emotion that compels them to act. They want to connect to your offering in a personal way.

To make personal connections, first you must treat the visitor as an individual, addressing her personal wants, fears, and desires.

Whatever your market, it is also desirable to show humanness to present some degree of personality for the visitor to identify with.

KEEP IT ABOUT THE INDIVIDUAL VISITOR

At all times, remember what will sell your offering. It is not you, it is not what you do or sell, or its features. It is the *benefits to the individual* who is buying. Always address the individual.

> *"Don't think of people in the mass. That gives you a blurred view. Think of a typical individual, man or woman, who is likely to want what you sell."*
>
> CLAUDE C. HOPKINS, SCIENTIFIC ADVERTISING

It can help to imagine that you are telling a friend about something you have found that you think could really benefit them. What language would you use to talk with your friend? Use that same language in your web copy.

Be clear whether you are selling your product or service, or selling yourself. If your service is personal, such as coaching or therapy, you are very much part of your offering. But you should always link every aspect of the offering to the visitor.

In your language, speak to "you" the reader. Talk about them, their needs, what they can get, much more than you talk about yourself. Talk *three times more* about them than you talk about you. Note how the introduction in Figure 8-9 does not mention the service provider at all. It's all about "you."

Being you-oriented also requires showing deference, acknowledging that they are in control. You respect their choice, and it is your job to give them the information they need in order to choose. Ask for too much commitment too early, before they've built up trust and momentum, and you will lose people. Serve their needs by giving them every reason to trust you and to choose you.

I mentioned Ken McCarthy's two filters—"So what?" and "Nonsense!"—in Chapter 7. Relevance is the key to bypassing the "So what?" filter. Behind "So what?" is "What does that have to do with me?" Let all your content answer that question.

FIGURE 8-9 The main intro panel on my design for BankLoans.com is packed with benefits and mentions "you" or "your" three times.

BE REAL

It is much easier to convince when you stick to what is true, and to demonstrate the facts through stories.

To test this, take a few minutes and browse other sites in your sector. Look at which of them present slogans and catch-phrases, and which tell real stories. Which approach appeals personally to you? Which trips your "Nonsense!" filter? The same approach is likely to work for your prospects too, who are real people like you.

If you were telling someone face to face about your great business, you would not make embellished claims, you would tell stories that he or she would understand. You would talk about the way you treat your customers, what your products let people do, and why they love them. Do the same when selling online.

Ville & Company, the London management consultants I introduced in Chapter 5, have a positioning based around their personal, flexible approach, which distinguishes them from the bigger firms. Figure 8-10 shows a callout from my home page design, which is written to come across as direct, personal, and authentic.

How we Work

We believe that our philosophy and way of working is distinctive and enables us to deliver greater value to our clients...

Find out how »

FIGURE 8-10 This language sounds personal and accessible.

BE HUMAN

Try writing as yourself, not as some disembodied voice. Consider using "I" rather than the royal "we," so people can connect emotionally with you. Creating the feeling of a relationship is particularly important to strong-I and strong-S personality types.

Add photos of real people: yourself or your team. Stock photos stand out a mile and lack credibility. One of our partners even shows a photo of one of their call center staff alongside the phone number on their web site, together with the text "This is Louise—she really works here."

If you make a promise or guarantee, consider adding a graphical *signature*, which represents you and strengthens your word. (For identity protection reasons, you may not want to use your real signature!)

Figure 8-11 shows a design mock-up I did for the online fashion clothing retailer Goddiva.co.uk home page. The header block features an editorial-style introduction from a real person with a face and a signature, creating a personal and friendly feel.

FIGURE 8-11 A personal introduction from the site editor echoes magazine style, and will be familiar to the target market.

Another powerful tool is to tell your own *personal story*. (This is particularly useful for strong-S personalities, who most want to feel they can trust you personally.) What motivated you to do what you do? Why are you passionate about it? Revealing your own reasons gives other people something they can really identify with.

Figure 8-12 shows my suggested redesign for a marketing site run by Tim Marsh, who produces books on cycling in France. Tim's personal account at the top of the page will connect with people who share his sense of adventure and passion for cycling.

You don't need to make yourself look good, just trustworthy. They're not buying you—they're buying your offering. Look back at your real story, and think what you can tell to help people understand why you're talking to them:

▶ "I was really struggling to find anything in my area to solve this need, so I decided to set it up myself."

▶ "I personally wasted thousands of dollars before I found this way."

▶ "I really felt I had been ripped off, and knew there must be a better way."

▶ "I want to help other people avoid the mistakes I made."

▶ "I've made every mistake it's possible to make. I have learned these time-saving techniques through 20 years as a practitioner, and I want to share them with you."

FIGURE 8-12 My redesign for Tim Marsh's ebook sales site opens with his personal story, communicating Tim's passion to the visitor.

Stories like these will keep your visitors feeling they are connecting with another person, not a disembodied brand, which will ease their fears and help them to trust you and your offering.

Build Interest

Assuming your web page is affirming the positive signs people want to see and helping resolve their doubts and objections, the path to conversion should be clear of rocks and holes.

That is not always enough to get people ready to take action. You also need to *compel them forward*, and get them to the point where they really *want* what you are offering.

> **NOTE** *The advertising industry uses the acronym AIDA to describe the process of building an ad. AIDA stands for Attention, Interest, Desire, Action. Keeping your visitors engaged requires* interest *to be maintained and* desire *to be built, in order for them to be ready to take the next action.*

Standalone advertisements have to do this in one sitting. They must usually identify one type of audience at one point of awareness, and try to get them all the way to conversion. You are not limited by those constraints. You can create experiences for many types of audience at any step on the Awareness Ladder. The immediate goal is only to help them reach the next step.

Each step requires attention to be stimulated, then trust and interest to be built as you lead up to the next action, which is to take the next step.

For each page on your site, consider what current level of awareness it addresses, and the next level you want visitors to reach. What is required to bridge the gap? What will draw people through to the action? What will generate and build interest and desire?

Copywriters have a few techniques to get people to keep engaging:

- ▶ Keep it fresh
- ▶ Keep delivering value
- ▶ Keep the scent

Keep It Fresh

Avoid your content sounding familiar. If anyone thinks "I've read this before," you've lost them. For a message to have an impact, it should occur as new, get their attention, and seem worth reading.

To be more specific, though the message should be new, the *style* of your content *should* be familiar. Use the language of the person you are addressing.

You are probably not representative of your target audience, so do not write for you. Write for them, in their language. Talk about what they find interesting, not what you find interesting.

Your *content*, however, should come across as fresh. Whatever you are telling me, it should feel like I have never heard this before. To keep my attention, your message should be distinctive, remarkable, and unique.

Above all, avoid using the same marketing speak and buzzwords that your competition uses. If everyone in your sector stands in line, copying each other's communication and values, and you stand in line with them, why would someone choose you? If you stand out, you will be noticed and people will have a reason to discover whether you offer something special.

Bolwell's Edge RV is a ground-breaking caravan, which gave us the freedom to keep the style of the whole site fresh and modern (see Figure 8-13). The brochure download page uses the kind of direct and personal language that is becoming more common on the Web.

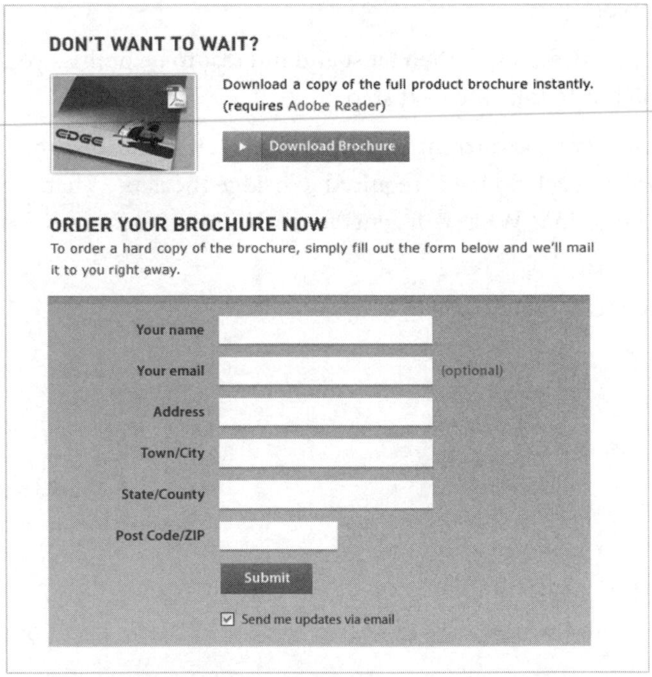

DON'T WANT TO WAIT?

Download a copy of the full product brochure instantly. (requires Adobe Reader)

▶ Download Brochure

ORDER YOUR BROCHURE NOW
To order a hard copy of the brochure, simply fill out the form below and we'll mail it to you right away.

Your name _____
Your email _____ (optional)
Address _____
Town/City _____
State/County _____
Post Code/ZIP _____
Submit
☑ Send me updates via email

FIGURE 8-13 The brochure download page from the Bolwell Edge web site uses friendly language that's straight to the point.

Keep Delivering Value

The only purpose of a headline is to get you to read the first sentence. Each sentence should both communicate value and also make you want to read the next one. What keeps us reading is "What's in it for me," whatever that is. Every paragraph should suggest more value to come, so that your visitors feel they are getting value, and will keep getting more value by reading more.

Try finishing sentences or paragraphs with a question, which creates uncertainty and makes me want to read on to get the answer. Why does this work every time?

It works because no one likes not knowing. (See what I did there?). A simple way to get people to read on is to continue one sentence with the closing thought of the previous sentence. For example, I might tell you that sentences are like playing dominoes.

In the game of dominoes, you have to match each piece with the same number of dots as the previous piece. That's what that last sentence did. The previous paragraph ended with the mention of dominoes, which was slightly intriguing. "How is it like dominoes, Ben?" The very next sentence gave you the answer, picking up with "In the game of dominoes...".

But that's not all...

Great, you're still reading! If you want people to read all your content (which you do), don't fulfill your promise too early. Keep a bit back. If your headings or introduction give all the answers, people may think they don't need to read on to find out. What keeps me reading is the offer of value.

> "One way to arouse interest is to give free information as well as sales talk in your copy. In doing this, your advertisement should be arranged so that the free information comes first and the sales talk second. If the sales talk is placed first, the reader may never reach the free information section."
>
> JOHN CAPLES, TESTED ADVERTISING METHODS

Unlike the ads John Caples wrote, when you apply the Awareness Ladder to create web pages arranged in concentric funnels, you don't have to have to have the sales talk on the same page.

Keep the Scent

Each page should get attention with a promise of value, and must then proceed to deliver that value. While this applies at the page level, it can also be true in the big picture. If a visitor has come to your site to achieve some specific goal, ensure the scent of that goal is present on every page.

Whatever you promise should generate *positive reasons* to move forward. The language of possibility usually beats negative or fear-based copy. Creating a dream and making it seem *achievable* will be more compelling than serving up a nightmare scenario and making it seem *avoidable*.

> *"People are seeking happiness, safety, beauty, and content. Then show them the way. Picture happy people, not the unfortunate. Tell of what comes from right methods, not what results from the wrong. For instance, no toothpaste manufacturer ever made an impression by picturing dingy teeth. Or by talking decay and pyorrhea. The successes have been made by featuring the attractive sides."*
>
> CLAUDE C. HOPKINS, SCIENTIFIC ADVERTISING

For example, one of Joe's sites may serve visitors who arrive interested in finding a way they can prevent hair loss. Depending on their search, they could conceivably arrive at a number of points on the Awareness Ladder. They might be searching on the general topic, or wanting to know about what treatments exist, or asking whether surgery is a realistic alternative option.

At whichever point they enter, they only have one goal: "A hair loss treatment that will work for me." So every page Joe publishes should contain the *scent* of the resolution of that need. That goal is what drives visitors to keep reading. They need to remain convinced that the way to get the value they want is to read on.

Put yourself in Joe's shoes. Let's say you have a Step 2 article, "The Only 3 Ways Proven to Stop Hair Loss."

Don't list the three ways at the top! Someone who reads that may think, "OK, now I know enough, thanks," or, "Yup, I've heard of those. Nothing new here." These are both failures. (Why? Because they have not kept the prospect engaged and brought them to the next level on the Awareness Ladder.)

You might start by talking in general terms about the three solutions. "You may have heard of hair transplants, laser treatment, or natural remedies. But which actually work, and which are a waste of money?" (The mention of wasting money will spark a sensation of fear in some prospects, which could get them to keep reading.)

You might mention that there are many more that have either not been proven to work, or have been proven *not* to work.

Mention the third best way first, and end on reasons why this may not be right for everyone. (That will make me read on, because I'm getting value and there is more to come, I just know it.)

Do the same with the second solution, and finish with, "However, the cost of this technique can put many people off. Is there a solution that's been proven to work and does not require such a big investment?" (That will make me wonder whether you're going to give me the answer I wanted—the free information that was promised in the headline.)

Finally, tell me about Joe's Miracle Hair-Gro. Explain how it is supposed to work. Mention the reasons why people are hesitant to try it at first. Tell me about the dozens of stories you've heard about its effectiveness. Say how affordable it is and link to other articles that go into more proof. (You could even link to places where you can buy Miracle Hair-Gro now.)

Then the job is done. You have persuaded a visitor to read the whole piece, with the promise of free valuable information, and you have delivered that information. Along the way, you have differentiated your offering from the alternatives he might have considered. In other words, you have successfully helped your visitor from one level of awareness (Step 2: solutions exist, but not aware of yours) to the next (Step 3: aware of the product and some of its benefits). You have also provided a link for him to take the next steps (Steps 4 and 5: getting convinced that this product is the one for him) with an option to proceed to buy.

But you have not sold! This is important. If you had finished the article with a "Buy Now!!!" button, the article could lose its credibility. Anyone reading through, or skimming or skipping to the end, would realize the page is selling a product, which does not match the promise made at the top. Owners of other web sites would also be less likely to link to a selling page. Always take people up one rung at a time, and you will retain trust and credibility.

Make It Easy

Finally, there are many ways to make it difficult for someone to engage with your web site. I'll describe the common mistakes, and how you can avoid them.

Consistency

Hyperlinks must keep their promises. If someone clicks a link, the page he arrives on should be the one he expected. An easy way to achieve this is to match the link text to the heading of the target page. If a link says, "How you can cut your energy bills," and the next page hits the visitor with the headline "How You Can Cut Your Energy Bills" there will be no doubt he is on track.

Many e-commerce sites suffer from this kind of disconcerting experience. Often, clicking "Add to Cart" or "Proceed to Checkout" from a sales page can feel like the visitor has just been teleported somewhere onto a different site (which in many cases is true). Making sure the target page feels like you are still on the same site will decrease cart abandonment rates. If you can, show the same branding, layout, or color scheme, and repeat the names or pictures of the products he or she wishes to purchase.

Be Brief

If your language is clever and complicated, only clever people will get it. However, everyone can understand simple, clear language (even clever people). Replace any difficult or long words with shorter, clearer alternatives.

Readability expert Rudolph Flesch taught that the easiest sentence to take in is only eight words long. A sensible average is 16 words. Any sentence of more than 32 words is hard to take in.

Use short, simple sentences that pack a punch. (Note: that's just eight words.)

> "… And the same applies to paragraphs. Vary them, but keep them short, containing only one or two thoughts—especially the first one. A long opening paragraph is daunting."
>
> DRAYTON BIRD

NOTE *"Always try to remove unnecessary words wherever you possibly can without losing the meaning of what you're trying to say."*

Or I could say:

"Remove words wherever you can without losing meaning."

Which one did you understand? Which gets you to the next sentence quicker?

Use Simple Language

Use plain English. This will be more accessible to everyone, especially those for whom English is not their first language.

Use as many words as you need to communicate your message, and no more, as my landing page for Rjenda.com shows in Figure 8-14.

> *"Vigorous writing is concise. A sentence should contain no unnecessary words, a paragraph no unnecessary sentences, for the same reason that a drawing should have no unnecessary lines and a machine no unnecessary parts. This requires not that the writer make all his sentences short, or that he avoid all detail and treat his subject only in outline, but that every word tell."*
>
> STRUNK & WHITE, THE ELEMENTS OF STYLE

FIGURE 8-14 This landing page for rjenda.com is extremely concise.

Although they seem shorter, avoid contractions, like don't, shan't, can't, and she'll. They actually take slightly more brain power to decode than "do not," "cannot," and "she will."

Use active voice (A does B) rather than passive (B is done by A). This will make sentences that are shorter and easier to understand. Compare:

▶ "Sentences that are shorter are more likely to be understood by readers."

▶ "Readers understand shorter sentences more easily."

Make Text Readable

If your text is hard to read, do you think more people will read it, or fewer? If people don't read your text, how will they become convinced?

SPACING

Spacing around an element makes it easier to identify. That's why you get spaces between letters in words, bigger spaces between words, and yet bigger spaces between paragraphs. They make it easy to see where one thing ends and the next begins.

In our web designs, we avoid reducing letter spacing in body text. If anything, we occasionally increase it. We frequently add extra spacing between paragraphs. (You can safely reduce letter spacing in very large heading text, which often looks better without sacrificing readability.)

NOTE *I did a test and reduced the space between paragraphs on one article for a few weeks. The average time on page went down 9.5%, because people gave up reading. Adding extra paragraph spacing increased time on page by 15%.*

SIZE

Try increasing font size in body text and headings. A significant minority of people have some vision impairment. In some markets, you will find it is a majority. Larger text is no harder to read for those with perfect eyesight, but it may make it *possible* for a valuable proportion of your market to engage with your content.

NOTE *In another test, I reduced the body text size on another article. Although average time on page actually went up (probably because it was still readable, but slower to read), bounce rate increased by 5.5% (which meant one extra visitor in eighteen chose not to engage with the site).*

LISTS

If you have a few items to communicate, bulleted lists are often more appealing. Lists are often more accessible than paragraphs. They present content in manageable bite-sized chunks, which will be easy to understand. Bullets in the form of check marks create positive momentum, as the examples in Figure 8-15 show.

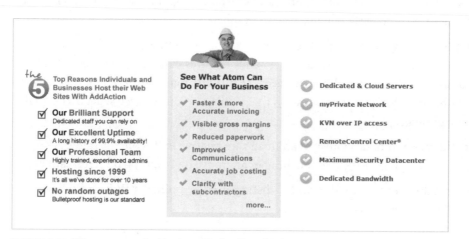

FIGURE 8-15 When communicating benefits in a list, check marks feel positive and uplifting.

CLEAR HEADINGS

Use subheadings within your text to highlight useful words. Headings help someone scan the page to find out if it is interesting, so using clear headings can increase engagement. Try to make your headings give the shape of the body text, without telling the whole story.

The text size must be significantly larger than body text for the heading to stand out.

> **NOTE** *I tested reducing the heading size of H2s and H3s in one article. Average time on page went down 5.5%.*

CAPITALIZATION

Using SOME capitalization will draw attention. Like any noticeability factor, using all caps makes text less readable, more likely to be overwhelming.

(On the flip side, you may deliberately choose to reduce readability to get people to skip over terms of use, legals, small print, and so on.)

Imagery

Images can sometimes tell more than text. For example, graphs or charts can describe a trend more succinctly than a table full of numbers.

Good quality imagery can make the difference. If all e-commerce vendors use the same low-quality catalog shots, sourcing better pictures can make the product seem more desirable. Showing multiple views of the product may show the item in an even better light, and also give an impression that somehow your service reflects the quality of the photography.

Ensure the size and noticeability of an image are relative to its content value. Also "zoom in" to emphasize the real meaning of an image by cropping off irrelevant areas.

Icons can help to draw attention and to distinguish key points or links from body text, as Figure 8-16 shows.

FIGURE 8-16 Icons draw the eye to useful next steps, and can also work as cognitive shortcuts.

Audio and Video

As broadband Internet access becomes the norm, more sites are using multimedia in place of static text and images.

The benefit of audio, video, and animations is that they can allow the visitor to sit back and watch or listen instead of having to read and scroll. Some people understand much better by listening or viewing than by reading.

Some information can be explained more directly and simply through moving visuals. Video walk-throughs can also replace lengthy screenshots and text.

Try not to depend on audio or video exclusively to deliver your message. Always offer an alternative for those using alternative browsers, such as phones and text-to-speech readers.

Avoid using multimedia gratuitously because it can drain attention. The fundamental rule is to use it only where it enhances the experience and communicates more information more easily.

Unnecessary Steps

Any step can only have a sub-optimal conversion rate. Provided you have included all the information a visitor needs in a logical sequence, are there any steps that you can remove to increase overall conversion?

Although gathering visitor information can be a worthwhile goal, forcing people to register or provide their e-mail address in order to get what they want can also be a big rock in the road. Unless you have given them enough reason to believe they will achieve their goal, they are likely to give up.

Figure 8-17 shows two versions of the home page for Rankmill.com—the original and our redesign. Rankmill lets anyone create their own top list of anything, and publish the list on their web site. The site's major goal is to get visitors to create their own list. We had the idea that the "Create your own Top" control in the left-hand column was not descriptive enough, and could be made more appealing.

We flipped the page over, moving the "Create your own Top" into the main section, and other people's top lists over to the left column. Although the functionality was identical on both pages, the original version generated zero new lists from 196 visits, and the new version got 11 from 183 visits. The redesign did not remove an unnecessary step, but it certainly made the goal action *feel* more achievable.

Forms

When you do need to request information, it is *generally* advisable to keep your input forms as short as possible.

Oh, and 99% of "reset" buttons should be removed (the ones that set all of the values in a form back to their original blank state). When did you last use one yourself? Very few forms benefit from a reset function, but clicking a button accidentally could be extremely inconvenient.

Figure 8-18 shows a nice, clear form design that follows one of our standard design patterns. The labels are right-aligned (to keep them close to their respective fields for people using screen magnifiers), fields are sized to a fixed number of lengths, and there is sufficient spacing between each item to help you match the labels and fields.

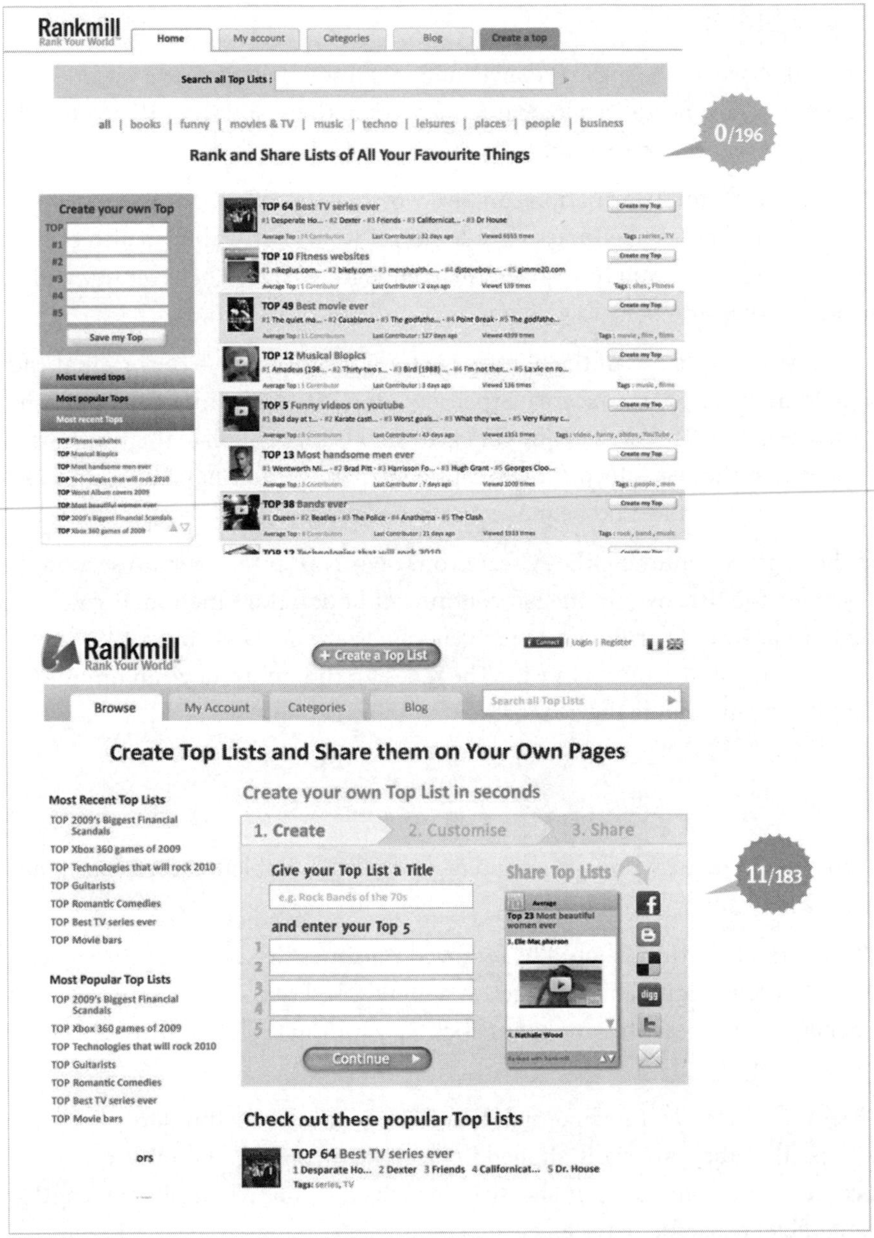

FIGURE 8-17 Changing the priorities on Rankmill.com instantly boosted conversions from 0% to 6%.

Organization Information
This information is used on your Payment Receipts.

Organization Name	
Organization Website	
Organization Phone	
Street Address	
City	
State or Province	
Zip / Postal Code	
Country	Australia
Category	Business
Organization Logo	Browse...

You may upload images in JPEG, GIF, BMP & PNG Formats.

FIGURE 8-18 Data entry forms should feel simple and easy to complete.

In place of a long form that asks for every possible piece of contact information, try a simple variation that just asks "Your name / Your message / How can we contact you?"

A common problem is whether to break up a long form into smaller steps. There is no right answer to this. I have worked on sites (such as online divorce applications) where long forms suggest a thorough and serious approach.

Will people be encouraged by seeing "Step 1 of 6," or will they be put off? Will more people complete the process if they are not told in advance how many steps there are going to be?

Only testing will give you reliable answers to these questions.

Dead Ends

Avoid leading your visitors to any point from which they cannot easily move forward. Dead ends are likely to leak visitors.

Even if you think you have given everyone the options they should need, consider whether you can provide safety nets to catch those who have not yet found their next step forward.

There are different types of navigation links. Your site-wide navigation at the top of the page serves as signage to tell visitors what is available on the site. Inline links give them opportunities to jump to what they want, to choose a different thread of conversation, or to break out to get additional information.

One common safety net is the now commonplace "super footer nav." You have seen these, often half a page deep and containing lists of rich links to articles in addition to the standard copyright and privacy links, as illustrated in Figure 8-19.

Here is another kind of navigation. Because real estate at the bottom of the page is cheap, designers have realized they can show more, longer links. Not only do these links create more chances to hook a visitor's interest, they can also create site-wide links that contain more keywords than the shorter navigation at the top of the page, where space is at a premium.

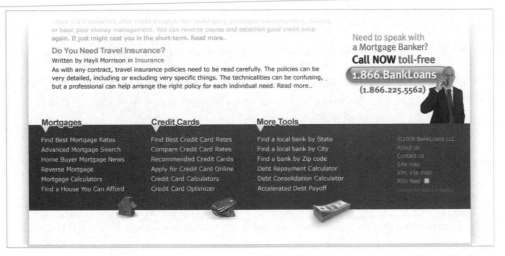

FIGURE 8-19 A "super footer nav" gives a mechanism to serve visitors who have particular needs that have not been fulfilled elsewhere on the page, and provide rich links for SEO purposes.

You may also try providing a search function at the bottom of the page as well as at the top.

"Did we answer your question?"

A great tip is to put a simple Q&A section at the bottom of your content pages.

Include a form that asks "Did we answer your question? If not, please let us know." The form includes space to enter the unanswered question and (optionally) name and contact e-mail. When a request is received, simply publish the question and your answer in the Q&A section on any relevant pages. Figure 8-20 shows one of these forms on the Bolwell Edge Q&A page. Note that name and e-mail are not required, because we don't want anything to get in the way of collecting this valuable information.

FIGURE 8-20 A "Did we answer your question?" form is great for collecting unresolved questions.

These forms serve several useful purposes:

▶ Generate new content that may help answer questions that you are not aware of.

▶ Show visitors you care and you are listening.

▶ Give them a friendly way to expect to get answers to their questions.

They also capture the real questions of real people *in their own words*. You may think and talk using the internal language of your own sector. The words you use may not match the ones a man on the street would use when searching for what you do. So adding their exact questions in their exact language provides new keywords that you would not normally use. They are also already phrased in the form of questions, which could match the real questions people type in to search engines, helping you get even more relevant.

So, the method to keeping visitors engaged is to give each type of visitor the *positive signs* that tell them they are on the right path to get what they want, to resolve their *doubts and objections* along the way, and to present your content in a way that is *easy and compelling*.

If you achieve these, you will have a clear road and can build real momentum from page to page, eventually leading to conversion. Each step will require a commitment from your visitors. The next chapter looks at how you can get more people to keep taking those steps with compelling calls to action.

CHAPTER 9

Call Them to Action

The previous two steps—getting a visitor's attention and keeping him engaged so you can deliver your message—serve only one purpose: to get him to take the next step. Attention and engagement are essential, but they are worth practically nothing unless they lead to action. A call to action is literally a prompt and a mechanism to get your visitor to take the next appropriate action *now*.

Your web site will have small steps and big steps, small actions and big actions. Whatever the next step is, if it is not taken, you may lose that visitor. Each page on your site should have one or more specific preferred next steps:

- ▶ Sell or squeeze pages often have only one goal action—to get the visitor to commit to buy a product.
- ▶ On functional pages, such as subscription or checkout forms, the action is to complete the form successfully and proceed to the next step in the process.
- ▶ Most of your content pages should include prominent next steps immediately following the main content, which will take the prospect to an appropriate next page (usually one step up the Awareness Ladder).
- ▶ Other pages, like menus of content, galleries, search results, and articles, may have many possible next steps. These next steps are often low value, such as advertisements or links to move to another page of interest. In many instances, simply keeping people engaged with the site is an appropriate goal.

This chapter explores the factors that often hold us back from getting commitment from web site visitors, sets out the six main principles you need for compelling calls to action, and illustrates the tips with practical examples.

Classes of Next Steps

If every page on your site is an ad, what is the *sell* on each page? If a page does not seem to have a logical next step, try to imagine what the visitor's experience may be at that point, what she may be looking for, or what she might be ready to do, and then do what you need to do in order to let her do it with ease.

Actions and steps should lead directly to your web site's goals. Your site may have several different goals, and it is important to know which are the most valuable. A successful site delivers more people to the most valuable goals.

Closing Calls to Action

Most calls to action lead people toward closure in their current visit. Taking our agency's main marketing site (webdesignfromscratch.com) as an example, there are four types of final, closing goal:

1. Make contact with our agency regarding a web project.
2. Purchase an ebook.
3. Sign up for our newsletter.
4. Click an affiliate link or other advertisement.

Our site used to carry much more advertising that it does today. That changed when we figured out the average EPV (earnings per visitor) for each type of action, and realized that the value of the average visitor in terms of agency leads was 5.9 times the average ebook sale value, which in turn was worth about 15 times the average ad revenue per visitor.

The clear message we drew from this data was that we were *wasting attention* on advertisements. This realization caused us to reduce the level of advertising on the site and to focus more attention on the more valuable calls to action—those for our ebooks and the agency.

Of course, not all visitors may be in the market to take up your major conversion. It makes sense to provide those visitors with additional actions that can still deliver business value.

A major consideration should always be how to keep people moving toward your ultimate goals without losing them. If you can minimize the leaks in your system, you will maximize the conversions. The way to minimize leaks is to make your site so compelling that every visitor can find the next thing of interest on any page.

Non-Closing Calls to Action

Some visitors may be *in the market to* take up your main earning propositions (the ones that deliver immediate business value), but are not yet ready to do so.

Perhaps they are at an earlier point in the sales life cycle, and simply cannot commit today.

Rather than going all-out for one big sell, consider offering these people calls to action that require less commitment and still keep a lifeline to a possible future conversion. Getting them to sign up for a newsletter or to download ebooks or whitepapers are typical early-stage actions that may still bear fruit farther down the line.

Do not be tempted to rely *exclusively* on soft, non-closing calls to action. Your web site must cater to those visitors who return at a later stage, ready to take the next step. If it does not compel them to commit, you cannot expect them to do so. (That would be like dating for years, but never popping the question!)

Build Momentum

Although it is a mistake to get stuck before the conversion, it is also risky to try to go for conversion too early. Do not try to shoot people all the way up the Awareness Ladder. You cannot skip steps and expect people to be ready to commit. Each necessary step must be present, and the access to each step is usually a distinct call to action.

A call to action is not the last thing that happens in a visit. Any successful conversion will probably have many small calls to action along the way. Do not expect good results by proposing marriage on the first date. Just like in a courtship, if you are going to pop the question there will have been a lot of previous requests, starting with, "Would you like to go out for a drink? Maybe Friday?" This gives the other person time to find out enough about you to know whether you are likely to fulfill his or her needs. Experiences on the Web are no different. People need to know enough to be able to proceed with confidence when you finally invite them to accept the ultimate invitation.

> **NOTE** *The old home page of a client's site we redesigned featured several closing calls to action. In fact, the main headline on the home page was "Subscribe NOW!"— even before any benefits had been communicated! Needless to say, the old site had a very low conversion rate.*

All commitments have a natural cycle, with a beginning, middle, and end. Along the way, there needs to be a complete sequence through the steps of awareness. If those steps are delivered on different pages, there needs to be a call to action at each step.

Imagine that your conversion point sits on top of a hill. Your job is to lead your visitors up a steady climb, along a path that is as direct as possible. Yet, if the path up the hill is too steep, visitors may not have enough *momentum* to complete the last vital step. You need to take them through the sequence of awareness so that their experience is complete, while still ensuring that each step in the process is only as long as it needs to be.

Where your stats show low click through or conversion at a particular call to action, ask whether there may be a step *missing* (that is, the path is too steep). In this case, you may test adding more affirming positives or resolving more doubts. Walk the road yourself and identify each step of awareness. If they are not clear, ask yourself what is missing.

You may also consider whether the path is *too long* and winding. Are there steps that could be removed? Could you maintain momentum by combining two or more pages or steps into one? Does your path eventually lead to the point of conversion, or does it just go round and round?

Ensure that every page has one or more logical next steps that are timely and appropriate. Now you just need to make people *want* to take the steps. That's what this chapter will show you.

Six Tips for Crafting Compelling Calls to Action

Here are my six top tips for making calls to action that really convert for maximum impact:

- ▶ Ask!
- ▶ Be clear and strong
- ▶ Repeat the appeal
- ▶ Nudge them over the line
- ▶ Appropriate timing and placement
- ▶ Don't stop there

Ask!

The first essential tip for having calls to action that work is—have calls to action!

A sales process without a close will not produce sales. A web page without a next step is a dead end. When a system has stoppages that prevent flow, you get leaks. In the case of your web site, people give up when you make it anything less than easy to proceed, because it takes *work* or *thought* to find a way forward.

If you don't ask, how can anyone say "yes"? Don't be the kid who stands crying in the school yard, complaining that no one is playing with him, and when asked "Did you ask to join anyone's games?" sniffs "No."

MAKE IT EASY

Whatever the next step may be, your job is to make it *easy*. Do not assume for a moment that anyone cares enough to put thought into what to do next. When there is something to do now, tell them "Do this now" and you'll be amazed how many more people do it.

> **NOTE** *Always remember, you are talking to an "undecided." The "no" crowd is not going to convert, and the "yes" guys will convert anyway. The visitor you are building your web site around wants your offering to solve his problem. That's why he is here. All you need to do is show him the way.*

Do not fool yourself into thinking that visitors will find their way back again if they don't convert today. If your site doesn't compel them to action today, why would they take action next time?

Not having calls to action is the single most common failure we find in web site conversion. Your calls to action are your signage that point to rewards ahead. If you remove all the signs to conversion, the only people who find their way there will do so by accident.

Figure 9-1 shows the impact of providing a clear call to action where one did not exist previously. The goal of this page on Skinnerinc.com is to drive more people to submit a form with details of goods they wish to be evaluated for auction. The original page featured passive links to the next step ("Skinner Appraisal Services"), from where visitors could click again to access the form. Simply adding a call to action with clear benefits ("Get a Free Evaluation Today") that links directly to the form resulted in 284% more people submitting the evaluation form.

Overview   How to Buy   **How to Sell**   Lot Alert   SkinnerLive!   FAQs

SELLING AT AUCTION

Skinner, Inc., is one of the world's leading auction houses for antiques and fine arts and the preeminent auction house in New England. With expertise in over 20 specialty collecting areas, Skinner provides exceptional marketing for property and attracts educated buyers who bid strongly because they trust Skinner's reputation, expertise, and the quality of offerings.

Request an Auction Evaluation

Whether you wish to auction one object or an entire collection, contact the Skinner Appraisal Services department by calling 508-970-3000 to arrange an evaluation of your item(s).

Note: Obtaining an evaluation places you under no obligation to sell. There is no charge for an auction evaluation.

Determining Auction Estimates and the Appropriate Auction(s) for Your Property

The Skinner appraiser will evaluate your property in terms of its auction marketability and will provide auction estimates. This is a price range that an appraiser believes your property will likely sell for at auction.

Skinner takes special care to find the proper auction for your property. This means including your item with like material to attract interested collectors. Skinner staff will evaluate current market demand and provide adequate sales exposure time. Consignments are generally needed at least 2-3 months in advance of an auction.

Approximately two weeks before the auction, you will receive notice of the sale date, auction location, and the lot numbers assigned to your items that will appear in that auction.

Commission Rates and Fees
Skinner's standard commission rates for a seller are:
--10% for items selling for $7,500 or more;
--15% for items selling between $2,000 and $7,500; and
--20% for items selling for less than $2,000, with a minimum commission rate of $30 per lot.

ORIGINAL

Overview   How to Buy   **How to Sell**   Lot Alert   SkinnerLive!   FAQs

CONSIGNING TO AUCTION IS EASY WITH SKINNER

Skinner, Inc., is one of the world's leading auction houses for antiques and fine arts and the preeminent auction house in New England. With expertise in over 20 specialty collecting areas, Skinner provides exceptional marketing for property and attracts educated buyers who bid strongly because they trust Skinner's reputation, expertise, and the quality of offerings.

Get a FREE Auction Evaluation

Whether you wish to auction one object or an entire collection, contact the Skinner Appraisal Services department by calling 508-970-3000 to arrange an evaluation of your item(s).

Note: Obtaining an evaluation places you under no obligation to sell. There is no charge for an auction evaluation.

    Get a Free Evaluation Today

+284%

How we Evaluate your Property

The Skinner appraiser will evaluate your property in terms of its auction marketability and will provide auction estimates. This is a price range that an appraiser believes your property will likely sell for at auction.

Skinner takes special care to find the proper auction for your property. This means including your item with like material to attract interested collectors. Skinner staff will evaluate current market demand and provide adequate sales exposure time. Consignments are generally needed at least 2-3 months in advance of an auction.

Approximately two weeks before the auction, you will receive notice of the sale date, auction location, and the lot numbers assigned to your items that will appear in that auction.

FIGURE 9-1 Adding a direct call to action shortened the path to a key goal and delivered powerful results.

GET OVER YOUR RESISTANCE TO SELLING

Selling does not just apply to e-commerce sites. Money does not need to change hands in a sale. If you have a web site, you are selling something, whether it is a product, a service, an idea, or connections. You can do so actively or passively. (Hint, actively wins.)

What are you trying to do: sell, or not sell? If your purpose is to sell, sell without hesitation or shame! Use every tool at your disposal to sell and sell more. Do you already have too much business?

Active selling shows confidence, which generates confidence in your visitors. Imagine a friend asks you "Should I get one, do you think?" If you reply "Definitely!" she will feel encouraged and will probably go ahead and get one. If you do not answer, she probably won't. If you say, "Well... It's up to you," she won't. The same goes with the undecided visitors on your web site.

"Everyone likes to buy stuff. No one likes to be sold to."

DAVID OGILVY

We have all had experiences of being sold to so hard that we lose confidence in the seller. (Being British, I may be particularly cynical.) It is natural to develop a mistrust of selling. Do not confuse being "salesy" with selling. If you have this sensitivity, it may help to view your role as "helping people to buy" rather than selling (just as long as you do it).

Unless you help them buy, they won't buy. And they *want* to find a solution. They want to buy. They are your target market, they need what you offer. That is why they are here. Because they are undecided, they need your assistance to decide, so help them buy.

At every step, do not leave your visitors to guess, tell them what they can do next. And, when, the time is right, be sure to pop the question.

> **NOTE** *Go through your site now and notice how many pages have no obvious next step.*

Be Clear and Strong

The second biggest conversion sin is having *calls to action that don't call*.

Calls to action should be obvious, bold, and direct. To make a link or button direct, its content should say one of only five things:

▶ What I want to *get*

▶ What I want to *do*

▶ What I want to *know*

▶ What I want to *happen*

▶ Where I want to *go*

If any call to action does not fit into one of these categories, change it so it does. So change "Click here to get our current brochure" to either "Current brochure" (get) or "Download our current brochure" (do).

Also avoid vague standalone verbs like "Browse." Nobody comes to any web site just to browse. Tell me what it is I'm going to *get* by browsing, for example, "Browse Articles."

Similarly, "Read more" is not a very compelling call to action. I don't go onto a web site for the pleasure of reading, I read in order to get something I want. A link that points to the thing I want, like "Full article" or "How it saves you money" is much more promising.

> **NOTE** *"Click here" is not a call to action, because I will only take action with a reason, and clicking is no reason. Remove the "Click here" from any link, and it will be clearer and more direct. (The only time I ever use "Click here" is when it is not at all obvious that the target is clickable, which should never really happen.)*

FRONT-LOADING

Always try to get the most meaningful and impacting words at the beginning of any link, sentence, or paragraph. This will get them more directly into people's heads (especially those who are scanning).

I have one concrete example of front-loading in action. I tested various calls to action linking from our About Us page to our Contact page. The text "Talk to Us" beat "Next: Talk to Us" by 16%. Why? The only difference is removing the filler copy and front-loading the action word.

COMMAND

If you want your friend to go ahead and call someone, which would compel action, saying "Maybe she might like a call" or "Go ahead and call her"? The second one with the command calls for immediate action.

Another reason that phrasing your calls to action as commands is simply that people do what they're told. (In a famous psychological experiment run in 1974 by Prof. Stanley Milgram, 65% of participants delivered what they believed to be dangerously high electric shocks to actors, simply because they were instructed to do so by an authority figure.)

> **NOTE** *A simple proof of this theory is to look at pay-per-click ads on Google search results. I just searched for "family tree." Of the top five results, three started with an imperative: "Trace Your...," "Create...," and "Build your...." Try the same test with pay-per-click ads in your own markets.*

ApartmentSmart.com markets affordable housing solutions across the U.S. We worked with them to increase conversion rates across the web site. Figure 9-2 shows two versions of the main property detail view. A few minor changes, including making the main calls to action more obvious and easier, helped generate a 30% increase in applications via the web site and by phone.

In Figure 9-2, our redesign is on the bottom. It has a more explicit and upbeat call to action, which acknowledges the visitor's authority ("Send Message" is more positive than "Submit"). Because generating phone calls is one of the site's objectives, making the phone number prominent, and adding the reminder "Call FREE," also encouraged visitors to take that next step.

PITCH YOUR LANGUAGE APPROPRIATELY

A commanding tone is not always best, depending on the context. Figure 9-3 shows a number of variations of calls to action we included at the bottom of all our articles, which invite readers to contact our agency to discuss their web project. The results varied widely.

An emphasis on listening produced much better results than a direct order. The more personal "We'd love to hear... Contact one of our team today" creates a direct human connection, whereas "Contact Scratchmedia now!" is far too abrupt for the context. There are no golden rules. Only testing will prove what works best for your pages.

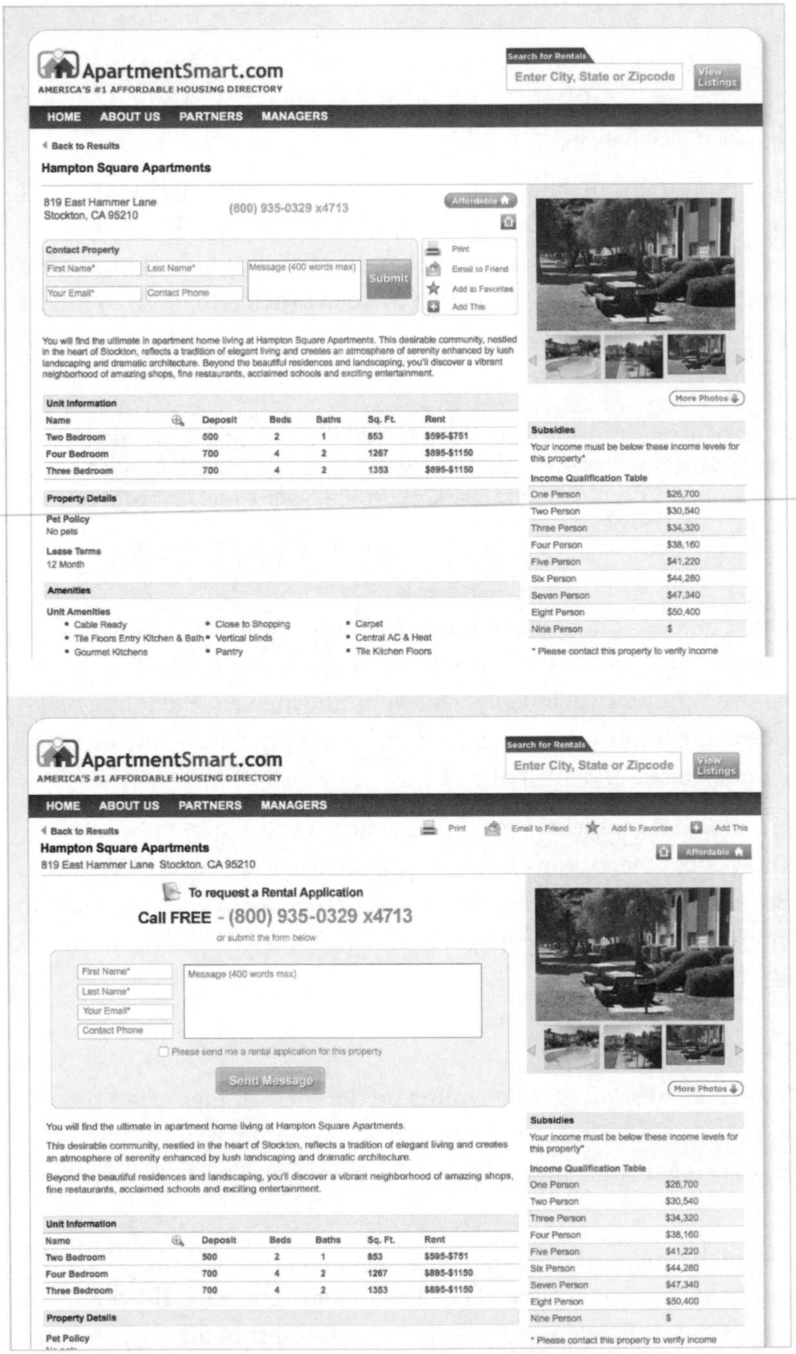

FIGURE 9-2 Making the form and phone number more prominent in the ApartmentSmart.com user interface generated a 30% increase in requests for applications.

FIGURE 9-3 Various ways of phrasing the same call to action produced a variation in results.

MAKE CALLS TO ACTION NOTICEABLE

Calls to action will be used more if they are noticed. You can apply basic graphic design techniques to make your calls to action stand out.

- ▶ Big elements are more noticeable.
- ▶ Elements with space around them stand out more clearly.
- ▶ A call to action that sits right in the natural flow of the page, in the main content area, or following the content just viewed, is more likely to be seen.
- ▶ Any element that has a bright color that is not used elsewhere on the page will stand apart.
- ▶ Applying 3-D effects, like beveling, gradients, and drop shadows, will make a link look more like a button. A button is a mental shortcut for "something I can press," and there is something about an appealing button that makes you want to press it.

We have numerous examples where making calls to action clearer produced significant improvements in conversion rate. In one of our earliest tests, we replaced a text call to action with a massive orange button and got an instant increase in click through of almost 150%, as shown in Figure 9-4. Though the original call to action should have been noticeable, because it is on a bright yellow background, the same color was used to highlight text on the page, so the call to action just didn't stand out. Our shiny button was three-dimensional with larger text, and looked different than everything else on the page.

We achieved useful improvement when we tried to increase the conversion rate of Zefyr.net, a site that markets online accounting software for small businesses. Figure 9-5 shows the before and after results of a simple change to a call to action on the home page. The goal is a click through to the Free Trial page.

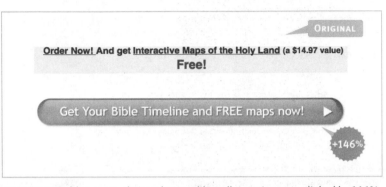

FIGURE 9-4 Bolder, more obvious button-like call to action gets clicked by 146% more people.

The original call to action was one of two similar links in blue and had the text "FREE 30-DAY TRIAL." Simply changing the color of the call to action to orange helped it stand apart and produced a 28% increase in click through. Just changing the link text to "Try now free" produced a 43% improvement. Together, both changes resulted in a 56.7% increase in click through over the duration of the test.

SHOW ONE CLEAR PATH FORWARD

Imagine you are in a room with one door. When you want to leave, you will proceed through that door. If you were in a room with 10 doors, you may leave through any of the doors. The more doors there are, the less likely you are to take any one particular door.

All the calls to action on your web pages are doors to other places. If you have lots of doors, you should expect people to use them. If you want more people to leave in one direction, you have a few simple options:

1. *Remove all the other doors.* (This is how squeeze pages work. They give some free information to get your interest and then offer only one way forward. If you want what is on offer, you have to take the only available door.)

2. Make the preferred door more *accessible, obvious, and inviting.* If a doorway is wide and well lit, it will be easier to walk through. (Make it easy and obvious using the noticeability factors described earlier.)

3. Position the other doors *away from* the preferred door. You are also more likely to take the first door you come to when you are ready to leave. (If you want people to take one particular action, do not place alternative calls to action near it on the page.)

FIGURE 9-5 Making the call to action stand out using color plus using a commanding text increased click through by 56%.

Repeat the Appeal

A call to action is more compelling when it fulfills the desire and promise that your message has set up. There must have been some appeal that first captured the visitor's attention, which you have reinforced and amplified through creating a mental vision that affirms what the visitor wants.

What has driven the visitors to the call to action is "what's in it for me." The call to action should strengthen the scent trail. So let it remind them that the realization of the promise is right behind that button or link.

If you have built the promise of easily reducing your credit card payments, the call to action should not say "Click here to find out more." It should say "Show me how I can slash my card debt today!"

If you are promising a free report, instead of "Register here," let the button shout out "Yes! Send me my FREE Report Today." (This time, the visitor is issuing the command, which gives her a feeling of power.)

Figure 9-6 shows another call to action we improved on the Zefyr site. The previous "Trial" page used a green arrow for the "next" link. We changed the arrow to a much bigger and more obvious button that read "Start my free trial now." This resulted in a 112% improvement—more than doubling the conversion rate of the form!

If you have overcome an important objection, such as "no risk," repeat it in the call to action with "Start My No-Risk Free Trial Now." If the visitor may be concerned about shipping speed, you can also counter this on the call to action with "Send Mine Today for Guaranteed Delivery in 48hrs."

USE YOU-ORIENTED LANGUAGE IN LINKS

Wherever you find yourself using links that are purely descriptive, consider flipping them to the reader's perspective with you-oriented language and benefits to him. Even at this point, he does not really care about you and what you do! Those internal viewpoints risk triggering the "So What?" filter. People only care about how it benefits *them*. So flip:

- ▶ "About Us" to "Your Team"
- ▶ "Testimonials" to "What Homeowners Like You Say"
- ▶ "Our Services" to "6 Simple Ways You Can Save"
- ▶ "Our Vision" to "Our Commitment to You"
- ▶ "How we work" to "6 Ways We'll Boost Your Profits"
- ▶ "Comparison Table" to "All Your Options Explained"
- ▶ "Why Choose Bigcorp" to "How Bigcorp Will Help You"

FIGURE 9-6 This more obvious call to action with benefit-rich language more than doubled conversions.

Notice how the last example uses *presumptive language*. Instead of offering "how we *can* help you," the position is "we *will* help you." This helps create the image in the visitor's mind of already being helped by Bigcorp. It is impossible to get commitment without any mental picture of benefits.

Figure 9-7 shows the power of benefits on a call to action; in this case, a headline on a cross-promotion shown at the bottom of articles. The name of my first book is "Save the Pixel," but nobody wants to save the pixel. The results show that they clearly *do* want to make better web pages.

FIGURE 9-7 Just adding benefits to the headline on this promotion more than doubled the click-through rate.

NOTE *Whenever we have added benefits to a call to action that did not previously feature benefits, the lowest increase in click-through rate we have achieved is 20%.*

FOCUS ON THE BENEFIT, NOT THE COST

Avoid language that focuses on what visitors will have to *do*, and instead focus on the *benefits* they will enjoy. Change "Fill in our application form" (which sounds like work) to "Start Earning $$$ Today." (Notice how words like "now" and "today" help the benefit feel instantly accessible.)

Though positive, upbeat language is generally preferable, you can use both the carrot and the stick. If the motivation is to avoid something fearful, consider using that in the call to action, such as "I'm Ready to Stop My Cravings" or "Start Protecting My Family Today."

Figure 9-8 shows three alternative calls to action to buy "Save the Pixel" as an ebook. The benefit in the second variation delivered a clear improvement. The third variation took the stick approach, and underperformed the flat original call.

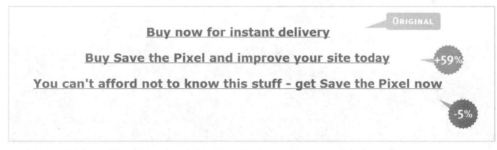

FIGURE 9-8 Adding a direct benefit produced a 59% improvement in click-through rate.

Try not to use language that suggests any cost to the visitor. The conventional and familiar "Add to Cart" seems to outperform "Buy Now" in most tests, probably for several reasons. One is that the idea of a shopping cart may make the site seem more professional and trustworthy. It also takes the focus off spending money and replaces it with a gentler idea of just putting something in your cart (and maybe choosing to remove it later).

In Figure 9-9, the main call to action prompts visitors to enter the name of their business into a box and click a button that promises "See Your Site Now." The promise is of immediate benefit with no work.

FIGURE 9-9 Notice how the main call to action in this redesign promises an easy process with instant results.

Nudge Them Over the Line

Sometimes, your call to action cannot provide quite enough energy to get people over the line. Due to lack of space, or lack of arguments, the button or link itself is not sufficient. People need a little nudge to take action now. There are several types of nudges you could use, including repeating key benefits and reassurances.

Figure 9-10 shows a medley of calls to action, none of which simply says "do this." They add "FREE," "Low PRICE," "easy," "just a few moments," "log you straight in," "toll-free," "Start NOW," "Call NOW," "no risk," "NO long-term commitment," any of which can serve to help the visitor over the line.

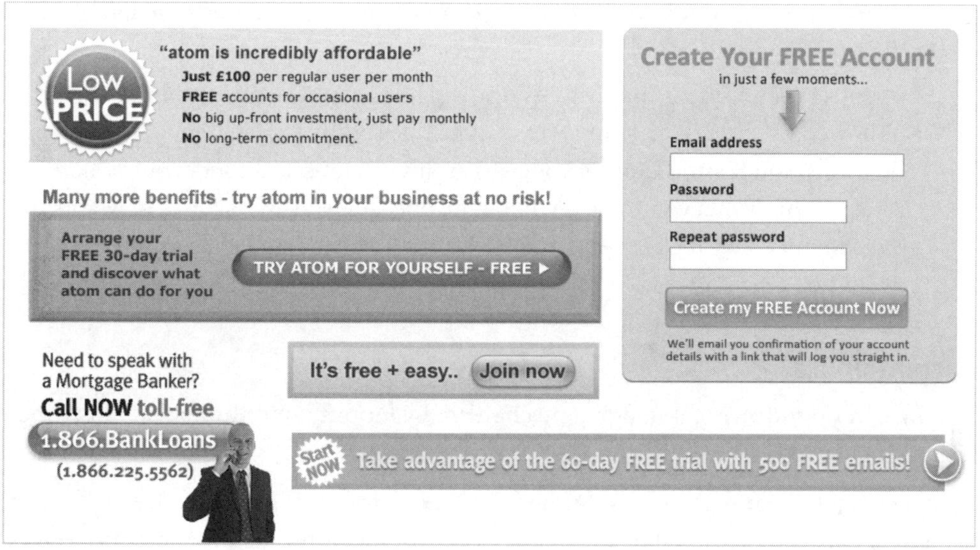

FIGURE 9-10 Various calls to action from my designs. Note the variety of techniques that prompt the visitor to take action now.

INJECT URGENCY

The most effective nudge of all is to inject *urgency*. The reason is, urgency simply tells you that you should act *now*. If you think about it, acting now is the only way you can get click throughs or conversions. Not acting now will never produce a conversion.

▶ The classic urgency tactic is to have a time-limited offer. This works just as well online as in stores "Hurry—Sale must end!" (Some online marketers dynamically set their offer always to end later today.)

▶ One of our clients runs a different "Ends today!" sale on each day of the week—every week! An undecided prospect who returns later in the week will see a different offer, and will assume that the previous sale has ended and been replaced with a new, equally appealing, campaign.

▶ Another very effective age-old marketing technique is to limit the availability of something, the "Only a few left in stock" approach.

▶ I've also seen dozens of tactics along the lines of "This information is so valuable I am only going to share it with a handful of people." As with the other techniques, whether or not the claim is true is not really important. All it needs to achieve is to sow the seed of enough doubt in the prospect's mind to help her decide it would be better to act now (because she was *probably* going to do it anyway).

▶ A softer technique is simply to list the top few reasons why I should act now, followed by the call to action. You can just be totally transparent and say "5 Reasons You Should Call Us Today." Yes, it's obvious and crude, but remember this person wants your offering to be the one that solves his need; he wants to be convinced with clear reasons, so why not go ahead and state exactly why he would be crazy not to accept!

PRICING NUDGES

Pricing can provide a great nudging mechanism by tapping into the appeal of getting something for less.

Even a classic sale or discount can provide that extra impetus someone needs. Be sure to show the previous price styled with a strike-through alongside the "new" price, as in Figure 9-11.

FIGURE 9-11 If you can claim to offer a discount, strike out the regular price to reinforce the saving.

It may also help to state how much the visitor will save by acting now. "Buy now and save $47!" Any implication that a price will not be available next time adds further urgency that could tip the visitor to choose to buy now.

REASSURING NUDGES

There may be a fear or doubt holding someone back from taking action now. If you can imagine likely doubts, or discover them through research, try countering them at the point of call to action. You are unlikely ever to lose a conversion by repeating your reassurances.

▶ If privacy is a concern, add "We respect your privacy."

▶ If safety is a concern, add secure shopping icons adjacent to each point of action (from "Add to Cart" all the way through the checkout process).

- ▶ If you accept multiple payment methods, show all the logos of every one you accept near your calls to action, in case someone is thinking "What if they don't take my debit card/Amex/PayPal?"
- ▶ If value could be questioned, add "Lowest price guaranteed—or we'll refund the difference."
- ▶ Sweeping guarantees can work great, such as "Buy now—100% satisfaction or your money back" in place of "Buy now."

Appropriate Timing and Placement

Sell online like you would in a face-to-face situation. You wouldn't try to force someone standing in front of you to commit to something she did not understand. You would lose credibility. The same holds true online—to a degree. The difference is that, unless you have a very linear sales page, you cannot be sure of the path your visitor has been on. So place your calls to action *at any and all points* where someone may be ready to take the action.

Calls to action don't necessarily have to be "above the fold" (meaning the area of a page most people can see without scrolling down), but they don't have to be just at the end of a page either. A page can have several calls to action, even the same one repeated many times (which our tests and others' have proved to be very effective).

What you need above the fold is *enough reason to continue*, but I would recommend testing including an obvious call to action above the fold.

In Chapter 8, I described how some personality types need more information, while others are more impulsive, so they will be ready to buy at different times. Just because long copy works in print ads does not mean it is the only thing that works. Long copy may suit more of the people more of the time, but you do not have to have just one call to action.

Strong-D and strong-I types want enough to get excited about, so give them the big claims followed by an early call to action.

Strong-S and strong-C types (in particular) want more reassurance, so they need more info. They will ignore the early calls to action, so present the facts and resolve the doubts and repeat the calls to action further down as well.

Figure 9-12 shows my latest sales page for "Save the Pixel," which features the primary call to action no fewer than five times, following each compelling reason to own the book. (Although the page may not be readable at this scale, note how the calls to action are obvious.)

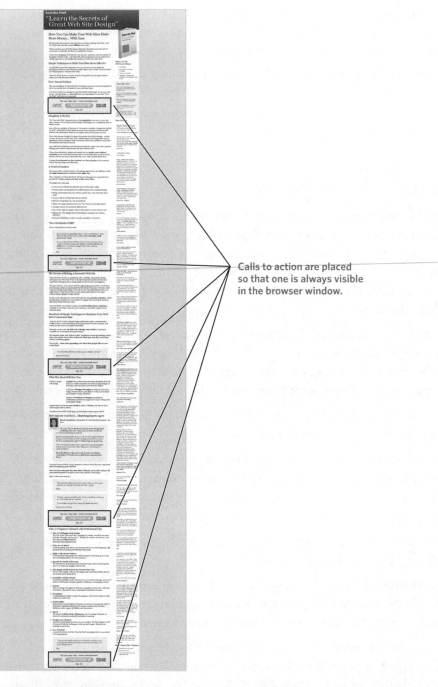

Calls to action are placed
so that one is always visible
in the browser window.

FIGURE 9-12 This long sales page repeats the call to action five times,
so that it is always accessible at the point the reader is convinced.

There is no right approach. Only your own tests will prove what combination of call to action timing and placement works best. Here are some tips to consider:

▶ If you use testimonials, try placing your first call to action directly after your first testimonial, which could be a confidence "hot spot."

▶ Another confidence hot spot is your guarantee. Try placing a call to action directly after any guarantee.

▶ For people who scroll all the way to the bottom of a page, ensure there is a call to action at the very end of your page. Most people should already be convinced by that point and will not see it, but anyone who does may use it.

▶ Try varying the text on calls to action. More impulsive appeals may work better higher up your page, with more conservative copy later.

EVER-PRESENT CALL TO ACTION

It is possible to always have a call to action on hand at the moment the visitor is ready to take it. One method is to use JavaScript or CSS to create a floating layer that never leaves the screen, even if the visitor scrolls. Though this could feel quite intrusive, it may work to optimize the clicks on a call to action, particularly for long pages.

A less objectionable fixed-position call to action is the fixed footer. You will have seen these on marketing sites, where a strip is permanently fixed to the bottom (sometimes top) of the page. Wherever you scroll, this strip remains visible with its persistent call to action.

CATCH-ALLS

If all your main calls to action fail, you should still aim to recover as much value from a visitor as possible. Here are some great ideas for mechanisms to catch people who are still undecided, so you can learn how you could have served them better:

▶ Live chat is a common catch-all. This could be an online text chat, or even just a phone helpline. Putting an open call to action to call in with any questions or issues gives all visitors a path to resolve their own needs, and also gives you valuable insight into what your page isn't doing right. Make it part of your call script to find out exactly what pages the visitor has tried before calling you.

▶ Show common Q&A or FAQs at the bottom of all relevant pages, followed by the "Did we answer your question?" form. As with any feedback mechanism, consider what you can do to make it easier for future visitors to help themselves (sometimes known as Level Zero Support).

▶ If you are willing to wring every possible conversion out of a sales page, you could even consider a pop-up catch-all call to action (which may be annoying but very effective). These are activated by some simple JavaScript, which, when the visitor tries to shut down or leave the page, shows a message that tries one last time. "Wait! Are you sure you don't want to take up our amazing offer? You will not get another chance. We'll even give you X, Y, Z!"

CAPTURE DETAILS FOR YOUR MAILING LIST

A newsletter sign-up form can be a useful catch-all, and very valuable for your business. Even if someone is not ready to accept your offer today, they may do so in the future. But if they leave now as a stranger, you may never hear from them again. You should *always* capture a visitor's contact information, even if you don't know what to do with it yet.

Compare the value to your business of a stranger you never met with someone who has volunteered to receive messages from you. *Autoresponders* will let you write a sequence of e-mails, which can be delivered automatically at set intervals.

The easiest way to get visitors to subscribe to a newsletter is to give them something *for free*. When I changed the newsletter subscription call to action on webdesignfromscratch.com, adding the offer of 50 free web design secrets in your e-mail, *subscriptions jumped tenfold*.

Whenever a visitor subscribes, I do no additional work. I have written a series of 50 autoresponder messages in my e-mail subscription manager (AWeber, www.aweber.com). They receive one secret every weekday for the next 10 weeks.

It's a great example of a win-win:

▶ The subscribers get a lot of free information, which builds their trust.

▶ It keeps my brand at the front of their mind.

▶ In these e-mails, I have at least 50 opportunities to pass on a message. Some contain sales messages for my other products, or affiliate links to other products I may promote. In all cases, the offer is appropriate to the content of the free information.

▶ Furthermore, when I have a new offer, I have a ready audience of thousands of friendly, trusting, prospects, who look forward to receiving my communications.

Give people something for free when they sign up for your newsletter. The call to action in Figure 9-13 is at the bottom of the page, where space is cheap, so it can employ a bucket-load of noticeability factors (large, bold, colorful, high-contrast, dynamic arrow and check mark, plus 3-D effect on the button).

FIGURE 9-13 Your end-of-page call to action can capture details for your mailing list.

Don't Stop There

My last tip for calls to action could dramatically increase success. It follows the same idea that selling to existing customers costs a fraction of selling to a new customer. In brief, don't ignore further calls to action once a goal has been reached. On your web site, the person most likely to take up an opportunity you present is likely to be the person who has just said "yes" to a different opportunity.

As you have probably seen on Amazon, once you have added a product to your basket, it offers you more products you may be interested in. And, after you check out, you get yet more offers.

Consider what further calls to action may be appropriate *upon completion of each goal*. Use these suggestions as starting points:

▶ After someone has made a purchase, offer him other stuff to buy or pre-order.

▶ Consider up-selling and cross-selling. When a visitor has added an item to her shopping cart, tell her how she can save money by adding more stuff, or tell her about accessories she should consider to go with her purchase.

▶ If she has downloaded a white paper, ask if she would like to subscribe to a newsletter so you can send her updates.

▶ If someone has just requested a sales call via a web form, warm him for a sale by offering a "Working with us" document or case study.

▶ Upon registering, could you suggest some easy tips to help a new member get started?

▶ When someone has looked at how to find your premises on a map, offer to send your details to his phone by text message.

▶ Are there natural affiliate offers you could place at the bottom of popular articles for people who have read all the way through and may be wondering what to do next to learn more?

▶ At what points on your site could you confidently invite visitors to send content or offers to their friends?

Put It All Together

The purpose of any page is to get someone to take the next step. There is *always* a next step, whether it is to pay, to commit to buy, to download, to register, to log in, to click a link, or to find the information you need successfully and then go away. Every page could have logical next steps. The first task is to figure out what they are and prioritize them so you can direct people to the steps that may actually make you money.

Once your page has gotten a visitor's attention and kept him engaged with compelling content that creates an image in his mind of how his life will be better, after you have shown him all the affirmative signs he needs to see and resolved his fears and doubts, you can confidently offer the next step.

Ensure you provide calls to action at any point that you would like someone to do something else next. Make these calls to action direct, confident, powerful, and clear. Get them to resound with the promise of what's in it for the visitor once she clicks it, by featuring the key benefits she will enjoy.

To make it more likely that people will accept these invitations, give them nudges, reminding them of more positive benefits, assuring them their doubts have been resolved, and creating urgency to compel them to act now.

In case one call to action is not sufficient, you can try putting them earlier in the flow (for impulsive personalities) as well as at the very end of the page (where there's nothing to lose). Test all the content, placement, and design factors over and over.

You should not stop the moment someone completes one goal. If someone accepts your call, take the opportunity to offer her something else to do. And if she doesn't accept, put in place mechanisms to find out why, so that you can offer a more watertight service next time.

Part I of the book showed you how to review your markets and offerings, flipping what you do to the external perspective, which multiplies your marketing *breadth*. Through applying the Awareness Ladder you discovered ways to address all your markets at multiple points in the cycle, increasing your *depth*. You have seen how you can create a structure for presenting compelling content that engages visitors at any point and funnels them toward your goals.

So far in Part II, you have seen how to capture your visitors' attention, keep them engaged, and encourage them to take action, so that you can lead them confidently up the steps of awareness.

The next chapter *applies this whole toolkit*. I will take you through applying the Awareness Ladder once more, showing how you can apply all the techniques from Part II for maximum impact.

CHAPTER 10

Executing Your Web Site Strategy

You now have all the tools you need to boost your web site's traffic and conversion rate dramatically. But what should you do first to get the best results? How do you decide what kind of content to build when? This chapter gives you the direction you need to use all the tools covered to best effect.

Every web site is different. As the case studies in Chapter 5 demonstrated, the right strategy depends not only on the composition of the market but also on the *context* of your proposition to each market. That is likely to be different in each case. What's more, your web site will probably have many markets (each defined by a different problem), and each one could require a unique approach.

The process for building a highly successful web site is:

▶ Target early opportunities
▶ Create core content
▶ Add more funnels
▶ Generate traffic
▶ Consider Step 0
▶ Keep going!

Any new web site should follow this sequence. How much you do at each level will depend on your situation and your goals. I explore a range of considerations in this chapter using a real-world case study. The worked example comes from a client who approached Scratchmedia wanting to set up a brand new web site to promote their new virtual server hosting business, on a limited budget.

I'll show you how I applied the principles in this book to design a site structure that targets specific search markets, based on keyword research and the Awareness Ladder. This structure will not only reach profitable initial markets and channel them through compelling propositions to conversion, but also provides a platform for continual growth.

If you are creating a new web site, or completely rebuilding an existing site, you have the benefit of starting by researching the most attractive markets, which should give you the quickest return for your initial work. Most web site owners do not have that luxury. You may already have a site with inbound links, which you obviously don't want to lose.

If this applies to you, you will need to work with the structure you already have, certainly adding new funnels, but also re-working and re-linking your existing content in a concentric model, so that all your pages work together.

Web sites are not fixed structures. They are pages loosely linked together, and those links can be removed, rearranged, and built upon. Resist the temptation to treat your site's current structure as untouchable. When your core funnels work well, your site will work well, so you may need to make some significant changes while keeping your filenames the same. With good research, you will be able to make the required changes with confidence.

Target Early Opportunities

Whether you are working on a new site or an existing one, it is exciting to discover new potential markets. You just need to address any new markets in a logical and orderly way. The starting point for this is keyword research. Keyword research is a simple and powerful exercise that really can make the difference between time spent profitably and time wasted.

If you already have a web site, look at your existing funnels first. Does your site leak visitors at important points? If you start to put effort into attracting new visitors now, will most of them be lost through a leaky system? If so, you should certainly work on your existing funnels first, to get the maximum benefit from new traffic.

Simplify first to remove unnecessary distractions, insert powerful appeals that your target prospects can identify with, and ensure you have appropriate calls to action at all the appropriate points. When your stats tell you your existing system is working, it will be time to turn up the pressure by reaching out for more traffic.

Define Your Offerings

List the problems your products or services solve. As I showed in Chapter 3, each of these corresponds to a potential new market. Flip each product or service into what it does for the customer—a solution that you can market as a proposition.

Start with "How to," so an anti-virus software product becomes a "How to ensure your computer keeps working, keeping you productive," and a box of chocolates becomes a "How to make her feel really special."

It is always better to base decisions on what is already there in people's minds. The external perspective is where you will find real opportunities. Apply this knowledge to create benefit-driven content, and make sure you find out what benefits previous customers have found from your solution (or similar solutions). Ask them to describe these benefits in their own words, and talk to the people who talk to the customers. Those real benefits could prove to be more compelling than the benefits that you imagine people will get from your solutions.

Keyword Research

Take a few minutes to research each problem. Type some probable starting questions into a search engine and browse the first few results. What is being asked? What issues are people looking to solve? If you get ideas for alternative phrases, write them down. (Review Chapter 2 for more tips on carrying out keyword research.)

Your aim is to discover where the bulge in the market is. How many people are searching on the problem (Step 1), how many are aware that solutions exist (Step 2), and how many are looking for specific types of solutions (Step 3)? Your keyword research data will give you facts to reinforce your own assumptions.

The first result from your content strategy is one or more attractive Step 2 pages. You can't have any Step 1 landing pages until you have Step 2 pages to drive traffic to. You may use a Step 1 phrase as your starting point, which describes a problem that you can solve. This research should lead in turn to possible Step 2 or Step 3 phrases. You can then dig deeper into those specific areas.

NOTE *Most of your competitors will focus on Step 3. "Warm" prospects already actively looking for solutions are more likely to result in a sale. Knowing this fact creates opportunities for you to attract prospects at earlier points in their awareness.*

Using WordTracker (wordtracker.com) or Market Samurai (marketsamurai.com), run several rounds of keyword research tests to generate actual numbers on what people are searching for today. Both keyword research packages give you the facility to generate alternative suggestions, which you should certainly use to help you discover new opportunities.

Core Content Keyword Research Case Study: NTG Net

Danish consulting firm NTG Net (www.ntgnet.com) provides server virtualization solutions for businesses. The service allows customers to use external virtual servers in place of internal physical servers, for file storage, e-mail, or applications. NTG Net has a huge amount of experience in VMWare (the market leader in virtual server technology), so its offerings are all built around that platform.

NTG Net's experience and professionalism mean that it can deliver an excellent solution, but it is not the cheapest on the market. (In fact, it does not want to compete on price, because that will not deliver its ideal target customers—professional organizations looking for a provider they can trust.)

The company is setting up a new web site to market its virtual server hosting services. My initial objective was to identify the best keywords to use for the initial core content for the site. My starting point in this case was the Step 2 phrase "VMWare solution provider" (which describes the generic solution).

As the results in Figure 10-1 show, people are looking for a wide variety of specific technical solutions, in a wide variety of contexts. However, there are a couple of interesting early-stage queries in the results: "virtualization benefits" and "benefits of virtualization."

In this case, I added an extra column to the spreadsheet—a "Relevance" rating of between zero and five, which indicates how relevant that particular search term is to the client's offering. I amended my calculation to estimate the potential attractiveness of each term, based on the sum of all the traffic estimates, multiplied by the relevance rating, and divided by the title competition. The results are ordered by this field.

The client and I gave lower relevance ratings to terms that are too vague or could derive from multiple needs. We were only looking for terms that indicate that someone is (or could shortly be) in the market for this type of outsourced virtualization solution.

Depending on your scope, and the opportunities you discover, you may go through this part of the process several times. Your end result should be at least one target term for Step 2 content.

	SEO Traffic (Broad)	SEO Traffic (Phrase)	SEO Traffic (Exact)	Title Comp	Relevance	Calc
esx 4	2,775	1,519	33	13,000	3	99,860
virtualization benefits	137	75	33	1,310	5	93,298
esx performance	250	75	22	1,240	3	83,932
esx backup	374	75	26	1,720	3	82,852
benefits of virtualization	50	26	22	832	5	58,810
esxi server	374	136	12	4940	5	52,834
vm esx	683	112	26	4,950	3	49,764
install virtual machine	250	50	7	1,300	2	47,105
virtual server host	167	33	18	2,400	5	45,500
esx monitoring	112	40	26	793	2	44,807
esx server	2,279	1,864	205	29,200	3	44,661
server virtualization technology	26	22	22	706	4	39,977
manage virtual server	8	4	3	130	3	33,923
migrate vm	61	26	2	790	3	33,813
server virtualization	1,250	835	205	34,900	5	32,800
monitoring esx server	18	2	1	132	2	32,455
set up virtual machine	22	10	7	121	1	32,281
migrate virtual machine	40	26	8	749	3	29,607
virtual machine performance	75	50	22	1,010	2	29,026
virtual machine software	205	167	61	3,030	2	28,554
virtual servers	835	559	167	22,100	4	28,271
vm monitor	137	61	40	1,690	2	28,083
microsoft virtual server	559	457	112	12,100	3	27,970
server virtualisation	112	91	61	2,850	3	27,764
virtual machine server	457	50	18	4,250	2	24,686
esx server 3.5	205	112	10	2,670	2	24,445
vm workstation	457	307	50	3,420	1	23,775
vm monitoring tools	5	5	5	60	1	23,100
virtual machine infrastructure	12	5	4	296	3	20,858
virtualization management tools	8	7	7	245	2	17,486
monitor esx server	26	5	1	363	2	17,355
esx tools	205	40	33	3,430	2	16,188
virtual machine monitoring	18	8	5	390	2	16,154
virtualbox centos	250	75	18	4,360	2	15,721
virtual machine management	75	61	33	2,300	2	14,682
virtual machine defrag	5	2	2	71	1	13,606
vm management	91	50	40	2,740	2	13,182
virtual infrastructure management	14	12	10	549	2	13,158
install vm	374	61	2	3,810	1	11,465

FIGURE 10-1 Combined keyword research results for "VMWare solution provider"

Create Core Content

In addition to the initial Step 2 landing pages, you will need content that describes your offering and its benefits, plus a way for visitors to convert. It is possible that these could all be the same page. In the case of NTG Net, I proposed the structure shown in Figure 10-2:

▶ A single Step 1 page, on "Virtualization benefits." This has reasonable world-wide traffic (over 200 daily visits for #1 position) and relatively low title competition (1,310).

▶ A single Step 2 page. The focus is my original starting phrase, "Virtual server host" (traffic over 200 and title competition of 2,400).

▶ A single Step 3/4 page that emphasizes the benefits of this offering. "Best virtual server host" could be a good target phrase. This will also be the site's home page.

▶ And finally a conversion or goal page (Step 5), which in this case will be a contact page. There is little benefit in targeting this page for attracting search traffic, so "Contact NTG Net" would be appropriate.

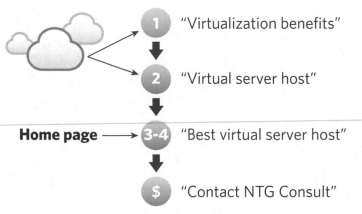

FIGURE 10-2 My initial content backbone for the NTG Net web site.

Get Clear on Your Context

In your own keyword research, you will notice that pages could work at different steps, depending on *the question being asked*. For example, the phrase "virtualization benefits" could be seen as Step 4, in the context of "virtualization" in general.

However, the context here is *this client's particular offering*—providing a virtualization service. I am looking for people who may be in the market for that offering. In that context, someone searching on "virtualization benefits" is only at Step 1, because they are not yet looking for a specific *provider*. They must have a problem to solve, and are clearly aware of virtualization as part of their solution. Their next logical steps are:

▶ Choosing whether they should use virtual servers, which leads to the problem of how best to go about it (Step 1, in this context)

▶ Choosing whether to outsource their server management (a general solution, Step 2)

▶ Go on to look for this specific solution provider (Step 3)

This structure gives the new site a *content backbone*, which fulfills my two initial objectives:

- ▶ To provide a useful initial funnel
- ▶ To provide a platform for growth

Your site will likely need a different structure. It is likely that you will have multiple offerings (whereas this client has one main umbrella offering). You may have several ways of describing your solution, which could give you multiple Step 2 entry points. You may not have identified an attractive Step 1 problem page. Different offerings may even demand distinct funnels with multiple Step 5 conversion pages. All of these patterns are valid.

Whatever your starting context, you must always have, at a minimum, at least one clear progression *from one or more entry points* (which match what people are looking for), leading through all the steps *to the point of conversion*. When you start with a clear content backbone like this, even if it is very simple, you can quickly start to add more funnels.

Common Features of Every Page

As Chapters 6 through 9 described, every page on a web site must get visitors' attention, keep them engaged, and make a compelling case to take the next step forward. If every page does that, your site should efficiently lead all genuine prospects through every step on the Awareness Ladder so that they convert. Here is a quick summary of what makes a compelling web page experience:

- ▶ Every page must promise value from the first glance. This should definitely apply to your main headline, and may include imagery, animation, or video content.
- ▶ Visitors should quickly see signs that they have arrived in the right place to get exactly what they are looking for. (They might find more than they expected.)
- ▶ The design of each page should match visitor expectations. So a professional service company should look immediately like a professional service company. A parenting community site should look like one. A cheap vacation site should shout out "cheap vacation!"

▶ Every page needs clear navigation that lets visitors know where they are, where they can go, what kind of site this is, what they will find, and what they can do here.

▶ Page content should be interesting, valuable, newsworthy, honest, and generous, which will encourage third parties to link to it.

As I explained in Chapter 2, you need to make each page appear to be strongly about your target search term (where applicable), to give it a competitive advantage with the search engines. Ensure the keywords or phrases appear in the page's title tag, in the H1 tag, and frequently throughout the content (good, natural keyword density, without sacrificing easy readability).

Step 1 Page: "Virtualization Benefits"

My single Step 1 page "virtualization benefits" can be the first of many that will feed traffic to the solution pages. This will be an article that offers a clear promise, and should deliver that promise while converting the visitor to Step 2 *in the site's context*— deciding that outsourcing their virtual server is the preferable solution.

When the visitor has been converted to Step 2, the page will present one or more links to the Step 2 page, which will discuss possible solutions to the question of how to outsource.

You will notice that, in this case study, the Step 1 pages are more loosely connected to the solution than "hair loss" is to "hair loss treatment." The research shows that not many people are actually searching for "virtual server host," which either means the market is small (which is not the case), or that there are numerous problems for which virtual server hosting is the answer.

If that is the case, it means that there are likely to be good markets at Step 1, but also that those markets have to be developed. Visitors who arrive in one context need to be converted to a new context—so that they come to view their problem as one for which *outsourced virtualization* is the solution. This shift in context is a step in qualifying them as a prospect for the web site's offering.

Step 2 Page: "Virtual Server Host"

Step 2 visitors are looking for a general solution to their problem. In this context, that means they want information on how or where to host their virtual servers.

The purpose of this page is to present NTG Net as a credible solution to the problem at hand. To achieve this, it may need to do two things:

▶ Frame the context of the problem to suit the offering.

▶ Then introduce this provider's offering as a good fit in that context.

This page will probably include a range of naturally related terms, to match Long Tail searches, including "virtual server hosts" and "hosting." Later, extra Step 2 pages can be created that target additional terms more exclusively.

Each Step 2 page will convert the visitor to Step 3—being aware that there is a solution worthy of consideration. The solution that is presented does not necessarily need to be NTG Net *itself*. A more finely targeted solution would be a *Step 3 proposition*, which should be crafted to match exactly what this particular visitor wants next: the virtual server outsourcing solution that is right for him.

The main call to action (on-link) should describe the proposition: "Best virtual server host" (or whatever Step 3 offering most closely fits the prospect's current need and awareness).

Step 3–4 Page: "Best Virtual Server Host"

Visitors arriving here are looking for the best virtual server host, whether they have come through a funnel on the site, or they have followed an external link. They enter at Step 3 (aware of the proposition, which is "how this service could solve your problem") and their *immediate need* is to reach Step 4 (convinced of the benefits to them).

The only purpose of the page is to deliver on that promise. Always bear in mind that visitors really *want* to find the right solution for them. That is why they are on the Web today. Assume that they are warm, but undecided, and simply need to have all their questions answered.

Because this page is covering both Steps 3 and 4, it will aim to go beyond convincing of benefits to convincing the visitors that they have no reason *not to accept this proposition now* (taking them to Step 5).

> **NOTE** *Although the content focus of this page is close to the Step 2 phrase ("virtual server host"), there is a natural progression from finding a host to choosing the best one, and the close relevance will only benefit the SEO relevance of both pages.*

This Step 3 (specific solution) page can also be the site's home page, because it accurately describes the whole company and its brand proposition. (The focus of this page *may* change later, following further keyword research, when new content requires a different focus, or if the company were to expand its offerings.)

I might consider adding the modifier "best virtual server host *for business*" to help segment the market. Because the client does not want private customers, distinguishing the proposition early both encourages target prospects that they are in the right place and disqualifies those who are not in the target market.

STEP 3: PRESENT THE PROPOSITION

Visitors already believe that what they find on this page *may* meet their needs, so the only objective is to raise their awareness to the next step—*convinced* that it could be what they are looking for.

The job of Step 3 content is to affirm all the positive signs prospects may be looking for, and also to counter the full range of possible concerns. Prospects must find clear affirmations that this solution will suit their business, will meet all their requirements, and that they will not have to worry if they choose this option.

For example, prospects should be left with no doubt that:

▶ They will get friendly, professional assistance to select the most appropriate service.

▶ Their virtual servers will be managed by highly trained and certified experts.

▶ If their needs change, the service will adapt to their needs, so that they always have enough capacity but are never paying for capacity they don't need.

▶ In the rare case of a hardware failure, their data will be protected and back online within a short timeframe.

▶ They can afford this solution—in fact, it is a sensible investment.

In other words, all the visitors' boxes are checked.

If there is a lot of information that falls into many categories, which may not all be applicable to every prospect, it may be better to break the content over multiple Step 3 pages, linked together into a Step 3 silo, which can provide more thorough information for those who need it, as shown in Figure 10-3.

Grouping and linking content together in this way allows prospects to browse horizontally, following their own preferences and needs. These other pages could be seen as secondary Step 3 content, probably linked from a primary Step 3 page (this core page). You may also find it beneficial to have specialized landing pages that focus on specific benefits, which will benefit from being linked together in a silo.

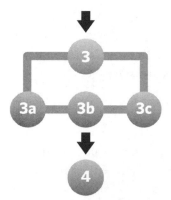

FIGURE 10-3 A Step 3 silo lets visitors browse the benefits and features that apply to them, until they are ready to proceed to Step 4.

STEP 4: BUILD DESIRE

Prospects at Step 4 are already aware of the benefits of the proposition. To get them to Step 5, where they are ready to take action, you must amplify the belief that their goal is within reach, and that accepting the proposition is the next step to achieving that goal.

The prospect wants this solution to meet his needs. He does not want to go back and look again. If you have shown him all the positive signs he needs and resolved all his doubts, you should have provided all the *content* required to make the final conversion seem sensible. At the end of Step 4 they should be confident that this is the only solution that they should accept.

But logic does not get conversions. The key to generating action is *emotion*. The focus of Step 4 is to build or to reinforce the prospect's mental image of a better, easier, happier, more successful life after he has solved his problem. Paint a picture of what life *will* be like on the other side of the door.

▶ Describe what it will be like when the goal is reached. Show the prospect how he will know he has made the right choice.

▶ Use assumptive language (such as, "When you hire us," or, "As soon as you open the box").

▶ Present testimonials that paint a picture of happy customers.

▶ Provide reassurances, trustmarks, and guarantees, which can help clear away any final doubts.

▶ Consider using a combination of carrot and stick. Limiting the window of opportunity or availability will help create urgency. In some cases, reinforcing the consequences of not finding a solution can help.

The final element of any Step 4 page is a strong and easy call to action that leads to the conversion page (which may be to sign up, place order, check out, or make contact). It is especially important at this point not to offer alternative exits. (In other words, you either go forward through this door, or you have to go back and start over.)

Step 5: "Contact NTG Net"

The purpose of Step 5 content is to make the final step *easy*, so there is no reason *not to* take it. Some sites benefit from including the final step below all Step 4 content, removing one click from the conversion path.

This site will have one primary call to action, which is to start a conversation with the provider through "Contact us." The contact page should support the prospect's conviction that he is making right decision, even if that involves repeating benefits or reinforcing the vision of success.

In this case, it may describe what will happen after he completes the form, "One of our consultants will contact you within one working day to find out more about your business and to discuss the options that suit your needs." Alternatively, the contact page could encourage the prospect to pick up the phone and state exactly what he needs. Both approaches emphasize the human touch, which can be particularly important to a service provider.

In general, I prefer to leave discussions of price as late as possible. Unless the prospect already has significant momentum, mentioning costs could give him a reason to quit the process. The more attention and momentum you can build, the more opportunity you have to convey benefits, which should mean that price becomes less of an issue.

> **NOTE** *For most brands, the ideal thought to create in the prospect's mind takes the form, "You pay a bit more, but..."*

Add More Funnels

When you have one complete funnel, which takes prospects from Step 2 or Step 1 right through to conversion, you have the backbone of an effective web site. You can now proceed to build more funnels around the core structure.

Keyword research will guide these next steps. The pivotal point of each funnel is Step 2: What solutions are people already looking for, and can you feasibly address those markets?

Additional Step 2 Pages for NTG Net

The original Step 2 page for NTG Net is "Virtual server host." Keyword research may reveal similar terms that describe the solution on offer, such as variations of "VMWare virtual host." Consider any alternative terms that match your core offering. If they have useful markets, it may be worth creating a variation of your core Step 2 landing page for each one. In the case of NTG Net's keyword research, other Step 2 terms that look appealing could include "manage virtual server" and "migrate virtual machine."

Next, I advise working down the list of alternative Step 2 terms, starting with the most attractive markets. If the market is strong enough, and you can match it with a proposition that leads to your products or services, address it with a dedicated Step 2 page.

You should also revisit your web research and keyword research on a regular basis to see if you can discover new niche terms. Keyword research is quick and a great value when you consider the investment required to make new pages.

You might also create new Step 2 pages in response to new Step 1 opportunities you identify. When new Step 1 pages are added in the future, additional Step 2 pages may be needed to provide more appropriate next steps, which might lead to pages like:

- ▶ "New host to migrate virtual servers"
- ▶ "Outsourcing virtual machine management"
- ▶ "Reduce cost of file storage"

In turn, each new Step 2 term may also provide an opportunity to create a new Step 3 proposition. For each additional Step 2 market, consider whether it will flow on naturally to existing Step 3 content, or whether you need to create a new Step 3 for each funnel.

Additional Step 1 Pages for NTG Net

There are two reasons to create additional Step 1 content:

1. As additional feeder pages for existing Step 2 content
2. Or where keyword research identifies new untapped markets

The initial Step 1 landing page for NTG Net is "Virtualization benefits." Further keyword research may reveal related terms, exploring how virtualization can help cut costs, manage budget, reduce risk, and facilitate growth. Each one could become a new Step 1 page, linking to the existing Step 2 page, "Virtual server host."

Related terms could all link to each other, in a similar way to how Step 3 (benefits) pages can link together. (In fact, selling the benefits of virtualization is a step toward accessing this market, so here I am doing a Step 3 exercise, but not in the context of the specific service being offered.)

From the initial keyword research, additional topics for Step 1, which indicate a possible early-stage prospect, could include:

▶ "Server virtualization" (and the British spelling "Server virtualisation")
▶ "Migrate virtual machine"
▶ "Virtual machine management"
▶ Specific technology, such as VMWare, EXSI Server, or VM ESX

If these terms provide a good match to an existing Step 2 page, such as "Virtual server host," they can link on to that page. If there is no useful Step 2 page, one needs to be created.

Generate Traffic

As soon as you have any content, you should start building inbound links. This should be part of your ongoing discipline. Initially, any links will help get your site found, but look for high-quality links from relevant, high-PageRank, old pages where possible.

You can create inbound links from off-site to any of your content, where you identify markets at the relevant level of awareness. But when you have built effective funnels, good reasons exist to focus on building links to Step 2 and Step 1 content:

▶ You have designed your funnels to channel as many prospects as possible to your goals. They should do that more efficiently than driving prospects to later stages in the funnel.
▶ There are often large, untapped markets at Step 2 and Step 1, out of the range of your competitors (because most sites start by talking about specific solutions, at Step 3).

Every Step 2 landing page needs other pages linking to it, both to provide direct traffic and gravity for search engines. Your Step 2 pages *may be* fed by one or more of your own Step 1 pages—if you identify significant markets at Step 1. The shape of your markets will dictate the strategy. There is little value in creating Step 1 content when there are more untapped but bulging markets at Step 2.

Whether or not you create your own Step 1 content, you can achieve quick results by creating inbound links from other web sites. This could be content that you create yourself, but more often it will be existing content.

> **NOTE** *View all content and link creation, whether on your own site or elsewhere on the Web, as saving for the future. Just like the effect of compound interest on savings, you may not see an immediate return, but the earlier you start investing, the quicker your investment will start to grow. Every page you can add a link on will get older over time, and its own PageRank may increase, meaning the value of the inbound link also increases.*

New Approach to Link-Building

In the old approach, link-building is a random numbers game. Lacking a coherent content strategy, designers and search engine optimization specialists tend to go just for traffic, building links from any pages they can find, based on keyword relevance alone (sometimes not even going that far).

The result is poor conversion, because the *immediate need* of the traffic is not well matched to the *immediate proposition* of the landing page.

Another common mistake when focusing only on subject matter is to create links between pages that are at the same step. For example, if you have a page about "virtual server host" and you look for other pages with the subject "virtual server host," you may be trying to link one Step 3 page to another Step 3 page. If the linking page successfully answers the prospects' immediate need for information, why would they follow the link to your page?

In the new approach, link-building is far more conscious and deliberate. You create inbound links from content that is relevant to both a page's *subject matter* and to its *awareness step*. Specifically, for each landing page, you will look for content that matches the page's *preceding* logical step.

So, for any Step 2 page, you should look for external pages that are focused on related Step 1 questions. In this way, you can know visitors' level of awareness and give them precisely what they are looking for next. Subject matter relevance may be slightly diminished, but conversion potential will be significantly increased.

> **NOTE** *The most effective strategies are often the most obvious. Refer your own content structure for ideas for inbound links. If you have created targeted Step 1 pages (based on solid keyword research) look for opportunities to build links from other pages with the same subject matter—and point the links to the same Step 2 pages that your Step 1 content links to. This will build relevance around the Step 1 term, which is exactly what you want.*

How to Find High-PR Links

Aaron Wall's site SEOBook (www.seobook.com) provides some very useful free SEO tools. In particular, I recommend two Firefox plug-ins: "SEO Toolbar," and "SEO for Firefox." Figure 10-4 shows the latter tool in action, showing the PageRank of every search result in a Google.com search. This lets me quickly target relevant higher-PR pages. (This example also shows the number of entries from DMOZ.org—the human-moderated Open Directory Project—which are viewed by search engines as highly trustworthy. You can configure the plug-in to show a variety of data for Google and Yahoo search results.)

FIGURE 10-4 SEO for Firefox tool from SEOBook, showing the PageRank of Google search results

Suggested Places to Build Backlinks

It is easier to generate backlinks from some types of sites than others. Here is a collection of techniques our team has used to good effect. Always be on the lookout for original opportunities, because the value of any technique will tend to decline as it gains in popularity.

FORUMS

Forums are great places to add backlinks. In addition to inserting relevant links in forum posts, most forums let you customize your signature, which is displayed after every post you make. When you have posted on a number of discussions, any links you put in your signature will instantly be displayed to readers and to the search engines on *every post you have made* on that forum, as shown in the example in Figure 10-5.

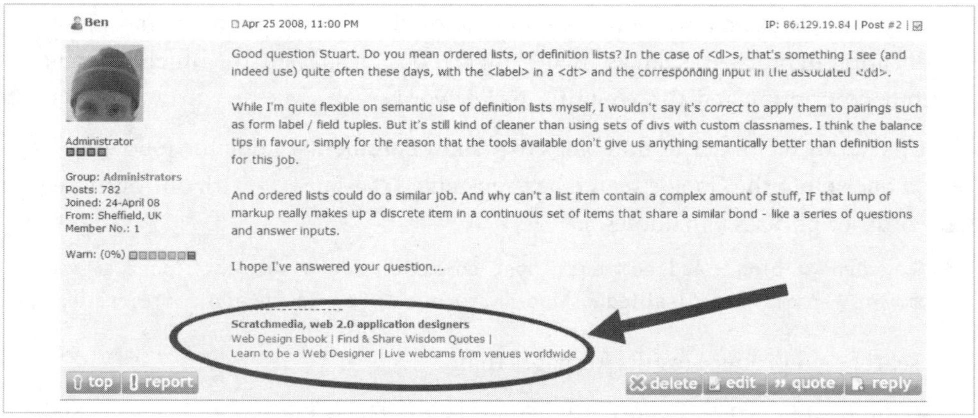

FIGURE 10-5 Every post I make on our forum creates four new backlinks. If I change my signature, it updates instantly across 1,000 different pages.

I recommend you join a few relevant forums. Having 1,000 backlinks from a single domain name is obviously not as realistic has having 50 backlinks from 20 different domains. Look for sites whose subject matter and domain name are as close as possible to your subject matter.

Be sure to follow the rules of any forum you join. Bear in mind these tips:

► Only post relevant, thoughtful content. Link-building on forums is very prevalent, and forum moderators are always on the lookout for people who only post short, meaningless messages for the purpose of generating backlinks. (On our forums, we delete gratuitous messages, and sometimes even delete user accounts, without warning or discussion.)

▶ Treat your forum posts as part of your brand's PR. The more value you can add, the more likely a reader will be to click one of your links.

▶ Do not customize your signature, or drop links into messages, until you have spent some time on the forum and contributed at least ten high-quality posts. Some forum software will not allow new members to add links, and you do not want to risk getting banned.

BLOGS

Many blogs allow readers to add their own comments to posts. Even if you cannot add links within comment content, you can often add your own web link, which is attached to your name. If you put your name as "Cheap software here," it is highly unlikely that your comment will pass moderation! I will often put my name and my qualification in brackets, such as "Ben Hunt (UI design specialist)," which is both an accurate description and also contains my keywords.

Use this handy technique to find blogs that allow comments. Copy the following search query into the Google search bar, replacing <<keywords>> with one or more keywords, or phrases ("in quotes"):

```
<<keywords>> blog +"add comment"|"post comment"|"add a comment"|"post a
comment" -"comments disabled" -"log in to post"|"log in to add" site:.ac.uk
```

This search will produce results for pages that:

▶ Preferably include some or all of your keywords/phrases and the word "blog" (add a plus sign to the start of any word that *must* appear).

▶ Include the phrase "add comment" (and variations).

▶ Do not include the phrases "comments disabled," "log in to post," or "log in to add."

▶ This example also uses the site: syntax to specify a preference for pages on domains that include .ac.uk (used by UK academic institutions, because academic sites are regarded as particularly trustworthy).

SQUIDOO.COM

Squidoo.com is one of a number of web-based applications that make it easy for anyone to create their own pages online without any technical skills. At the time of writing, it is also a PageRank 8 site (verify), which explains why a lot of site owners are using the site to create their own linking pages.

As an experiment, when working on the landing page strategy for Muazo (see the case study in Chapter 5), I created the page shown in Figure 10-6 on Squidoo in just 30 minutes. Its main heading matches one of my landing pages on Muazo.co.uk and it covers all the subjects of my other pages, and links to three of them. (Separate pages for each topic would have been even better.) The page is useful, easy to read, and provides three permanent inbound links.

You can also add links to your pages from existing Squidoo pages that support comments. Search Google for "site:squidoo.com" followed by your keywords.

FIGURE 10-6 My "Best Birthday Gift Ideas for Guys" page for Muazo on Squidoo.com

SOCIAL SITES

There are probably thousands of social networks and tools that let you easily create backlinks. Individual links are probably viewed as quite low in value. However, as search becomes more real-time, focusing on what's currently hot, concentrated social linking is likely to get more valuable.

If you focus on writing interesting and valuable content, promote it via any channels you can. Some of these also have browser toolbars (particularly for Firefox), which makes it quicker to post items. As a starting point, useful social channels include:

- ▶ Twitter (`twitter.com`)
- ▶ Facebook (`facebook.com`)
- ▶ My Space (`myspace.com`)
- ▶ LinkedIn (`linkedin.com`)
- ▶ Digg.com (`digg.com`)
- ▶ del.icio.us (`del.icio.us`)
- ▶ Reddit.com (`reddit.com`)
- ▶ StumbleUpon (`stumbleupon.com`)

Make use of any of your existing networks. You may also e-mail friends and colleagues and ask them to promote a page from their own accounts. If you have a mailing list, send announcements to your readers, and ask them to post links (where appropriate) on their own social networks, blogs, and web sites.

DIRECTORIES

Some online directories have strong standing with search engines. In particular, submit good pages to Yahoo! (`yahoo.com`), which is a paid directory, and the free Open Directory Project (`dmoz.org`). Listings on DMOZ can take a long time to appear, if you get listed at all, because the directory is moderated by people, but that quality also gives listings high value.

Most business sectors have their own free or premium niche directories. Search for "<< topic >> directory" to find those that are relevant to your subject.

CUSTOMERS' AND PARTNERS' SITES

It can pay to be bold and just ask for links from business connections. If you have customers or partners with relevant sites, send them personalized messages asking politely if they would be interested in posting a message and link to your content.

REVERSE-ENGINEER THE COMPETITION

A neat way to find good backlinks is to look at the pages that top the search rankings for your keywords and look at what pages link to them.

In your browser address bar, enter `http://siteexplorer.search.yahoo.com/search?p=` followed by the address of a top-ranking page. Alternatively, type `links:` followed by the URL into Google.

You will get a list of any results in each search engine's index that link to that page. Click through to the results to see which pages might be viable sources for links to your own content.

Consider Step 0

By definition, potential customers at Step 0 do not have a conscious need or problem, so they are not looking for anything, and you cannot identify them through keyword research. You must use common sense to imagine who might benefit from what you offer, and how you might effectively reach them.

At Step 0, you have to create problems, desires, possibilities, or needs in people's minds that are either new or are unexpressed. Effective Step 0 messages are interruptive. They will occur while people are doing something else, cause them to stop, and consider how the suggestion may apply to them.

It is still a good idea to focus Step 0 messages as far as possible. Ask what you already know about your market that could differentiate them from people who are clearly not in your market.

One simple technique is just to speak to their identity or role, or to mention some factor that a good proportion of prospects in any market might share. Notice how these example headlines both create the possibility of a need and distinguish their target audience:

- ▶ "What would happen if your server went down?"
- ▶ "3 things every new parent should be told"
- ▶ "Now you can eat what you want—and lose weight"
- ▶ "My secret tips to getting your dream job"
- ▶ "Is this the most economical SUV ever made?"
- ▶ "If you love the environment, this will drive you mad!"
- ▶ "The #1 web design trick for making easy money"

Depending on your demographic and your interests, some of these subjects may appeal to you, while others will not. That is the point. When you distinguish your market, you both include and exclude at the same time. The more people you exclude, the more relevant your message will appear to the right audience.

All these headlines hint at quick value, but require the prospect to read more. They are designed to create the awareness of some need or desire, and then to lead the prospect to Step 1 content. That next content can proceed to discuss possible solutions, assuming certain facts about the visitor's profile and her present need.

In some cases, the need may be non-specific, such as "I need to find out more about that" or "I could do with a laugh," in which case the task of the Step 1 content is to re-frame the context around a new problem or opportunity.

Once you have a message you would like to present, you have to put it in front of your Step 0 market, which means going out to them wherever they are. Here are a few suggestions for getting your message out to the world.

Advertising

Traditional advertising (outdoor, print, TV, and radio) is alive and well, and can provide good opportunities to raise awareness of a brand or product. They are most effective for promoting local businesses or name-brand goods. These media are not likely to give good value when you want to drive a specific market segment to a specific landing page.

Unless the prospect can immediately take the next step, there will be a high attrition rate. It is better to get your message in front of your potential customers via electronic media, which can present an immediate call to action that takes the prospect straight to your landing page.

As I mentioned in the Bolwell RV case study in Chapter 5, regular banner advertising can be a cost-effective way to reach a Step 0 market. The reason is that your target market at Step 0 is likely to be broad, which matches the blanket reach of a banner ad. Because you are paying for impressions, not clicks, you should identify web sites whose visitor profiles most closely match your target market demographic.

Pay-per-click advertising can also work well. If you know a lot about the demographic profile of your target customer, then Facebook may give good returns. On the other hand, if your market is more defined by subject matter, AdWords may perform better.

In all cases, it is important to distinguish your audience as accurately as possible and to serve them well-targeted messages.

Direct Mail

Direct mail is a mature industry, and still one of the most cost-effective marketing channels. Agencies will sell lists of names and addresses, the cost depending on the quality and level of segmentation. Many of the rules you already know apply to mailouts.

- ▶ Be distinctive (unusual, hand-written, or colored envelopes are more likely to be opened).
- ▶ Present one clear, powerful appeal, which distinguishes the target audience.
- ▶ Write simple, direct, accessible copy that delivers value while keeping the prospect reading. Communicate all the positive signs and resolve all the objections, and don't forget a strong call to action (which you can repeat several times).

PR and Article Submission

The most economical way to spread a message is to let other people do it for you. If you can make a compelling story, write it up as a press release and send it out to online and offline channels. Article submission engines, such as PRWeb (`prweb.com`) can help you distribute press releases world-wide. If a story is newsworthy, you may be able to generate a lot of inbound links for little effort.

Mailing Lists

Your mailing list could be one of your most valuable assets. Anyone who signs up to your mailing list has already been to your web site and is interested enough to volunteer to receive more information. That identifies them as a warm prospect for any message you may choose to give out.

I subscribe to dozens of online marketers' mailing lists, not because I am genuinely interested in the products, but because I enjoy seeing the range of approaches people try. I continue to be surprised at how frequently the best marketers come up with new propositions.

Do not take your mailing list members' attention for granted. Respect your readers' time, so keep your content and style fresh and interesting, or they may unsubscribe.

Previous Customers

Another simple and obvious method is simply to send communications to people who have bought from you before. They already know your brand, will give your message more attention, and are far more likely than the average new prospect to buy again.

Third-Party Mailing Lists

Until you have a decent list of your own, consider using other people's. I have had great success promoting products using this method. There must always be a win-win, so consider offering an exclusive discount to your partner's list, or agree to an affiliate revenue share with the partner. (I like to do both, so that everyone wins.)

E-mail messages can get forwarded beyond the original list or recipients. Mailing list software, like the industry leader AWeber (aweber.com), will tell you how many times a broadcast message has been opened. If you can create a message with viral value, it could be opened by more people than received it initially.

Ebooks

Another potential viral channel is the good old PDF ebook. These can give you great value. Instead of writing your "Ten top tips" as a landing page, consider writing it in your word processor instead, and giving it away for free to everyone who signs up for your newsletter. Ensure it follows the rules for good content (targeted, accessible, and interesting), is properly branded, and that it contains embedded calls to action that link back to specific landing pages. A useful ebook can find its way round the world and be seen by more people than you may ever reach through manual link-building.

YouTube

YouTube (youtube.com) is not only the world's second busiest search engine (after Google), it is also a great way to reach people who are "just looking." It is cheaper to make and publish video content than ever. Engaging and valuable video content can go viral and reach many more prospects than a plain old web page. Don't forget to tag any videos with your keywords and to include links back to your landing pages.

Keep Going!

The final step of your web site strategy is to go back and do it all again. There is no final step. As long as there are new markets that you can address with new propositions, as long as you can segment and refine your existing markets to target with more precision, you have opportunities to reach more people, to build new funnels, and to continue to improve the your conversion rates.

Every hour you invest in keyword research, content writing, link-building, list building, PR, tweeting, blogging, and generally being out there will only increase your investment in the great online marketing bank. Start now, and carry on.

Building an expansive marketing web site using the new concentric approach is guaranteed to bring you more traffic, and should dramatically increase your conversion rates. Now that every page has one logical next step, it is easy to monitor conversion in detail.

You should regularly check the click-through rates in every sequence of pages in every funnel. Because success is a function of traffic *and* conversion, it is vital to minimize leaks from your online marketing system. The final chapter introduces techniques for incrementally optimizing the conversion rate of any page, and introduces a powerful free tool from Google, which makes it easy to test alternative content and achieve significant and solid improvements.

CHAPTER 11

Optimizing Your Web Pages

If you have followed the complete process set out in this book, you now have a web site built around a content strategy based on keyword research, which you can be confident will bring good traffic.

You have designed multiple funnels and landing pages that target distinct markets at specific points in their awareness, which manage prospects' attention and guide them through to conversion, giving them the information they should need to make a positive choice to take action. You have set up Google Analytics with funnels that let you monitor click-through rates from each page to the next.

This approach will give you far better results than a site built around "first best guess." Your site is still based on multiple assumptions. What do you do when you spot leaks? How do you improve your conversion rates through funnels?

It pays to work on optimizing conversion, particularly from key pages at later steps on the Awareness Ladder, where your funnels converge. A 10% increase in conversion rate delivers the same impact as a 10% increase in traffic, and very often you can achieve significant improvements with just a few small changes—particularly when you first start to optimize your pages.

Blindly replacing what you have with another guess is not a reliable approach, because you cannot efficiently distinguish what works from what does not work. Even the best designers, copywriters, and marketers can't say what will definitely work best. I have described plenty of "best practice" methods, but no one can predict with certainty what will be best in any particular case. Human psychology is extremely complex. The only reliable way to know what will work for your web site is to measure what people actually do.

All you can do is *test, applying both creativity and analysis*. I recommend testing alternative copy, imagery, calls to action, and layout, wherever you suspect a page can be made more effective. This chapter introduces the process for optimizing any page on your web site.

Here is the general process:

▶ Analyze creatively what might be failing, and generate your best ideas about what might work better.

▶ Test the alternative approaches and evaluate the results to see if your ideas hold true.

▶ Repeat the cycle, making progressive improvements each time. Keep the improvements, and re-think the ideas that did not generate better results.

Our agency has delivered great results for a number of clients using the techniques in this chapter. We have used a few different software packages to implement and to monitor optimization tests. In this chapter I introduce Google Website Optimizer, one of our preferred optimization tools.

Google Website Optimizer

Google Website Optimizer (GWO) is a free online tool provided by Google that enables web site owners to execute two types of optimization tests on their content, to discover which of various options performs better *in practice*.

In this final chapter I explain how you can use Google Website Optimizer to run two types of optimization experiments: A/B split tests and multivariate tests. I share my tips on how you can use Website Optimizer to get meaningful and useful results—from my team's experience of running dozens of experiments on our own and clients' sites.

I summarize the mechanics of setting up experiments, because GWO provides excellent online help, plus the functional steps may change over time. I then focus on the overall approach and specific tips for using GWO to get useful results for your business.

Google Website Optimizer will let you display alternative content or styles on your web pages to different people and then tell you which alternative results in most visitors completing a specified goal. You access GWO itself through your web browser. You do not need to install any software, it is pretty easy to set up, and is totally free. It gives every web site owner the ability to test different approaches and to learn which performs best with statistical certainty in a relatively short time—an ability that simply did not exist a few years ago.

As I have emphasized throughout this book, you have tools at your fingertips today that give you far more power and speed than any previous generation of marketers could dream of. All you need to do to is to apply the same methodical approach to testing all your ideas, and you can achieve incredible results. These are not idle claims: We have literally *doubled the turnover* of businesses with a combination of creative design and analysis using GWO.

I should state that dozens of other powerful testing tools are available, which have their own strengths. GWO is not the only game in town, nor is it the best for every situation, but it enjoys huge popularity. I believe it is the best way for most owners of small and medium sites to get into conversion testing.

Testing in Parallel

GWO runs all test variations *in parallel*, which means different visitors are given different variations *at the same time*. This is crucial because it eliminates other influences, in particular time-based factors, which could negatively affect the validity of the experiments.

If you ran one page for a week, then another page the next week, you would not get valid results, because the *environmental factors* would be different from one week to the next. Say, for example, a popular site linked to your page on the second week, sending over a new group of visitors who have particular expectations. That group may be more or less likely to take the conversion action, meaning the playing field would not be the same from one week to the next.

The way GWO works is to use JavaScript code to select one page (or content combination) to serve to each visitor from a predefined range, so that all variations are shown to an approximately equal number of people.

It also ensures that the same visitor always sees the same content. If your visitor arrived on your home page, visited another page, and returned to the home page, and the home page suddenly looked different, it could be very disconcerting. For that reason, GWO saves a *cookie* on each visitor's client (browser) that identifies that visitor so that he or she can be served the same content next time.

How A/B Testing Works

A/B testing (also known as split testing) is the simpler of the two methods available with GWO. With a split test, you publish two or more alternative versions of a web page. Visitors are presented with one version at random, and GWO measures how many people proceed to a goal page in that visit. You get statistics that show the conversion/click-through rate of each page.

> **NOTE** *I must stress that the term "A/B test" may be misleading. You are not limited to just two alternatives, but can run any number of pages.*

Figure 11-1 shows a typical report from an A/B split test. (You can see the two actual alternatives I tested in Chapter 7, Figure 7-15.) I have highlighted a number of elements, as explained here:

1. You would use these controls to manage the test. Here, I have called the test "WDFS Contact A/B 2010-02-26."

2. The graph shows visually the relative performance of the variations over time. The lines will not appear until you have about five successful conversions for any variation. They will usually jump around early on in a test, when there are relatively few results, before flattening into parallel lines as the average conversion rates become settled.

3. In this A/B test, I am running two variations.

4. Every test has an original page plus one or more variations. Here, I have just one variation, titled "Redesign." It is possible to disable variations by selecting the checkbox and clicking the "Disable" button (currently grayed out). Disabling a variation removes it from the test, so no more visitors will see it. GWO does not let you re-enable a disabled variation. You can never disable the original page.

5. Here, both the original page and redesign are currently enabled.

6. The "Est. conv. rate" column shows the current estimated conversion rate. The first figure (1.13%) is the actual performance (equal to 11/970 from the final column). The second number (±0.5%) shows the calculated *margin of error* of the conversion rate. This means the final conversion rate of the original page could be between 0.63% and 1.63%, based on the data gathered to date, where the redesign could theoretically end up between 1.51% and 2.91%. Because there is slight overlap between those ranges, the test is not conclusive. The bars show graphically the relative potential performance range of the two options. The range of the redesign is higher than the original, but showing a small overlap. For this reason, the bar will be shown in yellow (meaning it is *statistically* inconclusive). A green bar would show a conclusive winning combination, and a red bar would indicate a clear loser.

7. The next column "Chance to Beat Orig." shows the statistical probability that any variation will outperform the original page. Here, because there are only two candidates, my redesign has a 96% chance of winning the test (which gave me enough confidence to conclude the test). It is important to note that this figure does not give the likelihood of being the best variation—only the chance of beating the original. The figure in the "Observed Improvement" column shows the current actual difference in conversion rate, compared to the original. Here, a 94.7% improvement shows that my redesign has achieved almost double the conversion of the original. The final column shows the actual number of conversions and the number of *impressions*, which means how many times each variation has been served to visitors.

You will quickly find it easy to scan the GWO report layout, even with multiple variations running, and quickly establish how the various alternatives are performing.

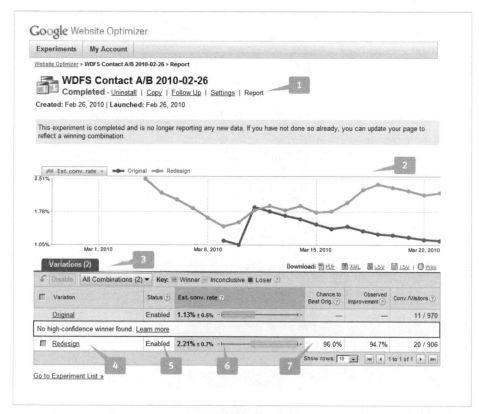

FIGURE 11-1 Report showing the results of an A/B split test

Creating A/B Tests

Setting up an A/B split test in GWO is simple, as Figure 11-2 shows (Google provides further good help within the tool itself, www.google.com/analytics/siteopt/):

▶ Give your experiment a useful title.

▶ Choose your original test page.

▶ Publish at least one alternative candidate page to test against the original.

▶ Identify your *goal page*. This is the page, which, when a visitor lands on it after having visited the original or alternative page, constitutes a success. This may be a next step, such as "Contact Us" or "Added to Cart" (in which case you are testing click through from one step to the next), or you may choose an ultimate goal page, such as "Thank you for contacting us" or "Confirmation of your order."

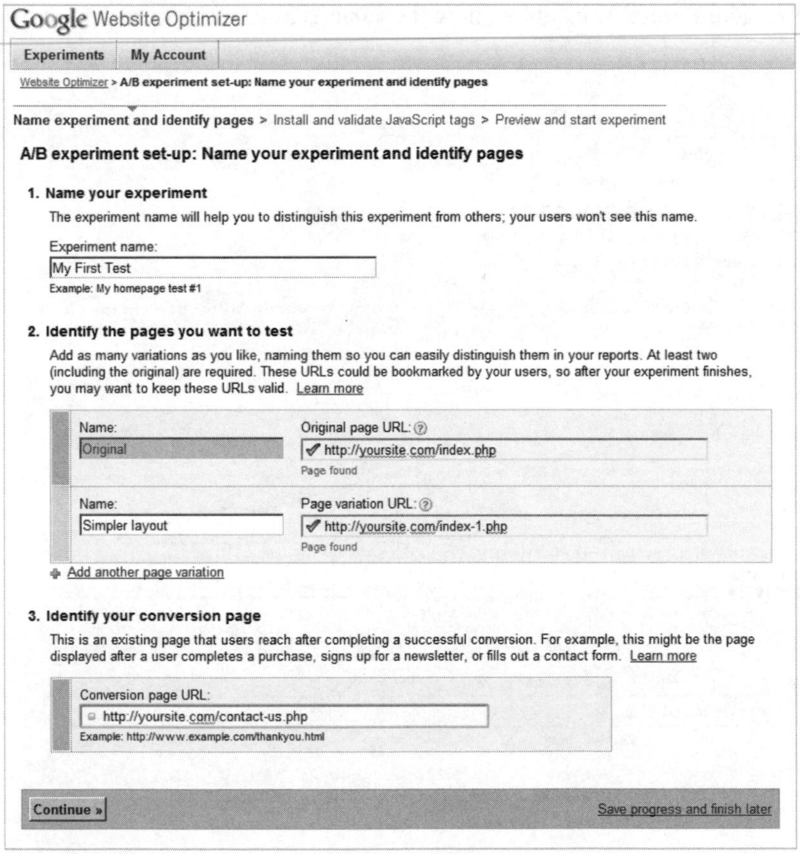

FIGURE 11-2 A simple form for creating an A/B test in GWO

How Multivariate Testing Works

Multivariate testing is more complex and powerful than A/B split testing. Success is not down to the performance of individual components. Rather, it is how well all the design and content elements work together that makes the difference. Our tests have proven this to be the case time and again.

If you have ideas for improving several different elements on a page, one option is to run a split test comparing the original against another version with all your changes implemented. Though you may get a result, that test will not tell you *which changes made the difference*. Half the changes may have a positive impact, whereas the other half may have a negative impact. A split test will not tell you which were helpful and which were detrimental, which is where multivariate testing comes into play.

In a multivariate test, the individual changes are served up at random to create many possible *combinations*. If you had three alternative headings, two alternative feature images, and three calls to action, a multivariate test would give you 18 different combinations ($3 \times 2 \times 3 = 18$). You could achieve a similar result by creating 18 separate variations with an A/B test, but it would take a lot more work.

The results will show you exactly how all the individual components impact the overall success rate, but this is less relevant than you may imagine. The real value in multivariate testing is that it compares how all the permutations work *in symphony*. This often gives a surprisingly different result than what you would expect just from looking at the relative performance of individual page sections.

 In GWO, multivariate experiments give you a second tab, which shows the average stats for all the page sections. Figure 11-3 shows both tabs in one of our multivariate tests.

Note that, on the "Combinations" view, the leading combination 22 is showing an 83.0% improvement over the original (which is the combination of all the original components). Combination 22 includes two of the original page sections and three variations. However, when you look at the average performance of the individual page sections on the "Page Sections" view, you notice:

▶ The "blue, closer" Image Link variation typically generates only a 0.51% improvement.

▶ The "no border" Product Description performs 0.87% *worse* than the original.

▶ The "centered" Product Nav is responsible for only a 9.56% increase in conversion.

These individual numbers clearly do not combine to make a significant 83% improvement in conversion rate. The reason is the symphony effect I mentioned earlier. After a year of constantly running multivariate tests, we now ignore the "Page Sections" tab entirely, and only base decisions on which *combinations* perform best.

Combination	Status	Est. conv. rate		Chance to Beat Orig.	Observed Improvement	Conv./Visitors
Original	Enabled	6.20% ± 2.9%		—	—	22 / 355
Combination 1	Disabled	15.0% ± 13%		73.3%	100%	5 / 40
Combination 25	Disabled	13.9% ± 14%		69.8%	85.2%	5 / 36
Combination 5	Disabled	11.9% ± 12%		65.1%	58.7%	5 / 42
Combination 9	Disabled	11.4% ± 11%		63.7%	51.5%	5 / 44
Combination 22	Enabled	11.3% ± 3.9%		92.9%	83.0%	38 / 335
Combination 2				87.1%	61.8%	34 / 339
Combination 16				82.6%	50.1%	32 / 344
Combination 20				82.6%	50.1%	32 / 344
Combination 26				82.5%	49.7%	32 / 345
Combination 8	Enabled	9.14% ± 3.5%		81.4%	47.6%	31 / 339
Combination 4	Enabled	8.77% ± 3.5%		78.5%	41.5%	30 / 342
Combination 28	Disabled	8.29% ± 4.7%		51.1%	1.66%	15 / 181
Combination 18	Disabled	7.93% ± 4.9%		47.9%	-3.16%	13 / 163
Combination 10	Enabled	7.85% ± 3.3%		70.0%	26.7%	27 / 344

Tooltip: Status: Enabled
Breadcrumbs: Original
Image Link: blue, closer
Product Description: no border
Right Column: Original
Product Nav: centred

Combinations (32) Page Sections (5)   Download: PDF XML CSV TSV | Print

Show rows: 15   1 to 14 of 31

Relevance Rating	Variation	Est. conv. rate		Chance to Beat Orig.	Observed Improvement	Conv./Visitors
Product Nav 1 / 5	Original	8.20% ± 0.8%		—	—	207 / 2523
	centered	8.99% ± 0.8%		83.4%	9.56%	208 / 2314
Breadcrumbs 0 / 5	Original	8.59% ± 0.6%		—	—	361 / 4201
	Hidden	8.49% ± 1.5%		46.6%	-1.19%	54 / 636
Image Link 0 / 5	Original	8.56% ± 0.8%		—	—	218 / 2547
	blue, closer	8.60% ± 0.8%		52.1%	0.51%	197 / 2290
Product De... 0 / 5	Original	8.61% ± 0.7%		—	—	234 / 2717
	no border	8.54% ± 0.8%		46.4%	-0.87%	181 / 2120
Right Column 0 / 5	Original	8.84% ± 0.8%		—	—	236 / 2670
	nicer heading, ...	8.26% ± 0.8%		23.7%	-6.55%	179 / 2167

FIGURE 11-3 Evidence of the symphony effect in action

You may notice a few more differences between the A/B test report and the multivariate report in Figure 11-3. Although I created only five alternative page elements, the experiment features 31 combinations (32 including the original permutation), because $2 \times 2 \times 2 \times 2 \times 2 = 32$.

The Combinations view shows several disabled combinations, displayed as grayed-out rows. You can tell GWO to disable losing combinations automatically, based on low statistical probability of success. Here, I have manually disabled a few that showed poor early performance, in order to push more visitors through the remaining options. The more visitors who view each option, the quicker you will get conclusive results.

The "Page Sections" tab shows a *Relevance Rating* score in the first column. This indicates which page section appears to have the greatest influence over the results. In this case, only the "Product Nav" section reports any meaningful impact, and that is still only 1/5 (because the average difference between best and worst variation is less than 10%). I find the relevance rating occasionally interesting, but rarely helpful. (In fact, the second best-performing combination uses the original Product Nav, and still shows a 61.8% improvement over the original, which seems to make no sense, and just proves the symphony effect again.)

Creating Multivariate Tests

The process of creating a multivariate test in GWO is similar to setting up a split test, in that you need to identify the page you want to test and a single goal page. Instead of creating alternative versions of the whole page, you will identify *sections of the page* for which you can create alternatives.

You will need to add the *control script* and *tracking script* on your test page, and add the *conversion script* to your goal page, just as in a split test. With multivariate tests there is another step. You need to insert a piece of JavaScript code into your page's HTML markup at the start and end of each section you want to test, as the instructions in Figure 11-4 show.

> **NOTE** *The inserted code includes a </noscript> tag that has no matching <noscript> starting tag. This means your markup will be invalid, but it's the way GWO works.*

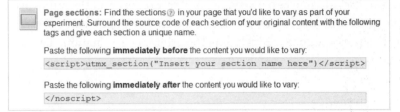

FIGURE 11-4 Identify page sections for a multivariate test in Google Website Optimizer.

You can name the page sections whatever you want. For example, if you wanted to test separately various combinations of your main page heading (h1 tag) and your first paragraph, you might add code like this:

```
<h1><script>utmx_section("heading")</script>
How Joe's Miracle Hair-Gro Works</noscript></h1>
<p><script>utmx_section("first para")</script>Joe's Miracle Hair-Gro has
been formulated using a unique secret blend of natural plant extracts,
etc.</noscript></p>
```

Note that the JavaScript tags wrap round the original content in each of the two sections. GWO will detect this content and use it as the original variation. Select meaningful names for the sections. Here, I have used "heading" and "first para."

Before you can continue from the step of setting up your experiment pages, you must have the JavaScript tags already in place on your test page. GWO will then pull in the original content from each section, and give you the opportunity to create one or more variations of each section, by typing or pasting in alternative HTML code. Figure 11-5 shows how this step looks. You can select "+ Add new variation" to create a new alternative variation for any section, which will start with the original content by default. You cannot edit the original variation for any section. (Note that in Figure 11-5 we are testing alternative CSS blocks, not regular HTML content, in order to change visual style properties, which is a valid and useful approach.)

In this first section of the chapter I introduced the basic mechanics of setting up split and multivariate tests. I recommend you start running your own quick tests as soon as possible, because you will quickly get used to how GWO works. You can test pretty much anything you think will make a difference. You will probably find it easy to get some apparent improvements, and you should learn something from each test. In the remainder of this chapter, I share more practical tips for getting the most out of Google Website Optimizer.

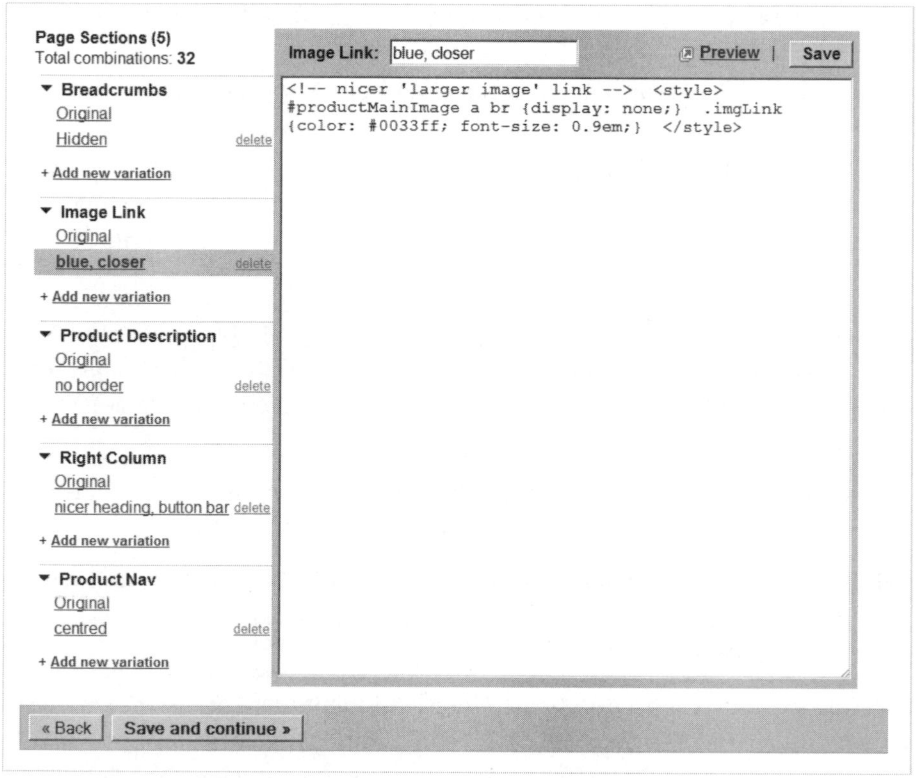

FIGURE 11-5 Creating variations for a multivariate test in GWO

My Optimizer Tips

Conversion testing is an extremely powerful marketing technique, and Google Website Optimizer is certainly a great tool, but you need to know how to use any tool to get the best results. Though GWO makes testing pretty easy, you still have many important choices to make in setting up and running experiments. I will offer what guidance I can, and your own experience will teach you much more (because you shouldn't take anything as the final word, right?)

When to Use A/B and Multivariate Testing

The first big question you will need to ask is what kind of test to use: A/B split test or multivariate test? The answer will depend on what changes you think a page needs.

If you are testing two or more totally *different approaches*, an A/B test will often be most appropriate. For example, if you want to test one version of your home page that leads with a cost-saving benefit versus a version that leads with a new feature, each would have a different headline, splash panel, and other content. Because there are really only two different variations, and testing combinations of the different content together would make no sense (that is, you have no reason to think a cost-saving headline with the new feature splash would convert better), an A/B test would be the right approach.

Another reason for going with a split test is if the number of variations is very small. If you want to try out three variations of an intro panel, it may be quicker simply to create three versions of the page (an A/B/C test) than it would to set up the same test in multivariate format.

If you want to test several different changes where the variations are broadly independent of each other, a multivariate test will probably be the right choice.

Figure 11-6 shows two combinations of a product page from the Towels Direct web site, the results of an ideal multivariate test. (This is the same experiment whose results are shown in Figure 11-3.)

We are testing five different page sections, which are independent of each other. The three significant changes that make up the leading combination are: the position and color of the "larger image" link; the centering of the "prev/listing/next" product navigation; and removing the line around the product description. Together, these three simple changes result in a 60% increase in conversion (add to cart).

FIGURE 11-6 The TowelsDirect.co.uk product page was an ideal candidate for a multivariate test.

We have found that sometimes a middle ground is required. This is where you have variations that could for the most part be mixed up, but where there would be inappropriate combinations that you would not want to be shown. In this case, it is fine to proceed to set up a multivariate test, and you can go ahead and disable any inappropriate combinations right at the start of the test.

Another situation where only a multivariate test will work is where technical reasons make an A/B test unfeasible. If your pages are generated by a content management system or e-commerce platform (possibly using parameters on the URL) it could be very difficult to create alternative complete pages. In this case, you can still use the multivariate method, and you can even re-create something like an A/B test by disabling all the combinations you do not want, as shown in Figure 11-7.

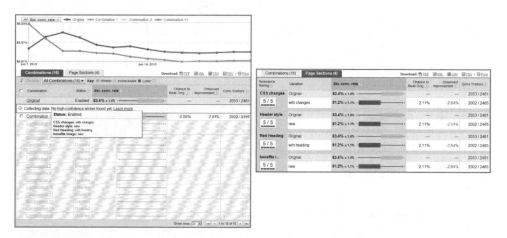

FIGURE 11-7 Using the multivariate method to create an A/B split test

The risk with this approach—and with A/B split testing in general—is that you can end up without a positive result and no clue as to how the individual changes performed. Figure 11-8 shows the two home pages we tested using the multivariate method, and the result is a marginal but conclusive 2.6% *decrease* in conversion rate (viewing a product page).

Here, I have made four changes: two different headers; showing or hiding the "Simply the Lowest..." heading; replacing the photo with the four panels showing key benefits; plus some CSS changes (including font size in the side nav). It may be that one or two of these changes delivered significant improvements, while the rest were detrimental, but because I did not run them as a proper multivariate test, I cannot know. Looking at the performance of each section in Figure 11-7, it is impossible to tell which page section changes were significant, because they only ran as a combination, so all seemed to have the same effect.

FIGURE 11-8 Two variations of the Fastlec home page achieved similar results.

Goals

The second decision you will need to make is what to use as your goal. The choice is usually between the *next step* and the *final goal*. For example, do you test the effectiveness of your service page by measuring the number of people who visit the contact page, or the number who actually submit a contact request? There are arguments for both approaches.

Ideally, you would always want to test a goal that has real business value, such as actual contact requests or actual sales. This is the most meaningful approach, because it looks at the whole funnel, the visitor's experience as a symphony. There is little point getting more people to click through to a next step if they are not proceeding to the final goal.

On the other hand, because there is attrition at each step of the funnel, people will drop off at each step in the sequence, which results in fewer completed goals. The fewer goals you get, the longer it takes to see useful results. The longer your tests take, the longer it takes to respond and to optimize the user experience.

In the case of the Fastlec home page in Figure 11-8, we used "viewing any product detail page" as the goal, which is not a conversion but an intermediate step toward conversion. This resulted in very high click-through rates—over 80%—which, combined with high traffic, produced a conclusive result in just 10 days. It could be argued that, although my variation produced a slightly lower click-through rate to product pages, it may still have generated more actual sales. In this example, it may have been worthwhile measuring conversions as sales.

There is no right answer to the question of what to use as a goal. I would offer three guidelines:

1. The higher your traffic, the more feasible it is to use more distant goals. If you have low traffic, you may get better results from running more short tests than waiting for a long experiment to complete.

2. Can you judge the impact of one page on the final conversion results? In many cases, getting more people to take one step forward can rationally be seen as a useful result.

3. How soon do you need to see results? If you have the capacity to run a new test every two weeks, there is little point setting up a test to complete in one week.

USING THE GWO DURATION CALCULATOR

Google provides a handy calculator that can help you predict the length of time it will take for a test to produce conclusive results (www.google.com/analytics/siteopt/siteopt/help/calculator.html). Just type in your best-guess figures, and the calculator will estimate the time your experiment will need to run.

Figure 11-9 shows three similar variations, which suggest how the input figures impact the duration of tests. The more combinations you have, the fewer page views you put through the test, the lower your conversion rate, and the lower the improvement in conversion rate you expect, the longer your experiment will take.

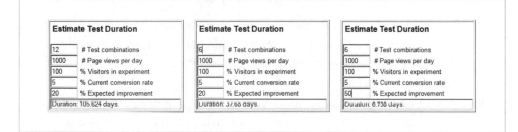

FIGURE 11-9 Estimating the length of experiments using the Google Website Optimizer Duration Calculator

You may get a useful result in a shorter time than the calculator predicts. You do not have to wait for conclusive data, because you may manually (or automatically) disable poorly performing combinations, or select a leading combination and move on to a new test.

One thing you should notice from the calculator examples in Figure 11-9 is the importance of keeping the number of combinations down, which applies for both split and multivariate tests. Halving the combination count from 12 to 6 here reduces the experiment length by two thirds.

USING AN EVENT AS A GOAL

Although GWO expects to find the conversion script on a particular page, you can also use a JavaScript event as a goal, which simulates a page load. To do this, look at the conversion script provided by GWO. It will have a line similar to the following one, which includes a 10-digit number:

```
gwoTracker._trackPageview("/1234567890/goal");
```

This is the method that needs to be called for the goal to register. You can then call it from any event, such as a simple click:

```
<div onClick='gwoTracker._trackPageview("/1234567890/goal");'>
```

Guidelines for Testing

When setting up and running your tests, remember these general guidelines.

BROAD STROKES FIRST

The most important tip is: Test broad strokes changes first. You probably have dozens of ideas of things you could tweak easily, but if your goal is optimization you need to get the fundamentals right first. Assuming you have defined a good funnel of landing pages, focus first on testing the following on each page:

▶ The overall *proposition*. It should be obvious what you are offering, and who you are offering it to. Your proposition should match at least one clearly defined need. If the page is not clearly *about* anything, test alternatives that project more direct messages.

▶ A strong *appeal* to catch attention. Your headline and most getable features should engage with the target visitors—at their awareness level—and get their attention with the scent of some immediate benefit. Test different headlines, early paragraphs, and primary imagery.

▶ Content to keep the visitor engaged. Can all the content justify its place on the page? Try adding or removing sections of content to see what keeps people's interest, builds their anticipation, and carries them through to the final step.

▶ *Call to action*. Every page should have clear next steps. Calls to action should be both compelling and consistent with the expectations you have created.

TEST YOUR BEST

Consider your alternatives carefully before you set up the test. Do not rush the creative thinking and do not test random guesses. Have a good reason for every alternative you include, because poor results will teach you little.

A good principle is to be clear on the idea you are testing before you proceed. Write down what you expect to learn from the test, and craft your variations accordingly.

I strongly advise you use your *best guess as the original combination*, because that is the one option you cannot disable while the test is running. We have run a number of tests where several strong combinations remain competing against a clearly weaker original combination. This results in lower overall conversions through the duration of the test.

POLISHING

When you are confident you have the broad strokes right, you can proceed to polish your content and design. As you move toward optimal performance, expect less dramatic improvements, but you may still find that even small visual and content changes can bring useful benefits.

Polish content by testing alternative wording. Shorten and rearrange sentences to be punchier and more readable. You can also try making keywords or phrases bold to draw more attention to them when people are scanning. Try adding more positive signs, resolving more possible concerns, adding extra useful information, or reinforcing your points with additional testimonials and evidence.

Polish content imagery by testing alternative images, showing multiple images, altering their size and position on the page, or by zooming in to focus on more important aspects.

There is often scope for tweaking general graphic design factors. Use the noticeability factors (position, size, boldness, contrast, color, dynamism, and 3-D effects) to draw the eye to more important features and away from less important ones. Pay attention to areas of the page that seem busy or obvious, and ask whether those areas support the dynamic flow of information.

Finally, consider whether any elements on the page can simply be removed. Taking away unnecessary content or visual design always leaves more attention for higher-value content.

INTERPRETING YOUR RESULTS

The best way to learn to read the results from GWO is through the experience of your own experiments. Running optimization experiments can be exciting and compelling. Try to resist the temptation to watch them on a daily basis to try to predict the outcome too early.

As with any numbers in business, ask whether the information you have gives you anything you can act on decisively. Until the stats are *actionable*, do not sit and watch them. Your time would be better spent coming up with new ideas for your next experiment.

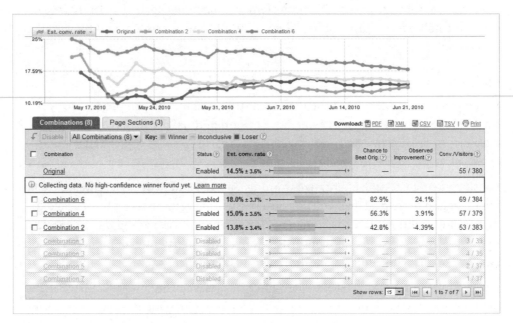

FIGURE 11-10 Sample GWO results. When should you disable a combination?

The experiment in Figure 11-10 shows a clear leader from the very start, which is very likely to be the winning combination, but beware of judging too soon. Figure 11-11 shows a different test where the original combination (indicated by the black line) seemed to be a clear leader in the first week. However, two combinations finally outperformed the original. The winning combination 5 was at one point the poorest performer. So avoid disabling combinations until the lines seem to have settled into a flat, parallel shape and have stopped switching order.

I tend to be quite aggressive in disabling combinations, preferring to complete an experiment as soon as I have a good idea of the likely winner. I will often immediately set up a new experiment to try to make further improvements. This seems to be a way to get quicker improvements than to wait for conclusive results each time.

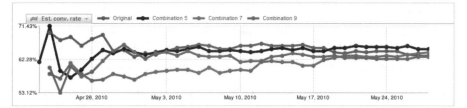

FIGURE 11-11 Let your graph lines flatten out before betting on a winner.

One final point to highlight is that, in my opinion, the "Chance to Beat Orig" figure is not particularly helpful. It would be much more useful to see a "Chance to Win" percentage. That would give a clearer picture on which combinations could safely be removed.

Some Limitations of GWO

Google Website Optimizer is a great free tool, but it is not the perfect solution for every site and every circumstance. Every solution has its strengths and weaknesses. Here are some possible weaknesses to consider.

One distinctive feature of GWO is that it is a *client-side* solution that requires JavaScript that runs in the visitor's browser. It will still work for about 99% of your visitors, which is more than enough to give you representative results.

However, the client-side method does mean that there are limits to what you can test. You are constrained to including all visitors to a page in your experiment. For example, you may prefer to show different experiments to visitors who are logged in, who have already purchased a product, or those who have not visited your site before. To achieve this, you would either need to direct those users to different pages, or use server-side code to display an alternative set of GWO JavaScript tags that belong to a different test.

Running a GWO test requires that you edit the client-side markup, which is not convenient for all sites, particularly where different sections of the HTML markup are generated by different server-side scripts or templates.

If you typically edit your page content in a content management system that uses a visual (WYSIWYG) editor, we have found that some of these can strip out JavaScript code when the content is saved.

GWO also forces each individual visitor to see the same content for the duration of the test (or while the cookie persists). For example, we ran a multivariate test to compare variations of callout ads for an ebook in the side column on our web site. Visitors always saw the same ad on every article. If that ad did not work for them, it would keep on not working for them page after page, which reduced the chances of showing an ad that would get a click through. Ideally, I would prefer to be able to tell GWO to show a random combination each time, but this is not currently possible.

GWO does not allow you to re-enable a disabled combination in A/B or multivariate tests. Nor can you modify any variation in a multivariate test—without stopping, copying, and re-starting the test. In this case, your statistics will start from scratch again. For this reason, it is very important that you take time to preview all the variations before you start a test running.

Creative Ways of Using GWO

Website Optimizer can also do more than it appears at first. Here are a few tricks that we have discovered.

> **NOTE** *Many more are available if you are expert with JavaScript. Check out Eric Vasilik's GWO Tricks at* www.gwotricks.com *to find out more advanced stuff.*

You do not just have to put regular HTML content in multivariate options. CSS style information can be really useful too. CSS has the added benefit of adding a layer of separation, which enables you to make changes while a test is running. If you know you are going to test four different styles, you can set the content of your variations as HTML using different *classnames*, such as:

```
<script>utmx_section("overall-style")</script>
<div class="style-brighter"></noscript>
```

You could create multiple variations of this div, each with a different classname. You do not have to specify what the classname "style-brighter" means at this point. Its properties can be set at any time in your style sheet, which means you can take more time to get the design right, even after the experiment has started.

Although GWO requires you to provide the address of one test page during setup of a multivariate experiment, you are not limited to running your test only on that page.

Copy the control script and sections onto other pages, and they will work everywhere. This is how we tested permutations of advertisements across 150 articles, simply by including the same code and markup in a single CMS template.

Likewise, you are not limited to having only one conversion page. You can include the conversion script on multiple pages, and any of those pages will count as a conversion. This can be useful if you are also running an A/B test on the conversion page (resulting in more than one copy of that page).

The Way of Optimization

Optimizing your click-through rates from each page to the next is the final technique in your web site optimization toolkit, and completes the new approach. I hope I have shown that this method is not a one-time exercise. It is an ongoing process that has no logical end. Do not be limited by the low performance of the old way. The Web is massive and still growing at an incredible rate. You have more potential customers than you ever imagined, and now you have the tools to reach them, to connect with them, and to help them discover propositions that deliver exactly what they need.

- ▶ It all starts with researching the real world. Keyword research shows you what people are actually looking for today, and gives you the means to keep discovering new markets.
- ▶ Multiplicity helps you turn your products and service into an ever-expanding range of finely tuned propositions.
- ▶ The Awareness Ladder lets you structure a content strategy that can address all your prospects, exactly where they are.
- ▶ The concentric model gives you a simple and logical structure that you can put into practice today, and which can grow organically at any rate you choose.
- ▶ You know straightforward techniques for catching visitors' attention and keeping them engaged with your content so that you can communicate your full message.
- ▶ Finally, web page optimization gives you a way to increase click-through rates through all your funnels and incrementally optimize the performance of your site.

I hope this book has inspired you to approach your online marketing with a new vision and energy, and—most importantly—never to stop getting your message to the people who need it. I wish you every success.

INDEX